Educating for Democracy

Case-Method Teaching and Learning

Educating for Democracy

Case-Method Teaching and Learning

Edited by

Robert F. McNergney
University of Virginia

Edward R. Ducharme
Mary K. Ducharme
Drake University

LEA LAWRENCE ERLBAUM ASSOCIATES, PUBLISHERS
1999 Mahwah, New Jersey London

Lawrence Erlbaum Associates, Inc., Publishers
10 Industrial Avenue
Mahwah, NJ 07430

Cover design by Kathryn Houghtaling Lacey

Library of Congress Cataloging-in-Publication Data

Educating for democracy : case-method teaching and learning / edited
    by Robert F. McNergney, Edward R. Ducharme, and Mary K.
    Ducharme.
        p. cm
    Includes bibliographical references and index.
    ISBN 0-8058-2483-9
    1. Case method. 2. Teachers—Training of—United States. 3.
Democracy—Study and teaching—United States—Case studies.
I. McNergney, Robert F. II. Ducharme, Edward R. III.
Ducharme, Mary K.
LB1029.C37E38 1999
370'.71'1—DC21   98-39825
                                                       CIP

Books published by Lawrence Erlbaum Associates are printed on
acid-free paper, and their bindings are chosen for strength and dura-
bility.

Printed in the United States of America
10   9   8   7   6   5   4   3   2   1

Contents

PART II: CASES

Preface

This volume advocates the use of case methods to promote democratic teaching and learning. What is meant by "case methods" and "democratic teaching and learning"? Why are these concepts important enough to merit a book?

Case methods designed for teaching people how to practice a profession help learners examine and solve problems as they reveal themselves in real life. Although the problems can be pedestrian and exhilarating at the same time, their study via "case methods" must be, as the phrase suggests, methodical. Case methods in education—like those methods used to prepare physicians, lawyers, and business people—force learners to attend to detail and to exercise judgment as they identify and solve problems. Although each has its own unique variations, case-method approaches in all fields promote careful examination of professional practice.

Our sense of "democratic teaching and learning" is probably best revealed in the writings of Thomas Jefferson. In a language that is now out of step with our sisters, he suggested in general terms the kind of education that helps people look to the future with some reasonable sense of optimism and power over their own lives. "Education ... grafts a new man on the native stock.... And it cannot be but that each generation succeeding to the knowledge acquired by all those who preceded it, adding to it their own acquisitions and discoveries, and handing the mass down for successive and constant accumulation, must advance the knowledge and well-being of mankind, not *infinitely*, as some have said, but *indefinitely*, and to a term which no one can fix and foresee" (The Rockfish Gap Report, August 4, 1818). Democratic teaching and learning, then, lead not only to a collective accretion of knowledge but to a perpetual dissemination, exchange, and refinement of knowledge among people. Case methods, as the chapter authors explain, can be organized and carried out to encourage this kind of practice.

Jefferson believed the people must retain the ultimate powers of the society; but he also believed that if a democratic society were to flourish, people had to be educated. "I know of no safe depository of the ultimate powers of the society but the people themselves; and if we think them not enlightened enough to exercise their control with a wholesome discretion, the remedy is not to take it from them, but to inform their discretion by education" (Thomas Jefferson to William C. Jarvis, 1820). Successful democracy depends on education that enables informed participation—a kind of democratic teaching and learning.

Neither teachers nor teacher educators working in isolation can ensure such an education. They need to work together, and even then they need plenty of support. Thus, we have organized the book into two parts to address these groups. Part I speaks directly to teacher educators. Chapters 1 through 5 suggest how and why they might use case methods at preservice and in-service levels. Teaching with cases does not come naturally. The approach seems to run counter in some ways to conventional practice, as some of the chapters indicate. Even though we have taught with cases for some time, our colleagues in Part I help us think anew about many issues related to teaching and learning with cases.

Part II, chapters 6 through 12, contains the grist for Part I—that is, a set of cases. These are designed to stimulate active consideration of democratic teaching and learning in elementary and secondary schools across the land. The cases can be and have been used successfully with both preservice and in-service teachers. They will be helpful in testing the ideas advanced earlier in the book.

Beyond some practical considerations, we address both teachers and teacher educators in the same volume, because writing for them as separate audiences—particularly in a book concerned with educational democracy—seems disingenuous. We do not want to pass up this chance to acknowledge that we teachers and teacher educators are more like one another than we are different.

ACKNOWLEDGMENTS

We owe our thanks to several people in particular who supported our work. Rose Duhon Sells, former president of the Association of Teacher Educators (ATE), appointed the Commission on Case-Method Teaching and Learning and charged us to produce an edited volume on how case methods might be used to support teacher educators, teachers, and students to advance democracy in America's public schools. Gloria Chernay, executive director of ATE, made the machinery of the organization work to see us through to publication. Naomi Silverman, our editor at Lawrence Erlbaum Associates, challenged our assumptions with wit and clarified our thinking with wisdom born of rich experience in the publishing world. Sandy Davis processed lots of copy quickly, professionally, and with unfailing good humor. Debbie Ruel, senior production editor at Lawrence Erlbaum Associates, coordinated everyone's efforts.

I

USING CASE METHODS
IN TEACHER EDUCATION

1

Teaching Democracy Through Cases

Robert F. McNergney
University of Virginia

Edward R. Ducharme
Mary K. Ducharme
Drake University

Thomas Jefferson argued strongly for education that would make individuals free and enable citizens to ensure democracy. In 1786, he wrote to George Wythe, "No other sure foundation can be devised for the preservation of freedom and happiness. Preach a crusade against ignorance; establish and improve the law for educating the common people. Let our countrymen know that people alone can protect us against the evils [of misgovernment]" (Boyd, 1953). Despite the various, differing views of Jefferson that recent revisionist historians have promoted, his understanding of the necessity for powerful education to provide effective governance continues to ring true. Contemporary America badly needs citizens educated in the values of democracy and the practice of effective citizenship that Jefferson enjoined.

The link between education and democracy transcends the centuries. Fenstermacher (1997) observes:

> In these times, many educational policymakers and practitioners give little consideration to the critical links between education and democracy. While this nation is in the

midst of cultural hurricanes engendered by bitter divisions over race, language, religion, and moral values, educational policymakers force the debate over America's schools into a teapot of comparatively puny issues such as academic standards, measures of academic achievement, and getting all children ready for school (although with hardly a thought to the point and purpose of the school they are presumably getting ready for). (p. 61)

What schools should be preparing students for is life in a democracy. Thus, 200 years after Jefferson wrote so compellingly of the need for powerful education, educational spokespersons like Fenstermacher echo the challenge.

LEARNING THE GAME

Some teachers understand the challenge of helping people learn to participate in community life, the cornerstone of democracy. They know students must practice making decisions and living with the consequences if they are to do the same when they grow up. Young people, some teachers argue, need opportunities to tackle large, unwieldy problems outside themselves, fail, try again, and win once in a while if they are to participate in the larger society. The opportunities to participate must be genuine; the decisions must have meaning.

Students must recognize and engage in real opportunities to work together on common tasks that they and others care about. "Service education" and "volunteerism" aim to accomplish such objectives, but these largely extracurricular efforts often miss the chronically uninvolved students. These approaches also deal with symptoms, not causes of problems. The Key Club paints the day-care center in the low-income neighborhood; no one asks why this should be done with volunteer labor or who should pay for the paint. The Glee Club sings to senior citizens at the care center; no one asks if the seniors like vocalists or why they live in this place, at this time, under these conditions. Such projects are largely "good works" in the traditional Christian sense of the term, not opportunities for engaging in civic problems. On the other hand, current society offers little in the way of activities guaranteed to contribute specifically to the public good; perhaps anonymous social acts are the best that one can hope for in this age.

Arguably, the most powerful finding from educational research conducted in the last half century is the positive relationship between students' involvement and their learning (Brophy & Good, 1986). As students increase their involvement, their learning grows. Greene (1995) describes just how rich and varied attempts to stimulate such involvement can be:

If teaching can be thought of as an address to others' consciousness, it may be a summons on the part of one incomplete person to other incomplete persons to reach for wholeness. It may be a challenge to pose questions, to seek out explanations, to look for reasons, to construct meanings. It may be a provoking of dialogues within the classroom space: What has to be done to find out why Haiti has been under totalitarian control for so long? What can be done over time to document the phases of the moon? What kinds of studies are required to make sense of the immigration crisis today as compared with the crisis of 1900? How can we determine the validity of first-person accounts? (p. 26)

Nearly a century ago, Dewey advocated the joining of education and real life. Tanner (1997) draws lessons from Dewey's laboratory school that have important implications for what education must be about. Tanner points out that, for Dewey, "Working together in close association with others on an activity meant that one's own work contributed to a common purpose and could build lifelong habits" (p. 3). This book is dedicated to the cultivation of lifelong habits of inquiry, service, and citizenship. We believe strongly that involvement is necessary to promote potent learning.

The relationship between learning and involvement is so strong and positive that researchers sometimes use estimates of involvement as proxy measures for learning; that is, when they observe students involved, they assume these students are learning. To be sure, most researchers examine relationships between involvement and academic achievement, not the relationship between engagement and learning how to participate in society. But there is no particular reason to expect the relationship between student involvement in community life and learning about being a good community member to be any different from spending time thinking about math problems and learning how to do them successfully.

Teachers must help students learn how to become productively involved in their education. Such involvement does not come naturally to everyone. Teacher educators must help teachers develop so they both know how and want to help students become effective community members. Postman (1995) comments:

> You cannot have a democratic—indeed, civilized—community life unless people have learned how to participate in a disciplined way as part of a group. One might even say that schools have never been essentially about individualized learning. It is true, of course, that groups do not learn; individuals do. But the idea of a school is that individuals must learn in a setting in which individual needs are subordinated to group interests ... the classroom is intended to tame the ego, to connect the individual with others, to demonstrate the value and necessity of group interests. (p. 45)

Teachers and teacher educators must be exemplars of providing services that extend beyond their jobs. Case-method teaching and learning can help educators and students focus on key problems, work together effectively, and connect learning with reality. Such learning can affect students and teachers for the rest of their lives. Learning directed toward improving society and helping others is connected with the 1990s emphasis on character education. Dewey noted, "The much and commonly lamented separation in the schools between intellectual and moral training, between acquiring information and growth of character, is simply one expression of the failure to conceive and construct the school as a social institution, having social life and value within itself" (quoted in Tanner, 1997, p. 23).

Many critics of American schools see them as largely autocratic institutions in which students go mechanically through the tasks that teachers assign to them. Despite generations of reformers going back even before Dewey calling for more student participation in their education, teachers and principals generally lead systems that do little to promote individual student autonomy. Barely a day goes by without someone in the popular press complaining about how Deweyan followers have produced settings in which students do what they want and teachers do not teach important knowledge—a charge inconsistent with Dewey's own views of learning as well as the views of those who understand his writing. Concurrent with these frequent general accusations, informed visitors to classrooms see largely lecture instruction and rote learning activities, scarcely Deweyan principles of education. Despite the caricatures of schooling that appear in the press and other media, students are scarcely involved in matters of their own education. Cases can provide meaningful involvement for students as they begin to wrestle with the issues that powerful cases raise.

Students must be much more intimately involved in their learning if they are to become effective citizens in the world's greatest democracy. They must have learning opportunities enabling them to be highly active participants. Schools themselves must become little centers of democracy where all the residents—teachers, administrators, and students—learn about leading, following, governing, being governed, and all the other aspects of democracy. The use of cases can promote a more democratic classroom, one in which all have access to the judging and analyzing processes. In cases, there truly is no *correct* answer, only well-reasoned ones.

CASES AS COMMON TASKS

The development and effective use of cases in education can be a powerful mechanism for teacher educators, teachers, and students to become actively involved in issues that affect their lives. A case focuses people on a common situation—one full of specific, interconnected issues. The case, a slice of life, represents not an idealized situation, but a representation of the way life is. Typically, a case story line or sequence of events carries readers from beginning to end. Characters enter at various points and interact to evince a set of issues, dilemmas, and opportunities. In general, the more complex a case is, the better. Complexity permits multiple levels of analysis on sometimes competing but always realistic problems.

The dimension of reality may outweigh all others in terms of importance; that is, a case must appear to be an accurate and engaging representation of life if readers are to take it seriously. Researchers use the term *face validity* to connote the same idea. When people read a case, they must believe that "on its face" the case depicts a real situation. The more people believe the situation is one they might encounter, the more likely they will be to engage seriously in unraveling its complexities.

A good case can supply common interests—a prerequisite, as Postman (1995) notes, to the creation and maintenance of a disciplined group. A good case instructor can use that case in a classroom environment where members of the group feel free to entertain new or unusual ideas without fear of censure. A case can help prospective and practicing teachers to think differently about ways of thinking and knowing. It invites discussion and controversy. Because there are no "right" answers to case issues, both teachers and students are liberated from the tyranny of the right-answer syndrome. The instructor who creates classroom conditions of psychological safety can extend people's thinking about matters critical to living in a democracy: understanding differences, choosing from alternatives, helping fellow students, simulating ethical thinking and acting, learning about history and its implications for daily life. Cases examined thoroughly in such environments can help students take on the personae of others, understand the complexity of moral decisions, and test beliefs and myths against the realities of life.

Other professionals reached similar conclusions years ago. The use of cases to train professionals began at Harvard Law School in 1870 (Merseth, 1991). Christopher Columbus Langdell, head of the law school at the time, introduced case methods in response to pressure for the reform of legal education. The time for such innovation was right. The study of law was not yet viewed as a legitimate academic discipline in higher education. The legal literature was immense, disorganized, and thus confusing to students and faculty alike. The prevailing apprenticeship model of training lawyers threatened to the existence of formal academic training (McAninch, 1993). The case method succeeded at Harvard Law. By 1915, case study was the preferred method in the most respected law schools of the time (Merseth, 1991).

In 1893, the Johns Hopkins Medical School began a radical approach to medical education: students received 2 years of instruction in the basic sciences and laboratory work followed by 2 years of rigorous clinical training with bedside learning. In their clinical education, students followed the progress of a number of patients until they were discharged or died. Medical students at Johns Hopkins learned to examine, diagnose, and treat actual patients, and this hands-on approach to medical education provided the foundation for the case methodology still used in medical schools today (McAninch, 1993). The Johns Hopkins model was widely adopted, but medical educators also made extensive use of narrative descriptions of patient cases in medical classrooms during the past quarter century (Saunders, 1991).

In 1908, The Graduate School of Business Administration at Harvard instituted instruction via the case method. Case methodology emphasized classroom discussion based on real-life problems. Some 10 years later, Dean Wallace B. Donham committed the school to case methods, providing enough momentum to ensure sustained use through the present day (Merseth, 1991, 1996).

Until recently case methodology in education received only limited use. In 1864, Sheldon used cases to demonstrate the use of the project method in classrooms at the Fourth Annual Meeting of the National Teachers' Association (Doyle, 1990). In the 1920s, the New Jersey State Teacher's College at Montclair developed a systematic collection of cases that were studied at the program level (McAninch, 1993). Casebooks for teacher education and cases appearing in methods texts have marked the professional landscape for the last 50 years or so.

In 1954, Bush produced a casebook examining the teacher–pupil relationship, and in its introduction he wrote:

> We are inclined to the view that the case method—long used in medicine and law, and more recently in public administration and business—will in the coming decades be relied upon increasingly in the field of education, both in the pre-service and the in-service training of teachers and administrators. That it has not been adopted more rapidly is primarily due to the lack of adequate case records suitable for instructional purposes (p. vi).

By 1990, proponents of case methods had carved a small but growing niche in teacher education. In March of 1990, the use of teaching cases made the front page of *Education Week* in a story that proclaimed:

> Long established as a pedagogical approach in schools of law and business, the case-study method is increasingly being viewed as an equally powerful tool for the training of teachers. Beyond its usefulness for injecting reality into an "ivory tower" setting, the technique is seen as a way to make abstract theory come alive for prospective teachers and help them practice the critical-thinking skills needed to deal with the complex problems they will face on the job. (Viadero, p.1)

For a variety of reasons, cases have taken root in teacher education, but have not yet become the preferred mode of instruction. Broudy (1990) contends that teacher education has not developed problems so general and compelling that a core curriculum of cases could be formed. McAninch (1993) argues that the teacher education community has not reached a consensus on how teachers ought to think about cases; the lack of professional consensus impedes case use.

Kleinfeld (1990) contends that cases, through the use of vivid detail, help students learn that cause and effect in the social world is like cause and effect in the physical world. Cases also help students frame educational problems; that is, they view educational problems as complex and ambiguous, not as simple situations that lend themselves to simple solutions. Because they share responses to a given set of problems, students develop a wider repertoire of actions. Cases help students become emotionally prepared for difficult situations. "The teaching case helps students realize that the world is more complex than they expected it to be, and they become more prepared emotionally for a world where things do not always work out as students think they should" (Kleinfeld, 1990, p. 50).

DIFFERENT POINTS OF VIEW

Nothing characterizes the essential nature of democracy quite like the existence of multiple points of view. Writing on July 4th, William Raspberry (1997) described the state of the nation as one of a set of islands—sort of racial and cultural enclaves—from which people intermittently venture toward the cultural mainland of America. America "works" when people take the plunge and arrive successfully on the mainland. When a few make it and encourage those who stayed behind to join them, more are sure to follow.

Few professionals must accommodate different points of view as often or in more ways than do teachers. Figuratively speaking, they must be able to bring their students to common ground time and time again. Having 25 students in a room means there can be 25 views on every topic. Although no teacher can keep in mind the imagined perspectives of 25 students at once, all teachers can acknowledge and behave as though there are many perspectives in their classrooms. Teachers' interactions with parents reinforce the importance of being able to understand that others live and act with a set of values different from their own. The use of cases presenting the complexities of democracy can help students to begin the necessary changes that may result in a nation that not only sanctions its diversity but honors it.

Teaching through cases enables students to identify important issues and express different opinions in a safe environment. Often the lecture–recitation style of teaching and the rote learning it promotes discourage students from exploring alternative perspectives; students infer that learning is the acquisition of a common set of "facts" and a series of right answers to questions. They may learn not to question at all or assume that one right answer exists for every situation, independent of multiple points of view, interests, or values.

The success of case-method teaching and learning depends on the existence and recognition of different values. Values drive actions of characters in a case. Skillful instructors explore the characters' positions to stimulate reflection on case events. Sometimes they do so by making explicit otherwise implicit perspectives. For instance, in chapter 6 of this volume, the presence of Leslie Turner, the teacher, dominates the story. Readers can readily begin to understand how and why she behaves as she does. In contrast, the character identified only as "the principal" is less vivid, but may be no less important or influential than Ms. Turner. Similarly, in Hallenbeck's chapter, the off-scene administrators playing golf are central to the situation described. Careful case analysis can help teachers and students recognize such subtleties.

A seemingly minor character can be central to a case analysis—the principal who quietly orchestrates events in his or her building, the mother or father behind the scenes who pushes the child to excel at all costs, the colleague who needs desperately to please everyone. Any or all of these characters can play important if not immediately obvious roles in a case. The voices and perspectives of Raspberry's many enclaves can be heard, considered, and valued.

REASONED ACTIONS

Teachers, like other professionals, must take action based on the best knowledge at hand. Knowledge emanates from a variety of sources, not the least of which are classrooms themselves. These places where teachers make and derive the rationales for action, as Greene (1995) contends, offer many opportunities to stretch our conceptions of what it means "to know."

> Our classrooms ought to be nurturing and thoughtful and just all at once; they ought to pulsate with multiple conceptions of what it is to be human and alive. They ought to resound with the voices of articulate young people in dialogues always incomplete because there is always more to be discovered and more to be said. We must want our students to achieve friendship as each one stirs to wide-awakeness, to imaginative action, and to renewed consciousness of possibility. (Greene, 1995, p. 43)

There are, as Greene seems to imply, subtle dangers in advocating a kind of passionless, calculated action based on what we know. First, passably articulate but fundamentally goofy thinking sometimes masquerades as knowledge. The Facilitated Communication fiasco—bogus attempts to help autistic children reveal their innermost thoughts—comes immediately to mind (McNergney, 1995). The literature contains other examples of dubious "knowledge" cloaked in scientific gobbledygook used to justify a range of questionable actions.

Second, an appeal to reason often seems to squeeze out maverick behavior—the sort of action that defies convention but that works and that inspires innovation in the process. Postman (1995) correctly described the situation: "Because we are imperfect souls, our knowledge is imperfect. The history of learning is an adventure in overcoming our errors. There is no sin in being wrong. The sin is our unwillingness to examine our own beliefs, and in believing that our authorities cannot be wrong" (p. 128). Teaching and learning might be hopelessly mired in a torpor were it not for a few iconoclasts out there working against the grain.

Case-based teaching encourages students to think about why they might behave in certain ways in given situations. Case instructors urge students to seek empirical, theoretical, and practical ways of knowing not because they guarantee success, but because they are simply the best kinds of knowledge professionals normally have available. The case process has a way of making students hungry for information wherever they can find it—other informed sources, books, parents, studying the lives of children outside schools, etc. Professionals behave in certain ways because they have reasons for doing so. When those reasons are based on the best knowledge available, and the action that emanates from those reasons is competent, teachers are more likely to achieve desirable results.

IMPLICATIONS OF CASE-BASED LEARNING

Many, including Thomas Jefferson, have written of the need for an educated citizenry in a democracy. As a consequence of this perceived need, many and varied items have appeared in the curriculum. Hirsch, for example, suggests that the rote learning of certain facts, names, and events develops students for life in a 21st century democracy. We would not minimize the value of such knowledge; however, we believe much more than that is necessary. Students using the Leslie Turner case (chapter 6) cannot get far in their analysis without some substantive knowledge of the specific historical matters she uses in her class and wants students to study. This is an illustration of the use of facts in a specific context. Life in a democracy demands rich understanding of the contexts of facts and the historical implications. When students miss the facts and misinterpret concepts, they can miss the point entirely.

Submersion in a provocative case enables students to imagine things different from their own perspectives, to consider the implications of various policies or actions, and to learn of their peers' views. At the same time, they can—indeed, must—acquire knowledge and skills vital to living in a democracy. Cases can provoke students to face the many, often complex, demands of real life.

Cases too might affect when and how students use the knowledge they possess. Many young people frenetically make decisions when they are playing computer games in the privacy of their homes or in arcades. They decide, it seems almost intuitively, whether to "kill" this figure or that one. Little in the way of values considerations occur in these decisions. In other games, they decide which player will have the ball, which person will starve, which nation will thrive, and so forth. They make these decisions of no real consequence in isolation from others or, at most, with one or two other players. Effective use of cases in schools can force students to consider both actions and their implications for others. Teachers must provide young people with opportunities to work collaboratively, to share concerns about public and private issues, and to entertain questions of moment and meaning, even if only vicariously through collective analyses of cases. And teachers will not do so until they have had similar opportunities in their own professional preparation.

Implications for Teachers

A teacher can make the difference in students' lives. Curricular and instructional revisions and revolutions come and go, but the one-teacher-with-25-students model prevails. When the one teacher maintains an environment that is democratic—when the 25 participate and come to believe and act as though what they do matters to themselves and to others—chances for the 25 to live efficaciously and harmoniously in the larger world are improved.

Sounding as much like a history teacher as a president, Woodrow Wilson (cited in Ravitch, 1990) observed:

> When I look back on the processes of history, when I survey the genesis of America, I see this written over every page: that the nations are renewed from the bottom, not from the top; that the genius which springs up from the ranks of unknown men is the genius which renews the youth and energy of the people. Everything I know about history, every bit of experience and observation that has contributed to my thought, has confirmed me in the conviction that the real wisdom of human life is compounded out of the experiences of ordinary men.

Implications for Teacher Educators

If students of teaching must consider the likely effects of the actions they project in cases, then teacher educators too must consider the consequences of their use of cases to prepare people for lives in schools. Dewey (1910) might have foreshadowed such consequences when he discussed how educators deal with difficult situations in real life:

> Every vital activity of any depth and range inevitably meets obstacles in the course of its effort to realize itself—a fact that renders the search for artificial or external problems quite superfluous. The difficulties that present themselves with the development of an experience are, however, to be cherished by the educator, not minimized, for they are the natural stimuli to reflective inquiry. (64–65)

When teachers get some practice solving problems or cases, they learn how to learn from what they do—the best, most desirable consequence of all. The literature on teacher socialization suggests that the effects of much of what passes for teacher education today washes out after 2 or 3 years on the job. How much better if teacher educators could equip teachers with an attitude that problems were to be relished for what they would teach and could arm them with the skills to keep learning from real life.

This book presents cases and perspectives on the nature of case-method teaching and learning. We believe one of the main values of cases is that they enable individuals to connect with one another by focusing on common issues. In doing so, people learn about each other—another important benefit.

The cases in this text are the results of the teaching, experimenting, and writing of the authors. They contend that the cases are constantly in a state of evolution. What they submitted for publication is the present state of each case. As the authors use the cases in their teaching, however, they will undoubtedly continue to evolve. We urge you to read, study, and use the materials from this text. We also encourage you to write to the authors or e-mail them with your reactions to the cases, with descriptions of how you used them, and with examples of your own work with cases.

REFERENCES

Boyd, J. P. (Ed.). (1953). *The papers of Thomas Jefferson* (Vol. 10, pp. 243–245). Princeton, NJ: Princeton University Press.

Brophy, J. E., & Good, T. L. (1986). Teacher behavior and student achievement. In M. C. Wittrock (Ed.), *Handbook of research on teaching* (3rd ed., pp. 328–375). New York: Macmillan Publishing Company.

Broudy, H. S. (1990). Case studies—Why and how. *Teachers College Record, 91*(3), 449–461.

Bush, R. N. (1954). *The teacher–pupil relationship*. New York: Prentice-Hall.

Dewey, J. (1910). *How we think.* Lexington, MA: D.C. Heath.

Doyle, W. (1990). Case methods in the education of teachers. *Teacher Education Quarterly, 17*(1), 7–15.

Fenstermacher, G. (1997). The public purpose of education and schooling. In J. I. Goodlad & T. J. McMannon. (Eds.), *On restoring public and private life* (pp. 55–71). San Francisco: Jossey-Bass.

Greene, M. (1995). *Releasing the imagination.* San Francisco: Jossey-Bass.

Hirsch, E. D. (1996). *The schools we need and why we don't have them.* New York: Doubleday.

Kleinfeld, J. (1990). The special virtues of the case method in preparing teachers for minority schools. *Teacher Education Quarterly, 17*(1), 43–51.

McAninch, A. R. (1993). *Teacher thinking and the case method.* New York: Teachers College Press.

McNergney, R. F. (1995, February). Facilitator communication. *NEA Today,* p. 20.

Merseth, K. (1991). The early history of case-based instruction: Insights for teacher education today. *Journal of Teacher Education, 42*(4), 243–249.

Merseth, K. K. (1996). Cases and case methods in teacher education. In J. Sikula, T. Buttery, & E. Guyton (Eds.), *Handbook of research on teacher education: A project of the Association of Teacher Educators*(pp. 722–744). New York: Macmillan.

Postman, N. (1995). *The end of education: Redefining the value of education.* New York: Knopf.

Raspberry, W. (1997, July 4). Will system let blacks over color line? *The Daily Progress,* p. A6.

Saunders, S. L. (1991). *Evaluating a videotaped case of a beginning elementary school teacher and describing its use.* Unpublished dissertation, University of Virginia.

Tanner, L. (1997). *Dewey's laboratory school: Lessons for today.* Albany, NY: SUNY Press.

Viadero, D. (1990, March 28). Teacher educators turn to case-study method. *Education Week,* pp. 1, 18, 19.

Wilson, W. T. (1990). The American reader: Words that moved a nation. In D. Ravitch (Ed.), *The new freedom* (pp. 224–228). New York: HarperCollins.

2

Organizing Instruction for Case-Based Teaching

Mary R. Sudzina
University of Dayton

Editors' note: Case-method teaching is not meant for every course or every instructor. Mary Sudzina draws attention to many benefits of cases, but she also alerts potential users to the kinds of constraints they may face when teaching with cases and the decisions they must make to be successful. Cases must fit the course organization, content, and goals. When selecting cases, instructors must think about the sources of cases and the formats in which they are written. Both the presentation and discussion of a case can influence how students think about teaching and learning in a democratic classroom and ultimately how they might construct and maintain such environments.

Cases, as "slices of classroom life," offer preservice teachers challenging opportunities to experience situations vicariously and to reflect on educational issues that teachers face in today's classrooms (see Sudzina, 1999). Case analysis and discussions about cases can lead to preservice teachers' conceptual understandings and higher order thinking skills (Levin, 1995; Lundeberg & Fawver, 1994; Sudzina & Kilbane, 1992), reflection and collaboration (McNergney, Herbert, & Ford, 1994), advanced research and technology skills (Sudzina, 1995, 1996, 1997), increased retention of course content (Allen, 1994), and advanced moral reasoning (Allen, 1995). Case methods attempt to bridge the gap between theory and practice in teacher education (see McAninch, 1993; Shulman, 1992) through democratic teaching and learning activities. Teaching with cases requires that teacher educators plan for instruction and learning in ways that differ from traditional classroom experiences.

In traditional instruction, the teacher educator acts as the instructional leader and content expert, selecting a specific body of material for students to learn. The primary pedagogical format is usually lecture, coupled with assessment that relies on objective test measures including multiple choice, matching, and sentence completion test items. There is usually only one correct answer to a given question. Students must master much of the information by memorizing and comprehending it, but not necessarily by applying and synthesizing it. Teacher educators often have few clues about student misconceptions or gaps in content and comprehension other than incorrect test answers. When this kind of information does become available, it is often too late in the semester for the teacher educator to challenge or influence student misconceptions and attitudes. The traditional approach to instruction does little to foster students' abilities to reason democratically or to make fair and considered choices.

Case-based teaching, on the other hand, is a *constructivist* approach to instruction (see Sudzina, 1997). The teacher acts as a facilitator and mentor, helping students to examine a wide range of perspectives in an unfamiliar situation. Both the teacher and the student create meaning from the case information. Prior experiences, history, and knowledge affect how students grasp the issues and formulate actions in a specific case issue. Although some responses are better than others, there is typically no one correct answer to a given situation. The appropriateness of the response, the context of the situation, and the personalities of the case participants all play an important part in "what works."

Case-based teaching may appear to be more loosely organized and less demanding than traditional instruction. The students are more actively involved in the material than they are in traditional classes, and the teacher facilitates and shapes class discussion as needed, rather than lecturing for the entire class period. Case-based teaching is actually more difficult to do well because "learning to guide students into genuine understanding is *much more* sophisticated and demanding" (Eggen & Kauchek, 1994). In addition to communicating content, teachers using cases must also anticipate and mediate a wide range of student responses to issues. Teachers must also relinquish some control in their classrooms. Some teachers must curb their natural tendencies to take charge and direct the student case discussion by offering their own insights and opinions. Students can learn many important lessons about teaching—and life —when they struggle with the often messy and inexact nature of real classroom dilemmas. They learn that few problems are as simple as they initially appear and that easy solutions or "quick fixes" rarely result in satisfactory long-term outcomes for the teacher or the students (Sudzina, 1999).

The effectiveness of the case study method relies on the capacity of the case to generate student interest and the skill of the instructor to create a democratic environment for class discussion. Wassermann (1993, 1994) suggests that instructors must know the case, know the issues, prepare good questions in advance, know their students, know themselves, and gather relevant follow-up activities. From my own experience, organizing instruction for successful case-based teaching involves: case selection and case integration within the curriculum; instructor familiarity with skills of case analysis, discussion, and debriefing; and decisions about case applications, objectives, and outcomes.

PREPARING TO TEACH WITH CASES

Many decisions must be considered when integrating cases into the teacher preparation curriculum. First, the instructor must review course organization, content, and objectives for an appropriate match with case-based instruction. Second, the instructor must identify or write cases reflecting course goals and/or content. Finally, the instructor must review, and, if possible, practice strategies for teaching with cases before introducing cases into teacher preparation classes.

Course Considerations

Case-method teaching is a labor-intensive process. Teaching with cases requires time to analyze, discuss, reflect, and debrief case issues. Instructors must consider the length of the term, the number of times the class meets, and the length of the class session in determining the number of cases to analyze. Instructors must also decide when to assign cases and how much time to allot to class discussion. Assigning cases for research and analysis before class and using one or more uninterrupted class periods for discussion and debriefing often are more effective than analyzing cases "cold" in one or several brief time periods. When cases are assigned in advance, class discussion, interaction, and problem solving appear to be more thoughtful (Sudzina, Kowalski, & Weaver, 1994).

Course goals may include increased student collaboration and class participation, increased reflection and problem-solving skills, specific research and presentation skills, and the applications of a particular body of knowledge to issues such as cultural diversity, classroom management, and, as in the case of this text, educating for democracy. The reasons for using cases, their characteristics, and the students to be taught can affect how cases are integrated into the curriculum, facilitated, and evaluated. Some students, particularly traditional undergraduate students who test extremely well on objective tests, may balk at the inexact and unpredictable nature of case analysis and the teacher's new role as facilitator. Students may feel frustrated as they are asked to shift their cognitive focus from a memorization to a problem-solving orientation (Mostert & Sudzina, 1996).

Case Selection

A variety of case study texts highlight educational dilemmas (i.e., Kauffman, Hallahan, Mostert, Nuttycombe, & Trent, 1993; Kowalski, Weaver, & Henson,

1994; Silverman, Welty, & Lyon, 1992; Sudzina, 1999). Other resources include a case-based course on the World Wide Web (Herbert & McNergney, 1998). Instructors should consider case content, length, and complexity, and the number of the cases to be discussed over the course of the quarter or semester. A quick rule of thumb is to teach no more than one case a week. The usual time and content constraints of most courses prohibit serious consideration of more cases.

This text contains cases to foster teacher and student thinking about personal rights and freedoms in a democracy. These cases can be used to examine how everyday events become the objects of ongoing conversations about education in a democratic society. Instructors could also write their own cases about local issues (see Shulman, 1992), or have students write cases about issues and dilemmas encountered in schools (Sudzina, 1993; Sudzina & Kilbane, 1992). In these instances, the instructor and the students create the curriculum.

Teaching With Cases

Unfortunately, cases do not teach themselves. Even the most engaging case will fail to elicit thoughtful student discussion if the instructor is unprepared. Although teaching notes are helpful, instructors usually teach a case a few times before they become familiar with it. Practice helps instructors to deal with the variety and depth of case issues and perspectives and to anticipate the kinds of responses students might offer. When cases are assigned at least a week ahead of time, students have opportunities to think about the issues and prepare themselves for case discussion.

One way to initiate case discussion is to ask students to give a synopsis of their interpretation of the case. As students describe the issues, perceptions, and possible courses of action, the instructor writes these on the chalkboard or on newsprint. Part of the skill of case facilitation is to elicit as many different issues, perceptions, and solutions as possible without making value judgments. Questions such as: "Are there other ways that event might be interpreted?", "Can you explain how one might arrive at another assessment?", and "Are there any other details that might be important to help us understand this case?" can prompt students to think about the issues rather than jump to simplistic or hasty conclusions.

Instructors who generate good class discussions ask the *who, what, why, when*, and *where* questions and avoid interjecting their personal and professional opinions. Instructor opinions can control and direct the outcomes of case discussion. Part of guiding a discussion in useful directions depends on an instructor's ability to decide which comments are relevant and which ones are not. Students naturally make connections and discuss their own experiences in related situations; however, personal and anecdotal reflections often become tangential rather quickly. A savvy instructor helps keep the focus of the discussion on the case facts and issues at hand.

An instructor can intervene in case discussion to help students recognize an obvious issue, perspective, or solution that is integral to the case. An instructor might say, "When I look at all the issues (perspectives, actions) listed here, I wonder why no one has mentioned _____." Students sometimes need prompting when they are uncomfortable or reluctant to discuss certain issues, such as those involving bias, prejudice, or inequity in the classroom or in society. Instructors who teach democratically can model how to frame difficult questions, seek information, and communicate with others about sensitive issues.

Debriefing a case is similar to case analysis except that students have already prepared their analysis of the case beforehand. The instructor and students collaboratively examine the evidence related to case issues, perspectives, actions, and consequences to decide what might constitute "best practice." Knowledge about relevant theory and research often become foci in determining the feasibility and appropriateness of actions.

As preservice teachers become more experienced with case analysis, they become more reflective and less likely to settle on inappropriate courses of action. They understand that there is more than one way to approach an issue and that some responses have a greater chance of success than others. They also come to realize that what may work for them may not work for someone else. These subtleties can frustrate students unfamiliar with a democratic environment who are excellent test takers and are used to— and who expect—the instructor to be the main source of course information and the authority in decision making (Sudzina & Kilbane, 1992).

Case Analysis

Organizing for case-based teaching means having a plan to facilitate case analysis, discussion, and debriefing. The following conceptual framework can be applied across content areas, educational issues, and levels of instruction.

A Five-Step Process for Case Analysis. McNergney, Herbert, and their colleagues offer a five-step process for analyzing cases (McNergney et al., 1994; Sudzina, 1996; Sudzina & Kilbane, 1994). The five steps, based on Dewey's (1933) work, are sometimes referred to collectively as a process of reflection. Reflection, according to Dewey, involves defining a problem for oneself in one's own terms before moving, often uncertainly, to a solution. The five steps include the following:

- Identifying the issues and facts in a case.
- Considering the perspectives or values of the actors in a case.
- Identifying professional knowledge— knowledge from practice, theory, and/or research—that might be brought to bear in crafting a course of action.
- Projecting actions that might be taken in a case.
- Forecasting likely consequences, both positive and negative, of particular actions.

There are several benefits to applying this conceptual framework to case analysis. The steps mirror the developmental process of case analysis. The framework can be applied to any case dilemma. The steps provide an objective point of reference for addressing issues in field experiences. Ultimately, the steps provide a model for solving classroom problems as they occur.

I usually introduce this framework early in the semester, with a handout. I demonstrate how it is used to shape thinking about educational dilemmas, from the identification of the issues through the possible consequences of particular actions. I often assign a short and controversial case, such as *Out of Bounds* (Kowalski, Weaver, & Henson, 1994) for students to read over the weekend. Embedded in this case are issues that I will discuss in my educational psychology class over the course of the semester. These include: classroom management, discipline, motivation, intercultural communication, sexual harassment, and group learning. This case sets up the relevance of the course content in dealing with "real life" educational problems.

As a warm-up to learning about case analysis, I ask each student to rank the following for the case: three most important issues, three most important perspectives, three most relevant areas of research, three most appropriate actions, and three likely outcomes as a consequence of their actions. Each student shares his or her perceptions, and I list them on the chalkboard, along with the frequencies of the responses.

Assessing students' responses can be an enlightening experience. Although all the students read the same case, they all do not see the issues and perspectives in the same way. We often have 10 to 15 different responses for every item in a class of 25 to 30 students. Such results surprise preservice teachers, who assume their peers perceive classroom dilemmas in similar ways. I use this opportunity to reinforce the idea of multiple perspectives. I also like to see and hear what students think about certain issues without the pressures of formal evaluation. These sessions help me decipher student information gaps, disagreements, and misconceptions.

After presenting the framework, I use a handout that states my expectations for the written analyses and oral presentations that students give at the end of the semester. I assign cases to groups of two to five students. I also review the case analysis framework in class to make sure everyone understands what to look for in a case.

Identifying the Facts and Issues.   I ask students to brainstorm among themselves and list all the issues they can identify. They also examine and list facts in the case, deciding which are relevant and irrelevant. Then they must decide among themselves the most important issues, and of those, which need immediate attention and which might be resolved at a later date. Regarding those issues requiring immediate attention, students must decide if they would be willing and able to take action.

Identifying Perspectives and Values.   Role plays help students recognize multiple points of view in a case. Many undergraduates initially tend to identify with the perspectives of the student or the teacher in a case (Mostert & Sudzina, 1996). When students take the roles of nontraditional students, parents, or a principal, they can often "hear" the dialogue, and imagine the motivations, values, and perspectives behind the words of each of the players in the situation.

Identifying Professional Knowledge.   After identifying the case issues and perspectives, I encourage students to review literature relevant to the case. Left to their own devices, most students tend to shoot from the hip, or limit themselves to the resources at hand. I want them to explore the knowledge on various issues in the cases.

I require an on-line review of the literature, using ERIC on the Internet or one of the Netscape search engines such as Infosearch, Altavista, or Yahoo. I do so for several reasons: to increase student research and inquiry skills; to facilitate using technology as a tool to access expert opinions and/or the most current information on a topic; to get students in the habit of accessing resources to inform their practice; and to promote problem solving that involves the breadth of resources available on a given topic. I caution students not to accept everything they read, but to weigh the evidence in light of their own experiences, their peers' and others' expertise, and the circumstances of the case.

Formulating Actions.   Projected actions should be realistic—actions that students would be capable of undertaking as the teacher in the case. Again, role play can be a catalyst in helping students hear how their proposed actions might be received by the other participants in a case. I often demonstrate how the style and phrasing of one's speech can be just as important as its substance. The reverse is also true—the "correct" words can be said, but if they are vapid, the result can be a loss of credibility and diminished capacity to effect change. Language, communication skills, and nonverbal behavior all should be considered in terms of their effects on the choices of action and probable outcomes.

Considering the Consequences of Actions.   Even the most carefully reasoned actions may not have the desired consequences because of factors beyond the control of the teacher. In addition to offering their best solutions, students must recognize that for every action there is always a "best case" and "worst case" scenario. The actual result may well lie somewhere in between and might satisfy all or none of those involved. I encourage students to formulate contingency plans for a variety of responses from others in the case. What may seem obvious to one person may be totally overlooked by another. I caution students not to assume anything, but to be clear about what they think and the reasons for their particular choices.

Case Applications

Case-based teaching offers opportunities to integrate assignments, skills, and activities into a teacher education program.

Assignments and Activities.   Initially, an instructor may want to select cases that highlight particular issues and concepts, such as the rights of students and teachers in a democracy, and then space them throughout a course. The content of one case can provide background for the next case. One or two class periods per week might be spent on theory and content, and the other class period might be devoted to application of theory and content to a related case. The instructor could assume primary responsibility for orchestrating the case analyses or share these duties with students. Cases can also be introduced at midterm or later in the semester, after sufficient content has been taught and tested (Allen, 1994; Sudzina, 1993). The possibilities vary with course goals, time, content, and organization.

After the instructor has modeled case analysis, preservice teachers can select favorite cases from an assigned text or list of instructor-approved cases, analyze these cases, and present them for class discussion as a culminating assignment for the semester. Evaluation criteria can be based on the five categories in the conceptual framework for case analysis. A Likert scale, with scoring categories ranging from excellent to poor, can be constructed for each item and distributed in class. (I also add an additional item to assess case presentation skills.) The instructor and students can apply these criteria and provide feedback. After each case presentation, the appropriate space is checked off by students and faculty, and scores are tallied for each item. This approach is effective in guiding preservice teachers to think critically about what constitutes worthwhile case analysis and to focus on how to communicate that information to others.

Assignments can range from simply reading a case and preparing notes to developing full-blown case presentations including video, audio, powerpoint, overheads, activities, handouts, reviews of the research, and role-playing. Written analysis can range from a simple outline to an in-depth analysis complete with theoretical explanations and research citations. It is helpful for the instructor to model presenting one or two cases for overall class analysis and discussion before assigning groups of students to work independently on cases of their own choosing.

I also have students write their own case studies on pupils that they observed and/or tutored in field placements, being careful to protect confidentiality. Sometimes students describe a classroom dilemma they observed in the field, using the same format as the cases that they are studying in class (see Sudzina, 1993; Sudzina & Kilbane, 1992).

The social organization of the classroom in case analysis is also important. Case assignments can call for individualistic, cooperative, collaborative, or competitive goal structures, or any combination of the above. Cooperative and collaborative problem-solving strategies (see Johnson, Johnson, Holubec, & Roy, 1988; Slavin,

1995) should be taught directly to undergraduate preservice teachers because few are familiar with the specific concepts and organizational strategies needed for successful group or team learning (Mostert & Sudzina, 1996; Sudzina & Kilbane, 1994). The most effective group size for team analysis is usually four to five, although groups can be as small as three, or as large as six.

Cooperative and collaborative groups work well and offer much flexibility for classes that meet frequently. Independent case analysis can be productive for pretest and posttest assessment of issues and content. Competitive goal structures, such as case competition, can offer an additional positive professional development dimension when implemented within groups that have already mastered cooperative and collaborative case analysis and research skills (see McNergney et al., 1994; Sudzina, 1994b, 1995; Sudzina & Kilbane, 1994).

Case Competitions. A specific application of case studies applied to teacher preparation, the educational case competition can extend the boundaries of professional preparation beyond the confines of institutional walls and teacher preparation programs. Case competitions usually involve diverse teams of preservice teachers from two or more institutions that meet in person or on the Internet to analyze a case. The team with the most defensible analysis can be designated the winner. Or teams can compete against a set of external standards for case analysis. Such a criterion-referenced strategy offers opportunities to designate more than one top analysis.

However, winning is not the only or even primary motivation for preservice participation in a case competition. Incentives include opportunities to work with mentors, to participate in community building activities, to develop advanced writing, research, and technological skills, and to engage in dialogues about professional practice with experts and fellow preservice teachers and teacher educators at other institutions. A team of undergraduate preservice teachers from the University of Dayton participated in the Second Commonwealth Center Invitational Team Case Competition, held at the University of Virginia over 4 days in May 1993. I was their faculty advisor. Other participating teams included the University of Calgary, Hampton University, the University of Hawaii, and the University of Vermont. As a result of that experience, I suggest the following activities (see also Sudzina, 1994a, 1994b; Sudzina & Kilbane, 1994).

Because a criterion for team selection in the competition was that the team members be as "diverse" as possible to capitalize on multiple points of view, the Dayton team viewed team-building exercises as extremely valuable. For a team to work well together, a certain amount of familiarity, camaraderie, and trust must be developed. In preparation for the competition, we held "working dinners" in the student union that allowed members to share their career aspirations, family backgrounds, and areas of expertise with each other. Team members attended additional classes together that used case studies to test informally their skills of analysis and to critique case presentations. They audiotaped problem-solving sessions and then listened to the tapes to reflect on each other's contributions and areas of expertise. This is an excellent technique to use any time when helping teams of preservice teachers learn to listen to each other without interrupting and assess areas of strength and weakness in case analysis.

The University of Dayton team also dined together at their faculty advisor's house one weekend and analyzed videotapes from the previous year's competition. On another weekend, the team met in the library for 5 hours to simulate the conditions and time constraints of the written part of the case competition. The team presented its oral analysis to the Honors/Scholars section of a case-based educational psychology class, where class members acted as competition judges and provocateurs. Individuals were challenged to put aside personal differences to achieve team synergy. This process of working closely together resulted in a strong team identity among members. An unexpected outcome was the close personal relationships that developed among this diverse group of students.

The University of Virginia Commonwealth Center case competition proved to be a highlight of these preservice teachers' professional experiences (Sudzina, 1994b). Although the Dayton team did not win the competition, members expressed feelings of accomplishment. They observed others as role models and gained a heightened sense of what was possible to achieve as professionals. They wrote about the case competition (Sudzina & Kilbane, 1994), presented a panel about their experiences at a national conference (Sudzina, Ahlgren, Damon, Miller, & Young, 1993), and hosted a regional case competition at the University of Dayton the next year.

University of Dayton preservice teachers tied with University of Virginia students in the first virtual case competition on the Internet in April 1994. They also participated in another virtual case competition the next year conducted over the World Wide Web (see McNergney & Kent, 1995). These competitions were extracurricular, requiring that students participate in their free time. They had to acquire the requisite technological skills including e-mailing, word processing, and accessing Internet and World Wide Web sites. The University of Virginia provided the technological support and Internet and Web sites for these competitions.

During the Fall 1995 semester, Robert McNergney at the University of Virginia and I conducted a virtual case competition on the World Wide Web between two of our regular undergraduate foundations courses. The preservice teachers at both institutions divided themselves into teams and "met" on the Web by posting their photos and short biographies. The competition schedule, case dilemma, team responses, and judges' comments were all posted to a specific Web address (see McNergney, Kent, & Sudzina, 1995). All case responses were subjected to blind review. Students at both institutions then read each others' analyses and the judges' comments. Course feedback and student evaluations about this experiences were overwhelmingly positive.

Case-based teaching and case competition have come full circle in my classes, from an external enrichment experience for a few students to an integrated set of case assignments, with Web experiences, for all of my students. Preservice teachers at the University of Daytona now seek out case competition experiences. They see them as opportunities to test what they know against an "ideal" solution and to be involved in an intense mentoring experience. They like the idea of testing the very best that they have to offer in a safe, nonthreatening setting. They also enjoy working with other like-minded preservice teachers while increasing their technological and professional expertise. Access to the Internet allows case competition participants and individuals in other preservice courses and disciplines to meet on the Internet to share ideas and discuss issues they will ultimately face on the job.

SUMMARY

Case-based teaching offers teacher educators and preservice teachers opportunities to grapple with the real-life dilemmas that educators, parents, students, and administrators face in today's society. There is reason to believe that preservice teachers are better able to solve problems, collaborate, investigate, and retain course content when exposed to the case-study method. Unlike most traditional instruction, the role of the instructor in this democratic approach to teaching and learning is that of a facilitator, mentor, and guide to student learning. Students actively construct knowledge and meaning mediated by their own prior experiences and backgrounds. Teaching with cases requires some adjustments in the way course content is organized, facilitated, and evaluated in teacher education programs.

Organizing instruction for case-based teaching involves case selection and case integration within the curriculum, familiarity with skills of case analysis, discussion, and debriefing, and decisions about case applications, objectives, and outcomes. Presenting an excellent case does not necessarily guarantee an excellent case discussion. An instructor's ability to lead and facilitate a case discussion, based on a plan for analysis, makes or breaks a case discussion.

McNergney et al. (1994) offer a five-step approach to case analysis that can be applied across content areas and educational issues. This framework involves: (a) identifying the issues and facts in a case, (b) considering the perspectives of the actors (e.g., teacher, students, parents, principal) involved in a case, (c) identifying professional knowledge (practice, theory, and research) that is relevant to the problems in the case, (d) forecasting and formulating actions that might be taken, and (e) considering the likely positive and negative consequences of projected actions.

Cases can be custom-tailored to course topics and contemporary issues. An instructor can assign cases to complement course content and students can select cases to research and present for class discussion. Case analyses can be evaluated by the instructor, subject to peer evaluation, or evaluated by a panel of outside judges. The format of case analysis and presentations can be written, oral, or hypermedia, utilizing the Internet or World Wide Web. Teaching with cases offers the instructor and students multiple possibilities to work together to propose solutions to the most pressing educational problems in our schools and society.

REFERENCES

Allen, J. (1994). A research study to investigate the development of reflective thought processes of preservice teachers through the use of case studies in educational psychology courses. In H. E. Klein (Ed.), *Learning the doing–doing the learning: The art of interactive teaching.* Needham, MA: World Association for Case Method Research and Application.

Allen, J. (1995). *Case studies as a method of instruction to develop reflective pedagogical thinking of preservice teachers in an educational psychology course.* Unpublished manuscript, The College of St. Rose, Albany, NY.

Dewey, J. (1933). *How we think.* Boston: Heath.

Eggen, P., & Kauchek, D. (1994). *Educational psychology: Classroom connections (2nd ed.).* New York: Merrill/Macmillian.

Herbert, J., & McNergney, R. (1998). *CaseNET: Internet-based courses for teachers and other educators.* [On-line]. Available: http://CaseNET.edschool.virginia.edu.

Johnson, D. W., Johnson, R. T., Holubec, E. J., & Roy, P. (1988). *Circles of learning (2nd ed.).* Alexandria, VA: Association for Supervision and Curriculum Development.

Kauffman, J., Hallahan, D., Mostert, M., Nuttycombe, D., & Trent, S. (1993). *Managing classroom behavior: A reflective case-based approach.* Boston: Allyn & Bacon.

Kowalski, T., Weaver, R., & Henson, K. (1994). *Case studies of beginning teachers.* New York: Longman.

Levin, B. (1995). Using the case method in teacher education: The role of discussion and experience in teachers' thinking about cases. *Teaching and Teacher Education,* 11(1), 63–79.

Lundeberg, M. A., & Fawver, J. (1994). Thinking like a teacher: Encouraging cognitive growth in case analysis. *Journal of Teacher Education,* 45(4), 289–297.

McAninch, A. R. (1993). *Teacher thinking and the case method: Theory and future directions.* New York: Teachers College Press.

McNergney, R. (1995). *Project Cape Town: Education and integration in South Africa.* [On-line]. Available: http://curry.edschool.virginia.edu/go/capetown.

McNergney, R., Herbert, J., & Ford, R. (1994). Cooperation and competition in case-based teacher education. *Journal of Teacher Education,* 45(5), 339–345.

McNergney, R., & Kent, T. (1995). *Virtual case competition.* [On-line]. Available: http://teach.virginia.edu/~casecomp.

McNergney, R., Kent, T., & Sudzina, M. (1995). *University of Virginia-University of Dayton dual case competition.* [On-line]. Available: http://curry.edschool.virginia.edu/~casecomp/dual.

Mostert, M., & Sudzina. M. (1996, November). *Undergraduate case method teaching: Pedagogical assumptions vs. the real world.* Paper presented at the annual meeting of the Association of Teacher Educators, St. Louis, MO.

Shulman, J. (Ed.). (1992). *Case methods in teacher education.* New York: Teachers College Press.

Silverman, R., Welty, W., & Lyon, S. (1992). *Case studies for teacher problem solving.* New York: McGraw-Hill.

Slavin, R. (1995). *Cooperative learning (2nd ed.).* Boston: Allyn & Bacon.

Sudzina, M. (1993). *Dealing with diversity issues in the classroom: A case study approach.* Paper presented at the annual meeting of the Association of Teacher Educators, Los Angeles. (ERIC Document Reproduction Service No. ED 354 233).

Sudzina, M. (1994a, February). *Mentoring and collaborating with cases: Developing the skills and resources to compete in a national case competition.* Paper presented at the annual meeting of the Association of Teacher Educators, Atlanta. (ERIC Document Reproduction Service No. ED 374 124)

Sudzina, M. (1994b, October). *Consequences of preservice participation in a national case competition.* Paper presented at the annual meeting of the Mid-Western Educational Research Association, Chicago. (ERIC Document Reproduction Service No. ED 376 161)

Sudzina, M. (1995, April). *Case competition as a catalyst to restructure the teaching and learning of educational psychology.* Paper presented at the annual meeting of the American Educational Research Association, San Francisco. (ERIC Document Reproduction Service No. ED 382 683)

Sudzina, M. (1996, February). Integrating cases and technology. *The teaching of educational psychology: Trends, emerging issues, and new ideas.* Symposium conducted at the annual meeting of the Eastern Educational Research Association, Boston, MA.

Sudzina, M. (1997). Case study as a constructivist pedagogy for teaching educational psychology. *Educational Psychology Review, 9*(2), 199–218.

Sudzina, M. (Ed.). (1999). *Case study applications in teacher education: Cases of teaching and learning in the content areas.* Boston: Allyn & Bacon.

Sudzina, M., Ahlgren, K., Damon, K., Miller, B., & Young, M. (1993, October). *Competition, collaboration and case-based teaching: Reflections from an invitational team case competition.* Panel presentation, annual JCT Conference on Curriculum Theory and Classroom Practice, The University of Dayton, Bergamo Center, Dayton, OH.

Sudzina, M., & Kilbane, C. (1992). Applications of a case study text to undergraduate teacher preparation. In H. Klein (Ed.), *Forging new partnerships with cases, simulations, games, and other interactive methods.* Needham, MA: World Association for Case Method Research and Application. (ERIC Document Reproduction Service No. ED 350 292)

Sudzina, M., & Kilbane, C. (1994). New contexts for educational case study application: From the classroom to competition and beyond. In H. E. Klein (Ed.) *Learning the doing—doing the learning: The art of interactive teaching.* Needham, MA: World Association for Case Method Research and Application. (ERIC Document Reproduction Service No. ED 374 121)

Sudzina, M., Kowalski, T., & Weaver, R. (1994, June). *Case-based teaching: Reflecting on teacher education practices across content areas at two universities.* Symposium conducted at the annual meeting of the World Association for Case Method Research and Application, Montreal.

Wassermann, S. (1993). *Getting down to cases: Learning to teach with case studies.* New York: Teachers College Press.

Wassermann, S. (1994). *Introduction to case method teaching: A guide to the galaxy.* New York: Teachers College Press.

3

Making Connections: The Democratic Classroom and the Internet

Todd W. Kent
Princeton University

Editors' note: A. J. Liebling, noted journalist, said that the way to make sure you have freedom of the press is to own one. Democracy depends on access, and nothing provides access quite like the power of the press and the money to make it operate. Todd Kent makes evident how emerging technologies create access to mass communication for both the common man and every other common and uncommon person out there with a computer. But with the special opportunities of open access to instruments of mass communication come new problems. His case raises a range of issues that any teacher who is promoting student use of the Internet might have to face at one time or another. He suggests how technology can enhance democratic life in classrooms and describes possible implications of the use of new technologies for teacher education.

This case portrays issues involved with introducing the Internet into a classroom. Although making Internet connections is important, the most important issues underlying any use of educational technology are the human issues. Educators are most interested in how teachers and children are using specific technologies, rather than in what specific technologies they are using. This case illustrates how classroom teachers can make classrooms more democratic through electronic connections.

In June 1996, in a federal court decision overturning regulations intended to restrict the transmission of indecent material on the Internet, a unanimous three-judge federal panel in Philadelphia declared the Internet "the most participatory marketplace of mass speech that this country—and indeed the world—has yet seen" (Lewis, 1996). The need for free and active participation, a core notion of democracy, was embodied in this decision and later upheld by the U.S. Supreme Court. Firestone and Kopp (1994) further explore this connection between participation and the Internet: "The goals and workings of democratic societies can be variously expressed. We find that five core values must be balanced in one degree or another by the workings of government. The first four are liberty, equality, community, and efficiency. In each case, promotion of one value can take away from one or more of the others. A democratic process must also involve participatory access, a value that can enhance each of the others" (p. 19). Firestone and Kopp (1994) also state that, in regard to the Internet, "Universal access is a core concept, fostering both equity and liberty." If the judges are correct in their description of the Internet as an unprecedented market place for free speech, educators must examine their responsibility in educating students in its use. The education community must find a way to allow all children to participate actively in the Internet without falling prey to the distractions of an environment of free speech that includes inappropriate or low-quality material currently protected under the law. Public education has the potential to help ensure that access is not restricted to those children whose families can financially afford it.

Telecommunication technology in education can help build responsive communities of democratic discourse. The relationship between technology and democratic classrooms occurs on several levels. Harris (1994) describes four basic types of exchanges possible on the Internet: person-to-person; person-to-group; person-to-computer; and person-to-information archive. These four categories can be condensed into two general reasons people use the Internet: to access other people or to access information or services. Both of these functions are key components to a thriving democracy. In regard to the access of information and democracy, Jefferson (1810) stated that: "No one more sincerely wishes the spread of information among mankind than I do, and none has greater confidence in its effect towards supporting free and good government" (p. 387). In many other instances, Jefferson stated that the strength of a democracy resides in a well informed public.

The Internet allows individuals to publish information without the constraints of conventional publishing routes. Salvador (1994) observes that: " … many educators would argue that the value of the Internet does not lie merely in its ability to connect students to large amounts of content, which, incidentally, is already there without the help of traditional publishers, in the form of hundreds of data bases on every conceivable subject. Rather, say active on-line educators, the true value of the Internet lies in its ability to let students create and instantly share content themselves" (p. 38). Individuals' abilities to use the Internet to communicate with wide ranging audiences support another basic tenet of democratic education: free discourse among the members of the democratic community.

The importance of such discourse is emphasized in a model of democracy John Dewey advocated. Dewey (1916) proposed two basic elements in describing the Democratic Ideal: members of the community must have a large number of shared and mutual interests; there should also be free interaction between social groups resulting in change of social habit through meeting new situations produced by a variety of social interactions. The Internet is unprecedented in the history of technology for its ability to allow people from all over the world to communicate with each other. Serim and Koch (1996) observe that: "Many educators find that the Internet provides them with a professional community to which they had only limited access prior to using the Internet. On-line, they can easily meet teachers and experts in their field and find collaborators for student on-line projects and curriculum development. Mailing lists, newsgroups, and other collaborative spaces offer a forum for these interactions, making the exchange of ideas an ongoing opportunity not possible before the Internet" (p. 149). The kinds of new situations and interactions that students and teachers are finding daily on the Internet can stimulate democratic exchange, as the case that follows attempts to suggest.

THE CASE[1]

Part 1

Becky Weinstein sat at the computer quietly determined to learn to use the Internet in her classroom. She could give a sound educational rationale for introducing telecommunications to her sixth-grade class. Becky had read articles describing successful experiences with educational technology in some of the teaching journals; she had been to a conference the previous spring where one school's experience in getting on-line was described in detail. She believed that students should have more exposure to computers at school. The root of her recent conversion to technology, and she was a bit embarrassed to admit this to herself, was simply fear of being left behind. She had met a software developer at a dinner party who was very interested in the use of computers in classrooms. He talked about how the Internet was changing the ways people did business and how most of his correspondence was in the form of e-mail. He had asked how she used computers in her own teaching. The question wasn't *if* she used computers; the programmer assumed she did.

Becky was embarrassed to admit that, although her students had a weekly meeting in the computer lab, their computer activities were largely unrelated to their

---

[1]The names, characters, and events described in this case are fictional. The e-mail incident is a purely fictionalized account based, in part, on a true story described in an article by Rogers (1995). Several projects described in the case are drawn from actual projects posted on the Global SchoolNet Web site (http://www.gsn.org).

other class work. They did some word processing for an occasional academic assignment, but they spent most of their time playing with the drill-and-practice computer games. Becky often used this time to catch up on grading or her planning. She thought that having her students get time on the computer was important, but she questioned the value of most of the computer software. Although some software was creatively designed and entertained the students, other software was repetitive and quickly bored students. She noticed that most students enjoyed drawing with the paint programs, but for many keyboarding was painfully slow when they did any form of written work.

Becky grew defensive with the computer programmer, annoyed at having to explain herself. Becky had no formal computer training in her undergraduate teacher education program. She had attended a 3-hour workshop once, but found the content lacking—the workshop had focused on how to use hardware and software and had not addressed the integration of technology with curriculum. Becky had forgotten most of what she learned after a week or two. Once the school year had started, she had no time to learn how to use computers in her teaching. A good teacher, she perceived her lack of free time as a symbol of her hard work and dedication to her students. Speaking with the programmer, she was nagged by the thought that she must make the commitment to find the time. The longer she waited, the harder it would be to catch up, and her students were falling behind with her. It was a question of priorities, and learning more about computers and the Internet had simmered on the back burner long enough. Now, she wondered, what could she push aside in her daily schedule to make room for learning new technology? Who could teach her what she needed to know?

Becky met with the librarian, Ralph Langston, who spent an hour showing her how to use the World Wide Web. Because the library had a computer hooked up to the Internet, Ralph had become the de facto technology expert in the school. The computer lab also had one machine connected to the Internet, and that was where Becky was sitting. She thought a good place to start was for her students to use the Internet to learn more about the upcoming presidential election. Ralph had gone home after the last bell to pick up his wife from work, but Becky had his World Wide Web handout on the desk next to her. Becky opened up the Netscape program to begin her first "solo" on the Internet.

Becky was familiar with computers, but using them to make worksheets was very different from using them in her teaching. She used word processing regularly and in the last year had started using a spreadsheet for her grading. Becky also had her own e-mail account through the state Department of Education (DOE), but rarely used it. The DOE had recently rewritten the state standards of learning, infusing technology requirements throughout the curriculum. Simply by making the request, any teacher could receive an e-mail account and 1 hour a day free access to the Internet through the DOE computers. The DOE even provided disks to let teachers dial in from home. That might be a next step, if her old computer could run the software.

Becky's plan for her election unit was fairly simple. She wanted students to prepare reports about the most prominent candidates' positions. She would place students teams organized around the candidates for the presidential, congressional, and senate races. Each of the teams would research the positions of one candidate. She wanted them to use the Web as an information source. She would provide written guidelines for directing the students' research, and students could perform a scavenger search on the Web for information about their candidate. After the reports were done, she would stage a series of mock debates in her classroom, and then hold a mock election with her students the week before election day.

Becky brought up Netscape and clicked on the "Net Search" button. A Web page titled "Yahoo" came up; it had a little box and a button next to it that said "Search." She clicked on the "Search" button, and a screen came up directing her to enter one or two "key words." She clicked in the box and typed "election." A screen came up showing 229 matches; she scrolled down the list and was amazed by what she saw: many sites for both regional and national elections. She used the Bookmark feature to mark pages she might use, and then visited promising sites and marked the ones she liked. One site, called "Project Vote Smart," provided a wealth of information on campaign issues and citizen participation. She found pages from the White House, from newspapers near and far, and from local candidates' Web pages. She started to feel good about her project—there was more than enough information out there for her students.

Becky liked the Web. It was fairly intuitive; clicking the mouse on the locations she wanted to visit was easy. Becky did not like the waiting, however. On more than one occasion, she waited several minutes to visit a Web site only to get a message saying that the server had refused her connection. She would have to ask Ralph about that—the kids would get antsy if they had to wait too long to reach their sites. Becky also learned that it was very easy to lose your place. She lost the Yahoo page twice and had to start over each time.

She had been in the lab nearly an hour, and it was about time to go home. She decided to try one quick search, so she typed "vote" into the keyword box. This search was less rewarding than the search on "election." Becky realized that searching the Web was fairly similar to doing library searches. Getting the right key word was essential. Under the "vote" results, she saw some of the same sites that came up under "election." She also saw a site for voting on the hot football topic of the week. How many of her sixth-grade boys would pass up any site relating to football! Then she started seeing sites like "Screw the Vote," "Babe Vote '96," and the "Bikinis are Wee Contest." She also found a link to a site voted "the best 'XXX' site of the year." Becky felt her enthusiasm for the Web begin to fade.

Part 2

"Ms. Weinstein, Jeremy is being a dictator. He's not helping with the work and he's bossing everyone around," whined Phyllis. Becky enjoyed using cooperative learning techniques. She was running the project in the form of a large jig-saw. Each team of four or five students was to research one candidate, and then use computers to publish a press release outlining their candidate's position on a number of topics Becky supplied. Each member of the team was assigned a task. A campaign manager was responsible for keeping the team on task, meeting deadlines, and reinforcing the team's enthusiasm. The manager, following the research guidelines Becky gave out, would decide whether students had collected enough information on the various topics. That was Jeremy's job. There was a "campaign spokesperson" in charge of drafting and reading the final position sheet. That job belonged to Phyllis. Two "Web managers" were to collect the material printed from the Web and to make sure everyone on the team got an equal opportunity to operate the computer.

Becky began the lesson with a trust-building exercise in which the students exchanged lists of likes and dislikes. She thought the exercise had been effective. She had given Jeremy the job of campaign manager because he had a strong personality and was one of the brighter students in the class.

Becky walked Phyllis back over to her team.

"Jeremy, Phyllis said that you aren't helping out with the work."

"Ms. Weinstein, these guys just aren't doing their jobs, and I'm not going to do their work for them. It's my job to make sure we make the deadlines. They need to get with the program." ("Getting with the program" was a favorite line of Walt Marlow, Jeremy's football coach.)

"If he would quit pestering us every two minutes, then we could get our work done," Phyllis hissed.

"Jeremy, your job is to help keep the team on schedule and also to keep up team morale. It doesn't sound like you are doing either. Why don't you ask your teammates what you can do to help. That might help them feel better and also could help you get closer to getting the work done."

"I got stuck with a bunch of losers, and I'm not doing all the work," Jeremy replied.

"He hasn't done a lick of work, Ms. Weinstein." This came from Tommy, one of the quieter students in the group.

"I'm not doing your work just because you don't know how. He even has trouble working the mouse!" Jeremy shot back.

Tommy Jackson came from a single-parent, extremely poor household. His mother was a good, supportive parent who worked two jobs. Her three children fended for themselves at home most of their waking hours. Becky had tried to get Tommy into an after-school enrichment program, but Mrs. Jackson had to refuse. The only way Tommy could get home was by school bus, which left before the enrichment program started. In contrast, Jeremy came from an upper-middle-class home. He had a computer at home, and he was very proficient. In fact, several students in the class were obviously more adept at using computers and the Internet than was Becky. Becky had given Tommy the job of Web manager because he was very awkward on the computer. She hoped he would benefit from more time on the computer, something Jeremy certainly didn't need.

"Jeremy, using the Web is new to most of us. I'm going to give you the special job of being Web master of this team. If you can help your team become better at finding all the information you need, I'll give your entire team five bonus points. You get the points if the other members can find everything on the research guide."

Becky knew Jeremy was extremely grade conscious, and the five points would probably work.

"I guess so. But it won't be easy," Jeremy said. Tommy gave Becky a look that was not very appreciative.

After the position paper deadline, Becky planned to test the entire class on knowledge of their candidates' positions. All the teams' tests had a core of similar questions, such as "What is your candidate's position on abortion?" Becky also added two candidate-specific questions for each team's test. Teams that had average test scores of 80% or more also received five bonus points.

After the position papers were issued, Becky rearranged the teams into learning groups with one student representing each of the six candidates. Once in these groups, the students exchanged their position papers and practiced mock debates, moving through each of the research topics. The group task was to identify similarities and differences between the candidates. Becky then finished the project with a class discussion in which she rotated through the groups, calling up two students at a time representing opposing candidates. The students debated before the entire class their candidates' perspectives on a single topic she provided. Becky rotated through the groups until each student had performed. After this event, she passed out ballots for her students to vote.

Becky had become good friends with Ralph Langston. He soothed her fears about students accessing inappropriate material on the Web. Ralph said that he had tried some of the screening software in the library—"Netmommy" or some such thing—but he was not entirely happy with it, because it also blocked some appropriate sites. He thought a better solution was to limit the students to the sites on the Bookmarks list; because Becky had previewed each site on the list, there should be no problem. If students were limited to 20-minute sessions at the computer, they would not have much time to get into trouble. To cover herself, Becky sent home a letter informing parents that their children would be using the Internet to research the election project. The letter stated that the students would be supervised and would only visit approved sites.

On project days, Becky took the class to the computer room where the teams worked on their position papers. She had a research schedule where teams could spend 20 minutes at a time on the Web at one of the two connected computers—the one in the lab or the one in the library. Ralph had loaded her bookmarks on the library computer, and he had no problem keeping one eye on the kids as they worked.

Part 3

Becky was pleased with her first attempt at using the Internet. The students had gotten to information otherwise unavailable to them in the school's library. They seemed excited about using the computers in new ways; they loved their limited time on the Web. Becky believed that the students enjoyed seeing her flounder a bit. On more than one occasion, a student helped her when the computer hung up or when she had trouble locating a specific item on the Web. Although terrified at the thought of not being in control of her students, she realized that the problems she encountered were largely classroom management issues typical of any other class activity.

Becky was ready for a second attempt. She was becoming adept at using search engines to seek items on the Web. She was also relieved to find that although "adult" material certainly was present on the Web, it was not pervasive. Becky began one search with the terms "school" and "projects," and one of the links that came up was to the Global SchoolNet. For the first time, Becky really felt excited. Here was a Web site dedicated entirely to classroom education. One of the menu items was a "Projects Registry." This led her to a month-by-month listing of Internet projects. As she started to read the listings, she realized they were being posted by classroom teachers just like her. One project asked for other classrooms to build a "go-car" out of a set list of materials and then to share, by e-mail, the results of how far their car traveled using a single rubber band as a power source. Another project wanted classrooms in different parts of the world to compare how newspapers in their areas covered current events topics. A third wanted students in different locations to share information about local foods and produce.

Becky liked two projects in particular. The first directed students to go to a food store and collect information on the average cost of items on a supplied list. The students would then supply their results, via a newsgroup, to the project leader. Becky wanted to teach the sixth graders how to use spreadsheets, and she had been searching for a way to tie it to her own lessons. This project would introduce spreadsheets in a way that would keep their interest.

A teacher in Australia posted a second project that caught Becky's attention. This teacher wanted her sixth-grade class to exchange student-written versions of particular fairy tales to see how different cultures treated common stories. Becky liked the way the woman wrote the project posting. The description was simple, not technical at all, and the teacher seemed to be reaching out for help. Becky felt this teacher might be a kindred spirit on the Internet. She wrote down the e-mail address.

The Grocery List project was fairly straightforward. Becky divided the class into groups of three, and each group divided up the 18 items on the grocery list however they wanted. The students had to have a minimum sample of three brands for each item on the list. They brought their numbers to computer lab, and Becky showed them how to set up a spread sheet to do sums and averages. After each group finished its list, Becky let them post their results to the newsgroup.

For the Fairy Tale project, Becky paired the students to write their own versions of the fairy tales selected by the Australian teacher. Becky also had one pair write a version of a Paul Bunyan story to show their Australian key pals what an American fairy tale was like.

Becky faced a problem in using these projects: Her students had to access a newsgroup for the Grocery List project, and they needed to use e-mail to send and receive the fairy tales. Becky had an e-mail account through the DOE, but because of the cost of providing this service, the DOE limited the use of the accounts for all teachers to one hour a day. She wondered how she could manage both projects in the lab with one account and one connected computer. Ralph suggested she use an e-mail reader called Eudora, through which she could download the e-mail messages each morning and save them on a disk to read later. Then she could load them from the disk to any number of the machines in the lab. This software allowed the students to read mail and compose responses without being connected to the Internet. When they finished, Becky could take the disk out of the machine, connect to her account, and then upload all the messages at one time. Becky liked this idea because she could read the student work at her leisure and on any computer. She also liked students not being able to use her e-mail account directly.

The newsgroup was a little trickier to work with. Becky decided to open the newsgroup on her account and let each group post their own responses so they would have some ownership over their work. The e-mail address was hers, but the students signed their own names to their grocery lists.

Becky most enjoyed the exchanges with the Australian class. Her students sent messages to Australian project-mates as they finished their stories. When the Australian stories or responses came in, Becky downloaded them to Eudora and then transferred them to four lab computers for her students to read. Routinely, Becky would read through the stories first before loading them on several of the computer lab machines. She rarely used e-mail other than for this project, so the Australian messages were the only ones she received.

Becky typically came in early before school and downloaded her messages. Her class still met in the computer lab once a week, and she would load the week's mail from the Australian class on to the four computers in the lab. One morning Becky was running late and did not have time to read through each of the new messages she received that day. Her class was meeting in the lab that afternoon, so she put the mail on a disk and quickly copied the file to the four machines so that they would be ready for her class. She then ran from the lab to get to her classroom before the bell rang.

Becky had arranged the groups for the Grocery List and the Fairy Tale projects so that she could have half the class work on spreadsheets while half the class worked on word processing. With this arrangement, students would read mail, some would work at spreadsheets, and others would post their results on the Internet. Becky told four groups to start reading through the mail for the week, then she went over to the Internet machine to help a group log on to the newsgroup.

Sally Fisher came over to Becky and said, "Mrs. Weinstein, I think you had better talk to Angie." Becky looked over and saw that Angie was turning red and the students in her group were smirking and whispering. Becky went over to the group and asked what was wrong.

Angie started to say something, then bit her lip and pointed to the screen. Becky leaned over and saw an e-mail message dated that day. It did not have the Australian teacher's address, and it was addressed to Angie Economos. Becky read the message: "F—k you, you little bitch." Becky's knees felt week. She looked at the return address of the message and could not see anything useful. Becky couldn't understand how this happened. The message came to her e-mail account addressed to Angie.

Tommy Mulligan said, "I think Angie has a boyfriend on the Internet." The dam broke and tears started streaming down Angie's face. "Shut up, Tommy," sputtered Angie. "Yes, shut up Tommy," Becky said. Then it hit Becky. The week before, Angie had posted her group's Grocery List to the newsgroup. Someone must have gotten Becky's e-mail address and Angie's name from the newsgroup.

CRITICAL PERSPECTIVE

This case presents many issues, three of which seem most compelling:What does technology have to offer the democratic classroom? What implications does this case hold for teacher education? What, if anything, should be done about Angie's e-mail message? There are no definitive answers to these questions, but current knowledge can help in formulating responses.

Technology and the Democratic Classroom

Mosher, Kenny, and Garrod (1994) believe the explanation of a democratic school is inseparable from the rationale for such a school. They describe that rationale as having four primary principles: (a) democracy is vitally dependent on a responsive, educated citizenry; (b) children educated in democratic groups benefit personally as well as in terms of social development; (c) democratic participation contributes to the growth of minds; and (d) democracy has to be recreated in the understanding and behavior of each new generation of citizens or it is jeopardized.

In this line of reasoning, if children are to understand democratic values, they must be part of a democratic environment. Darling-Hammond (1994) observes that the dramatic changes in social and cultural context of schools are placing new demands on tomorrow's citizens: "This century's movement into a high-technology

Information Age demands a new kind of education and new forms of school organization" (p. 3).

There is little room in today's society for those who cannot manage complexity, find and use resources, and continually learn new technologies, approaches, and occupations. Increasing social complexity also demands that citizens understand and evaluate multidimensional problems and alternatives and manage ever-more-demanding systems.

These changes signal a new mission for education, one that requires schools not merely to "deliver instructional services," but to ensure that all students learn at high levels. In turn, the teacher's job is no longer to "cover the curriculum," but to enable diverse learners to construct their own knowledge and develop their talents in effective and powerful ways (Darling-Hammond, 1994).

Creating a more democratic classroom requires shifting power from the teacher to the students. The notion of democracy describes the location of power, loosely defined as the ability to make and implement choices, in a social structure. Authoritarian or autocratic structures have power concentrated in the hands of a single person or a selected few. A democratic structure diffuses the power of decision making to all the members of the population. Thus, as Darling-Hammond describes, the focus of teachers in a democratic classroom shifts from delivering a predetermined curriculum to providing a democratic environment in which students have a voice in the direction and construction of their own learning.

With a shift of power also comes a shift of responsibility. If students are to have more say in their own education, then they must assume more responsibility for that education. Leppard (1993), in describing the learning environments of democratic classrooms, states that: "Knowledge can rarely be transmitted from one to another as verbal statements in lecture form. Learners must engage with each other to gain knowledge and insight. Learners must take increasing responsibility for their learning. Teacher and learner are in partnership and the learner cannot expect to play a passive role" (p. 78).

When the teacher becomes a partner in learning, the responsibility for learning is shared. Interaction among learners is a key element in such an environment.

The facts of the case reveal that Becky Weinstein has already taken some small steps toward democratic learning. She values cooperative group work and established that pattern of learning before introducing technology to her classroom. Rolheiser and Glickman (1995) recognize the compatibility of cooperative learning and democratic classrooms when they write, "Although there is a range of effective teaching practices, certain ones are congruent with a focus on educating for democracy. One of the specific instructional practices that is aligned with the goals of democratic education is cooperative learning" (p. 199). Though Becky values group work and student interaction, she also maintains a high level of control over the learning process, as evidenced by constraining her students to investigate only the topics on the research guide she prepared.

Can technology help shift the responsibility for learning decisions toward the students? A longitudinal collection of qualitative data taken from classrooms in the Apple Classrooms of Tomorrow (ACOT) project revealed that teachers move through five stages of behavior—Entry, Adoption, Adaptation, Appropriation, and Invention—during the process of integrating technology into their teaching (Dwyer, Ringstaff, & Sandholtz, 1991). The impact of technology on classroom instructional paradigms increased as teachers moved through these stages. Interpreting the case in terms of these stages will be helpful in understanding how Becky has begun to integrate technology into her classroom.

The first stage, Entry, reflects concerns and issues involved with technical and managerial issues as teachers became familiar with the new technology. The style of classroom instruction during the Entry phase is predominantly the same before the introduction of technology. Becky Weinstein initially has her students using mostly low-level drill-and-practice software in their computer lab. Such practice relegates the computer to the level of a high-tech workbook for the students. Becky's comfort with computers is somewhat unusual. Becky becomes anxious, however, at the prospect of having to learn something new while she manages an already demanding schedule. Although Becky suffers anxiety as she faces new challenges, she remains open and enthusiastic about learning new technologies. Becky begins the case well established in the Entry phase of technology integration.

The Entry phase is followed by the Adoption phase. Here teachers focus less on technical issues and more on how to integrate technology with instruction to support the same instructional patterns that existed before the introduction of technology. (In the case of the ACOT classroom, these patterns consisted of lectures, recitation, and individual seatwork.) In the election project, Becky uses the World Wide Web primarily as an information source. Although she forms cooperative teams of students, this pattern of instruction is not new for Becky. She retains a large measure of control over student research and also over the format and content of the debate at the end of the project. Although the use of the Web is new to her and the class, Becky simply applies a previously established style of teaching to the technology.

The third phase, Adaptation, reveals an emphasis on the use of technology as a productivity tool. As students become more proficient at typing, computers become a means for attaining speed and efficiency in instructional activities.

The Appropriation phase became apparent in the second year of technology introduction in the ACOT project. This phase is characterized by teachers showing personal mastery of the technology as they begin to introduce new instructional strategies in their classrooms. Team teaching, project-based instruction, and individually paced instruction were some characteristics that emerged in the ACOT classrooms. In her second and third projects, Becky seems more confident with the technology and experiments with different project formats. Students use the computers to collaborate on their own fairy tales, but it is unclear how much discretion they had in choosing their own topics. The Grocery List project is a fairly rote exercise; Becky still retains substantial control over the decision making. Becky has not yet demonstrated a shift in instructional paradigm, and we would not have expected her to do so in such a short period of time. Becky does show concern for students taking "ownership" as they post their own Grocery List data to the newsgroup. This small event may indicate a willingness in Becky to begin the process of examining and redefining her own methodology.

The final phase, Invention, involves the creation of new learning environments in which learning is active, creative, and socially interactive. Control of learning shifts from teacher to students. During the Invention phase, teachers begin to question previously held conceptions regarding learning. In terms of establishing a democratic classroom, Becky must head for the Invention phase.

In Becky's class, students have the opportunity to interact with and learn from people of different backgrounds. The availability and immediacy of the information on the Web can help draw students closer to becoming active participants in the democratic process. As Becky becomes more familiar with the potential of these tools, she will begin to realize that her old paradigms are limiting her students. A more democratic paradigm—one where students take more responsibility for manipulating the tools of learning— will more likely yield higher levels of learning.

As an epilogue to this discussion, one might ask. Can learning be too democratic? Perelman (1992) argues the extreme: with the advent of new technologies, learning should be completely learner-directed. Perelman states:

> At its root, this technological revolution puts learning and education on a collision course. The essence of education is instruction—something some people do to other people, usually with required "discipline." The word *pedagogy* comes from a Greek verb meaning "to lead," and *education* itself is from the Latin word meaning "to lead forth." Both imply the active leader herding a flock of passive followers. But the essence of the coming integrated, universal, multimedia, digital network is *discovery*—the empowerment of human minds to learn spontaneously, without coercion, both independently and cooperatively. The focus is on learning as an action that is "done by," not "done to," the actor. (p. 23)

Perelman advocates student empowerment to the point of dropping the teacher from the learning partnership. He proposes a "microchoice" solution to educational reform in which each learner possesses a "microvoucher," much like a debit card, that allows the student to purchase learning on demand from a computerized network of educational service providers. Each student could fully direct his or her own learning at whatever pace is appropriate. Perelman argues that this combination of information and financial technology makes the traditional school building obsolete. The delivery of specific products and services for learning can be provided in the time, place, and form of the student's choosing. Technologically, the student can change "schools" as easily as switching TV channels, or can "attend" several different "schools" at once.

Perelman's view of education represents a nearly perfect educational democracy where designated classroom leaders do not determine choices and social interactions, but individuals do. History, however, offers few examples of pure democracies. When a citizenry embraces democratic ideals, the application of those ideals inevitably departs from a truly democratic form. A purely democratic educational system, such as Perelman's, may not necessarily be the adaptation of democratic values we want or choose for our classrooms. Nonetheless, he forces us to consider interesting possibilities.

Implications for Teacher Education

Becky Weinstein is a heroine. Her state Department of Education wrote technology into its standards of learning, yet the vast majority of teachers appear to have no formal technology training. Becky, like most education graduates, received little or no technology training in her teacher education program. In a survey completed for the Office of Technology Assessment in 1994, Willis and his colleagues reached two general conclusions: Teacher educators generally feel that technology is an important element in teacher preparation, and very few teacher educators teach with or about technology. Furthermore, more than half the recent education graduates surveyed said they were "not prepared at all" or "poorly prepared" to use technology. About 25% said they were "minimally prepared," and only 20% said they were "adequately prepared" or better (Willis, Austin, & Willis, 1994). Like most teachers, Becky was not prepared to integrate technology into her classroom, yet she was willing to face the unknown, with some degree of professional risk. If teachers are to use technology effectively in their classrooms, teacher educators must use and model technology in their own teaching. Education graduates need to learn how to use tools, but more important, they need to internalize good models of technology-based instruction.

Becky had attended an inservice workshop, but the content focused on the technology and not the integration of the technology into teaching. In a review of technology in teacher education, Willis and Mehlinger (1996) conclude that: "Most teacher educators agree that a stand-alone technology for teachers course is of limited value if it is isolated from the rest of the teacher education curriculum (Callister & Burbles, 1990) because the approach does not model how technology should be used in education" (p. 999).

Becky needs help in learning how to take advantage of new technologies in her own teaching. Teacher educators have had little to say about the effectiveness of instructional strategies, such as cooperative learning, with technology. Teachers like Becky need more information and support in using technology. Teachers less capable than Becky will avoid using technology altogether or flounder without help.

The school system also lets Becky down. The Department of Education passed technology components for its state standards of learning, yet we see little evidence of teacher education taking place. Becky is obviously unhappy with the quality of educational software in the computer lab and the limitations of two Internet connections. Most important, Becky lacks support. Ralph is a de facto technology expert, but providing support for teachers in their instructional use of technology is not typically the school librarian's job. Becky is on dangerous ground by allowing her students on the Internet with no school policy to support her. Many school systems are beginning to enact Acceptable Use Policies that govern student conduct while conducting activities over the Internet. Such policies, however, are not universal. Teacher educators should help preservice teachers understand these issues and give them the knowledge to make professionally defensible decisions. To do less will invite policies that are reactionary and piecemeal.

Becky's performance is remarkable given the lack of support for her efforts by the education community. Expecting all teachers to follow Becky's example is unrealistic. There is no substitute for adequate teacher preparation in technology.

The E-Mail Terrorist

Several projects depicted in the case are based on real projects described in the Global SchoolNet Web site (http://www.gsn.org). The obscene note is a fictionalized depiction based loosely on a true incident described by Rogers (1995). He gives an excellent perspective on resolving such problems (see http://www.gsn.org/teach/articles/email.ballad.html). Becky is at a juncture: She can react to the e-mail by trying to insulate her class to societal realities, or she can act democratically. The Internet is largely an unregulated body; community standards of behavior for the Internet are set not so much by legislation, but by the daily conduct and interactions of its members. As a member of the Internet community, Becky has the responsibility to pursue the matter and to address improper conduct. Because this e-mail assault was enacted against her class, she should involve the class to whatever extent is possible. Self-regulation is essential to a thriving democracy, and Becky's students should be part of the process of resolving this incident. In addition, this event offers an ideal opportunity to engage parents, teachers, and students in framing a community dialogue to establish an understanding that permits students to explore the Internet responsibly, that is, with age-appropriate safeguards. The incident offers an opportunity to prepare the learning community to cope with the realities of undesirable events when they occur.

In the actual incident described by Rogers (1995), the sender of the e-mail was tracked down through the help of system administrators. The sender of the message was an older student, who through the cooperation of various members of the Internet and school communities, was able to learn a valuable lesson in community responsibility. Dewey (1897) notes " ... the only true education comes through the stimulation of the child's powers by the demands of the social situations in which he finds himself. Through these demands, he is stimulated to act as a member of a unity, to emerge from his original narrowness of action and feeling, and to conceive of himself from the standpoint of the welfare of the group to which he belongs" (p. 363). Both the sender and the recipient of the e-mail have the opportunity to learn a great deal about the community in which they live, and such learning captures the essence of a democratic classroom.

REFERENCES

Darling-Hammond, L. (1994). Reframing the school reform agenda: Developing capacity for school transformation. *Transforming school reform: Policies and practices for democratic schools.* NCREST Reprint Series. National Center for Restucturing Education, Schools and Teaching. Reachers College: Columbia University.

Dewey, J. (1897). My pedagogic creed. In K. Ryan & J. M. Cooper (Eds., 1992), *Kaleidoscope: Readings in education.* Boston: Houghton Mifflin.

Dewey, J. (1916). *Democracy and education.* New York: The Free Press.

Dwyer, D. C., Ringstaff, C., & Sandholtz, J. H. (1991). Changes in teachers' beliefs and practices in technology-rich classrooms. *Educational Leadership, 48*(8), 45–52.

Firestone, C. M., & Kopp, K. (1994). Sustainable democracy, *20/20 vision: The development of a national information infrastructure.* Boulder, CO: National Telecommunications and Information Administration, Dept. Of Commerce, NTIA Special Publication 94–28.

Harris, J. (1994). *Way of the ferret.* Eugene, OR: International Society for Technology in Education.

Jefferson, T. (1810). Letter to Hugh L. White and others. In A. A. Lipscomb (Ed.), *The writings of Thomas Jefferson, 12,* 386–388. Washington, DC: The Thomas Jefferson Memorial Association.

Leppard, L. J. (1993). Teaching for democratic action in a deliberative democracy. *Social Education, 57*(2), 78–80.

Lewis, P. H. (1996). Judges turn back law intended to regulate internet decency . *The New York Times on the Web.* [On-line]. Available: http://search.nytimes.com/web/docsroot/library/cyber/week/0613cda.html.

Mosher, R., Kenny, R. A., Jr., & Garrod, A. (1994). *Preparing for citizenship: Teaching youth to live democratically.* Westport, CT: Praeger.

Perelman, L. J. (1992). *School's out: A radical new formula for the revitalization of America's educational system.* New York: Avon Books.

Rogers, A. (1995). Ballad of an email terrorist . [On-line.] Available: http://www.gsn.org/gsn/articles/email.ballad.html.

Rolheiser, C., & Glickman, C. D. (1995). Teaching for democratic life. *The Educational Forum, 59*(2), 196–206.

Salvador, R. (1994). The emperor's new clothes. *Electronic Learning, 13*(8), 32–46.

Serim, F., & Koch, M. (1996). *NetLearning: Why teachers use the Internet.* Sebastopol,CA: Songline Studios, Inc. and O'Reilly & Associates, Inc.

Willis, J., Austin, L., & Willis, D. (1994). *Information technology in teacher education: Surveys of the current status* (A report prepared for the Office of Technology Assessment). Houston, TX: University of Houston, College of Education.

Willis, J. W., & Mehlinger, H. D. (1996). Information technology and teacher education. In J. Sikula, T. Buttery, & E. Guyton (Eds.), *Handbook of research on teacher education: A project of the Association of Teacher Educators* (pp. 978–1029). New York: Macmillan Library Reference.

4

The Power of Multimedia Cases to Invite Democratic Teaching and Learning

Victoria J. Risko
Peabody College of Vanderbilt University

Charles K. Kinzer
Peabody College of Vanderbilt University

Editors' note: Democracy depends heavily on access to instruments of communication. However, even access is not sufficient if the instruments exert unusual control over those who use them. The authors contend that the deliberate use of multimedia to enhance case-based instruction supports democratic teaching and learning principles by inviting preservice teachers to think critically about multiple sources of information and divergent viewpoints and to appreciate the value of collaboration. They suggest how technology coupled with case methodology can unleash the democratic power teachers possess and help them develop deep understandings of pedagogical content. Moreover, appropriate use of technology with teachers can demonstrate the value of critical thinking, collaborative learning, personal reflection, and respect for diverse perspectives—all critical attributes of democratically organized environments for children.

The idea of democratic classrooms suggests dynamic learning environments in which multiple viewpoints are heard and respected, where teachers and students support each other's inquiry and study ideas in depth and for varying purposes. There is a shortage of educational settings supporting these kinds of teaching and learning. Instead, instruction that develops students' independent thinking and respect for diverse viewpoints may be more of a myth than reality (Darling-Hammond, 1996) with few students prepared to analyze conflicting points of view and think deeply about complex issues affecting their life or real-world problems (Applebee, Langer, & Mullins, 1988; Commeyras, 1993).

Teaching for democracy has long been viewed as essential for preparing students of all ages to think critically about information they acquire and to value the roles others play in their own learning. Yet goals directed toward inviting students' participation in their own learning and helping them embrace different perspectives to guide their thinking are not realized in many elementary, secondary, or college classrooms. Many indicators, such as the reports from the National Commission on Excellence in Education (1983) and the National Assessment of Educational Progress (Applebee et al., 1988) suggest that schooling must change to achieve such goals. Lasting changes will not likely occur until we transform teacher preparation programs. Teachers must be prepared to develop learning environments supporting the kinds of democratic teaching and learning discussed in this text. Future teachers must understand how to create efficacious teaching environments and how to participate in them. If teachers teach as they are taught, teacher education programs must provide rich demonstrations of the teaching methods we expect future teachers to adopt in their own classrooms.

At Vanderbilt University, we are using multimedia cases (Risko & Kinzer, 1999) as an alternative to a lecture-based pedagogy. We use these cases in literacy methods courses to help preservice teachers understand the complexities of implementing reading and writing instruction in elementary classrooms. Our cases serve dual purposes as an *instructional method* for enhancing students' generative and collaborative learning and as a *demonstration* of strategies they could implement when they develop their own classrooms.

PERSPECTIVES GUIDING OUR THINKING

Several perspectives that relate directly to promoting democracy in the classroom guide our attempts to reform our literacy methodology courses. First, we believe it is important to change the cultural landscape of our college classes. We want to create a "climate of permission," an environment in our classes where both the instructor and preservice teachers *expect* to be highly involved in the sharing and analysis of ideas. In such a climate, learning is shared and facilitated by the members of the classroom community. This direction for our teaching is influenced by our understanding of sociocultural research grounded in demonstrations of how teachers and students collaborate and mediate each other's learning (Gavelek, 1986; Tharp & Gallimore, 1988; Vygotsky, 1978). We also believe that knowledge is best constructed through multiple opportunities for interactions among the instructor and students (Cazden, 1988; Eeds & Wells, 1989; Hynds, 1994).

Both teachers and students bring rich sources of background knowledge to share with each other during the analysis of our cases. We find that preservice teachers benefit by learning from the "most knowledgeable" members of the class. Given the particular experiences of each member, the designated "most knowledgeable" person will vary according to the topic under study (Risko, Yount, & McAllister, 1992). Usually, the instructor is the person most informed about the course content, but students often guide the learning of the group.

The following example illustrates how students help one another. A sixth-grade student told us that she went home every day after school and watched television for 2 to 3 hours while she waited for her mother to return from work. When many of the preservice teachers expressed dismay about this use of time, one reminded us of a class reading in which the author described "latchkey" children. She, too, was a latchkey child with a single mother, who was a teacher. The student described how she felt being home alone, and what she did with her time after school. This sharing of a perspective different from those of her peers helped them understand a concept that was unfamiliar, even though this concept was "developed" in an assigned class reading. In this type of exchange, the preservice teachers learn to rely on each other, to recognize the importance of collaborative efforts, and to extend their thinking about teaching and learning. Democratic instruction is developed through such so-cial exchanges—the exchanges that occur among preservice teachers by "interact-ing" with the teachers and students represented in the multimedia cases.

We believe that engaging students in shared problem-solving activities is a pow-erful way to develop students' understanding of diverse pathways for achieving problem resolutions. Our instructional approach, referred to as *anchored instruc-tion* (Bransford, Vye, Kinzer, & Risko, 1990), situates problem-based learning within video-based contexts. We use video-based formats to encourage exploration and sustained thinking about complex, authentic problems. Students engage in ac-tivities requiring them to conceptualize problems from the content embedded in the media. Asking students to consider data and identify problem characteristics, in-stead of responding to problems that the instructor defines for them, can help future teachers "wonder why things are, to inquire, to search for solutions, and to resolve incongruities" (Hiebert et al., 1996, p. 12). Instead of learning information often viewed as far removed from its application (or information that is not used when it is appropriate for problem solving), future teachers involved in such instruction think about applications of information as they acquire it (Risko, 1996).

Case methodology influences our approach to instruction. Christensen (1987) and Learned (1987) indicate that teaching with cases is a process-oriented approach that encourages problem formulation and problem solving. During the last decade, teacher education scholars (Merseth, 1991; L. S. Shulman, 1995) argued that future teachers often view content of college classes as far removed from their future teaching experiences. Theory and pedagogical content are often taught in lectures or decontextualized activities requiring little or no application to instructional practice. Such instruction can oversimplify complex information and inhibit future teachers' abilities to respond to real-world problems. Cases, often written in a narrative form, describe realities of classroom events and invite reflection (Kleinfeld, 1995; Merseth, 1991; J. H. Shulman, 1995; Silverman & Welty, 1995). Recent reform efforts in teacher education focus on the content future teachers need to succeed and the pedagogy that can enhance their ability to make informed decisions. Cases that represent problems associated with teaching and learning can engage future teachers in "reasonable reflective thinking focused on deciding what to believe or do" (Ennis, 1987, p. 10). Coupling case methodology with anchored instruction, we produced multimedia cases situated in actual classroom events. Our goal for these cases is to develop future teachers' critical thinking strategies and their ability to respond to multiple aspects of problems that occur in classrooms.

We draw on these perspectives to build democratic learning environments that support both "competence" and "community" (Darling-Hammond, 1996). We believe these environments must be created deliberately to build competence by helping students think deeply about issues they are exploring, examine information from many perspectives, and learn how and when to use newly learned information for responding to problems. Such environments build community by helping students value what others offer in shared-learning contexts. We want students to feel comfortable being "themselves" (Greene, 1984) as they share personal experiences and examine and react to the ideas of others.

DEVELOPING INQUIRY
AND COLLABORATIVE LEARNING

We developed a set of multimedia cases that represent authentic classroom events that occur during reading and writing instruction in elementary school classrooms. These cases are comprehensive. We present them in narrative formats. They display instruction across primary and upper elementary grades and invite critical thinking and generative learning. We do not intend the cases to serve as exemplars. In the following material, we elaborate each of these characteristics and conclude by explaining how these characteristics can support democratic teaching and learning.

Cases Are Comprehensive

Our eight multimedia cases contain various forms of naturally occurring classroom situations associated with the complexities embedded in literacy instruction. These include teacher–student interactions, peer tutoring, teacher and peer questioning, and student participation in various reading and writing activities. The cases were recorded in Grades 2, 4, 6, resource, and Chapter 1 classrooms in elementary schools. The classrooms are located in urban, suburban, or rural settings and involve children of different SES levels and cultural backgrounds.

Each case presents actual classroom happenings (the content was not scripted) and focuses on one unit of instruction the classroom teacher developed. These units were organized around teacher-selected themes or targeted skills and strategies. We present case-relevant information in interviews conducted with the classroom teachers, other teachers in the school, students, parents, and principals. Additionally, professionals across disciplines (e.g., literacy, classroom management, and special education) provide commentaries on the literacy instruction embedded in the cases. Print materials accompanying the video content contain teacher lesson plans, children's scores on assessment instruments, and samples of children's work collected from class portfolios. Four cases display classroom literacy instruction and are used in our developmental reading methodology course. The other four cases focus on literacy instruction (in classrooms and pull-out programs) for diverse learners. We use these in our remedial reading methodology course. Related readings supplement the cases.

Cases as Stories

Each case runs 1 hour and begins with a video story (12 to 18 minutes) about the teacher, students, classroom organization, and instruction. We refer to this segment as the anchor piece for the continuing story. It provides an introduction to how the classroom is organized, how instruction develops over time, the teachers' selection of materials and activities, and the nature of student involvement. We use narratives to mitigate problems we discussed earlier—future teachers can memorize multiple facts associated with teaching but are often unable to use this knowledge spontaneously when it is useful to do so. We agree with educators such as Egan (1989), who argue that narratives may be the needed link to ensure learning and application of information, especially when the information represents ill-structured domains such as teaching and learning. The stories of our cases provide connections across multiple sources of information that may otherwise be viewed as disconnected or irrelevant to the subject under study (Connelly & Clandinin, 1990; Knowles & Holt-Reynolds, 1991; Noori, 1995).

Cases for Generative Learning and Critical Thinking

An important feature of our cases is "embedded data." The rich source of information embedded in the cases invites students to define their own issues and generate a number of plausible solutions. We do not provide solutions in the case materials. No one tells preservice teachers what they should believe about the case; instead we invite them to formulate their own interpretations and conclusions. Our hypermedia software allows access to multiple kinds of information for an in-depth study of the cases. Preservice teachers analyze the classroom events for a teacher's methodology, purpose of instruction, characteristics of the texts, students' test performance, and classroom behaviors. They can also interpret the case-related perspectives provided through the interviews (e.g., teacher perspective, student perspective). The cases are sufficiently complex to allow for sustained thinking and problem solving over several episodes. We encourage students to examine the cases from multiple perspectives, and in doing so to apply their newly acquired knowledge in flexible and appropriate ways.

Students entering teacher education courses have different backgrounds and perspectives on teaching. We use cases to guide students to make new discoveries. Initially, we want students to view the classroom situations from their own perspective. Having done so, they experience changes in their own perceptions as they are introduced to new concepts in the case material, class readings, and through class discussions with the instructor and their peers (Risko, Peter, & McAllister, 1996). The shared knowledge that develops helps students with different backgrounds learn how they can contribute and how unique points of view can enhance the learning of the entire group. We urge students to think of alternative solutions for the case problems to move them beyond a "one-right-answer" approach to problem solving. We urge them to think about how diverse viewpoints enhance their own thinking.

Cases Are Not Meant to Be Exemplars

Video is traditionally used to provide "models" of exemplary instructional procedures that preservice teachers are expected to exhibit. Such instruction suggests students are to go and do what they have just witnessed. This kind of application is difficult to achieve in classroom situations different from those depicted in the video exemplar. Beginning teachers may not be able to adjust teaching procedures for different classroom contexts, or to analyze the problems they are experiencing. We tried to mitigate these problems when we designed our cases. Our cases present authentic situations illustrative of how teachers across the cases adjust teaching procedures for specific reasons (e.g., student responses, curriculum demands). The cases encourage preservice teachers to think about how they would *respond* to the problems the teacher is experiencing. We ask them to compare applications of teaching concepts within and across cases to promote flexible thinking and the taking of multiple perspectives. We believe that when future teachers think about how others might behave in similar situations, they are learning to think and behave democratically. As they analyze different uses of information, they are more likely to be flexible and open to a constant reexamination of their goals and objectives given the circumstances of the classroom events.

The following notions are salient to our case methodology. First, the comprehensiveness of the cases provides many choices of topics for instructors and students. Case analysis allows case content to be transformed and adapted to fit the needs of the group. Second, the stories of the cases provide powerful ways to talk about case content. Stories also establish ways to reference and cross-reference specific applications of knowledge. The knowledge most relevant is that which contributes to the selection of particular instructional strategies. Third, the embedded data used to invite generative learning and critical thinking can be used to help preservice teachers go beyond a literal analysis to form elaborated understandings of multiple factors that must be considered when forming instructional judgments. Last, these videos provide demonstrations that invite reactions and reflections. The design of our cases helps us develop learning environments facilitating critical thinking and community building.

POTENTIAL POWER OF MULTIMEDIA

Our cases are enhanced with videodisc, CD-Rom, and computer technologies. In this section, we describe benefits of using technology-based cases over written or videotaped cases. We then discuss how multimedia support our goals for democratic education.

Multimedia Cases Versus Written Cases

We present most of our case information on video because it allows us to represent multiple layers of classroom events and show how, occurring simultaneously, these events affect each other and affect teachers' instructional decisions. Video allows us to provide elaborate happenings as they occur in classrooms.

Although written cases contain descriptions of classroom environments, these are filtered through a case author or narrator and leave much to the imagination of the reader. The reality of the situation remains distant from the reader. In contrast, when students see and hear actual events as they develop in the classroom, they are better able to understand newly learned information in a context of real classroom activities. Preservice teachers make their own connections and interpretations of the events they observe. When students encounter situations that closely resemble those they will face later, they may be better prepared to make instructional decisions in real classrooms. Written cases provide descriptions of classroom environments, but when prospective teachers see students and events influencing decisions, and draw conclusions about the effectiveness of such decisions, they may be able to facilitate the transfer of knowledge into actual teaching situations. Furthermore, the preservice teachers are learning to make decisions that come from within, rather than to expect that curriculum decisions will be imposed from the outside. Opportunities to learn in this way are important for developing future teachers' capacities to deal with life in democratically organized schools and in society.

Multimedia cases yield another benefit. Videos present varied opportunities to construct relationships among multiple sources of information. Opportunities to observe the complexities associated with teaching and learning increase the possibility of solving problems. Many aspects of the classroom's physical and social environments are displayed—the specifics of which are left to preservice learners' interpretations in print-based cases. For example, our preservice teachers view one case in which a classroom teacher is required by school policy to team teach with a Title I reading teacher. They work together in the regular classroom to support the mainstreamed students who are experiencing learning difficulties. The teachers have several options for designing physical arrangements and instructional procedures. When considering these options, the teachers must weigh the importance of classroom configurations, grouping arrangements of students, students' visual or auditory handicaps, proximity of items such as the chalkboard, student misbehavior, knowledge of specific students' strengths, weaknesses, prior efforts, and so on. Because videos are dynamic and comprehensive, they facilitate students' ability to form detailed mental models of the problem situation (Johnson-Laird, 1985). And, as students analyze the various factors that influence teachers' decision making, they are learning how to use disparate sources of information as tools to aid their problem solving (Cognition and Technology Group at Vanderbuilt, 1990).

As we discussed earlier, another advantage of a multimedia presentation of information is its usefulness for generative learning. The preservice teachers' learning is guided by their own actions as they interact with the multimedia materials. We use Hypercard software on the computer to access multiple sources of information—instructional context, student test data and portfolios, teacher lesson plans, teaching materials—and for viewing a case for different purposes.

For example, we present one screen from our hypermedia materials. Across the top of the screen, the menu designates the available information. Depending on their goals, the instructor and students can access video segments representing instruction in the classroom of the selected teacher, view the related interviews, examine students' portfolio materials, analyze the teachers' lesson plans, refer to relevant readings, or view the instruction of another teacher to produce comparison and contrast sets of information. The hypermedia provide access to these multiple sources of information and demonstrate the complexities of case information.

Previously, we used written cases that seemed to oversimplify real-world, complex problems. These cases typically focused on one major problem and provided the author's view of both the problem and the solution. Because they provided information already interpreted by the case author, their use discouraged preservice teachers from examining information from different perspectives and from making decisions different from the one presented by the author. The linear format of these cases discouraged our students from making multiple connections across the cases and from noting contrasting information. Conversely, video and software presentations provide actual events and real artifacts. They require viewers to state problems in a content domain; that is, to develop personal descriptions, interpretations, and recognition of patterns. This process prompts preservice teachers to think democratically by stimulating interaction with diverse perspectives, both with the cases and among those who are studying the cases.

We use video and compact discs because they possess random-access capabilities. Scenes can be easily accessed and revisited. Democratic instructors encourage preservice teachers to make choices about topics and questions to investigate. For independent learning to occur, preservice teachers must access information, recognize its relevance, and relate concepts to each other. An instructor who wants to teach particular video content from a videotape needs a guiding "script" and cues on tape. Random-access capabilities facilitate the exploration of the same content from multiple perspectives and for different reasons. When students access common case materials for multiple reasons, they can integrate factors contributing to particular aspects of teaching and learning. For example, when preservice teachers return to information such as test scores to analyze a child's performance, and then again to study classroom arrangements and grouping patterns, they begin to understand how different decisions relate to each other. They notice that assessment and teaching information can jointly guide instructional decisions. They notice, too, the consequences of particular teacher decisions that are depicted in the videos.

In two recent studies (Risko, 1995; Risko et. al., 1996), we observed that preservice teachers developed more flexible thinking about teaching and learning as they progressed through the case analyses. The students initially analyzed case information with a unidimensional, narrow focus (e.g., children experience literacy problems because they are unmotivated). Their goals for teaching were simplistic and singular. They held inexperienced, global notions of how to evaluate, plan, and provide instruction for children experiencing reading difficulties. As they continued to discuss and analyze case issues, they reorganized their existing schemata, adopted new perspectives, and in the process, advanced their thinking beyond their earlier naive conceptions. The multiple layers of case analysis afforded by the random-access aspects of our multimedia cases contributed greatly to their ability to comprehend the complexity of problems that the cases posed and to develop a flexible approach to identifying a range of related factors and issues.

Videodisc and CD-Rom Technologies
Versus Videotape Applications

We can present information about the social and physical environments of classrooms through videotape. Without rapid and frame-accurate search capabilities, however, videotape can be used effectively once to show an entire case. It is too cumbersome to rewind the tape to a desired scene, to revisit scenes within the videotaped case to view them from different perspectives, to use a specific scene as an example in discussion, and to view parts of a tape multiple times to generate a set of behaviors, constraints, or principles. McLarty et al. (1990) indicate that the optimal implementation of video is to show a segment in its entirety once, and then to revisit appropriate scenes. Students typically look at video initially as "entertainment." Little analysis occurs during the first viewing. Then, when they discover a dilemma, specific scenes must be viewed and reviewed again, often as many as 8 to 12 times.

This review of scenes to solve problems and to trace decision making is not feasible with videotape technology. We found that videotape does not provide opportunities for exploration and for problem identification and generation at the level required for learning to occur. Print-based cases have an advantage over videotaped cases in this regard. In contrast to videotaped cases, print-based cases allow students to return more easily to specific parts and reread and reflect.

Teacher educators who promote problem solving try to help students notice characteristics of problem situations and define conditions under which to apply knowledge. Preservice teachers who would become problem solvers need multiple experiences to explore and apply factual and procedural knowledge. Videodisc and CD-ROM technology allows easy, rapid access to many sources of information—an access capability difficult to achieve with videotaped material. Such ease of access allows preservice teachers to combine information in ways that helps them foresee the effect of particular actions on teaching and learning outcomes.

Our multimedia presentations allow us to demonstrate that both the instructor and students can exercise many creative influences on the curriculum in college classes. Multimedia allow flexible interactions with available information and provide powerful opportunities for helping the instructor and students access materials to address and resolve instructional issues. Instructors do not "prescribe" content in ways that inhibit students' active pursuit of their own questions. Instead, instructors use content to support inquiry.

TEACHERS AS LEARNERS
AND LEARNERS AS TEACHERS

Perhaps the most important benefit of case-based instruction for promoting democratic instruction in college methods classes is that no single authoritative interpretation of issues and problems embedded within the cases exists. The analysis of cases allows preservice teachers to construct understandings of novel concepts and to confirm and modify existing understandings (Eeds & Wells, 1989; Leal, 1992). Case discussions promote positive attitudes among preservice teachers about their own contributions and about others' contributions to the learning. Students assume a variety of roles typically reserved for the teacher (McMahon, 1992; O'Flahavan, 1989).

Teachers of cases transfer the responsibility for learning to students, and students come to believe that they can control their own learning as they learn how to interact with one another (Alvermann, O'Brien, & Dillon, 1990; O'Flahavan, 1989; Slavin, 1990). We become instructors and mediators engaging students in interactions with one another and in reflection on the material. Our discussions about case content are intended to establish a community where it is understood that *learning and teaching builds from information everyone brings to the case and what everyone learns from the case* (Eeds & Wells, 1989; Peterson & Eeds, 1990). Learning comes from within the individual and is socially constructed and shared in the college classroom; neither the instructor nor any other member of the group imposes it.

One advantage of learning in problem-solving contexts is that students acquire information and knowledge about the conditions under which various concepts and facts can be useful (Bransford, Kinzer, Risko, Rowe, & Vye, 1989; Bransford, Sherwood, & Hasselbring, 1988; Risko, 1992, 1995; Risko, Peter, & McAllister, 1996). Our analysis of discourse that occurs during case analysis reveals a dramatic increase of high quality participation in class discussions. Students assume multiple roles as they address each other's ideas, as they generate connections across multiple texts and video materials, as they share personal experiences that explain ideas, and as they compare case concepts (Risko, 1992; Risko, Yount, & McAllister, 1992). Students improve their abilities to analyze classroom problems from multiple perspectives, to think flexibly about classroom problems embedded in our cases, and to apply content and procedural knowledge to their own teaching situations (Kinzer, Risko, Meltzer et al., 1993; Risko, 1991, 1992; Risko, McAllister, Peter, & Bigenho, 1994; Risko, Peter; & McAllister, 1996).

We find, though, that certain factors constrain the effectiveness of case-based teaching and its usefulness for promoting democratic teaching and learning. Collaborative learning arrangements do not always develop easily in college classes. Both instructors and students sometimes find meaningful dialogue elusive because the culture of "traditional schooling" is well established long before students enter college. From the instructor's point of view, lecturing can be comfortable; delivering a monologue presents fewer risks than encouraging dialogue. From the students' viewpoint, sitting passively in classes and taking notes instead of thinking can also be comfortable. Fox (1994) describes the problem as a reluctance of preservice teachers to voice their personal opinions because of a "fear of being wrong; a fear of being told you are wrong" (p. 395). Furthermore, as Delpit (1995) and others suggest, changing expectations and the culture of the classroom is particularly challenging when the instructor and students are ill-prepared to share their personal thoughts with others. Building a community that encourages participation and sharing around the analysis of cases requires openness to opposing viewpoints. Building such a community may take time, careful planning, and many opportunities to engage in discussions. As Welty (1989) suggests, effective discussions require "practice, practice, and practice."

The exploratory nature of case analysis requires the course instructor to adopt a role that supports students' active participation. Class discussions contain a series of "false starts" (Hartman & Allison, 1996) that can lead to important insights or false conclusions. The instructor must guide the learning events in ways that promote a careful study of case content while at the same time encouraging competing interpretations. The instructor must maintain a balance between an acceptance of different plausible interpretations of case information and keeping the discussion sufficiently focused (Grassman, 1992). It is important to help preservice teachers understand the consequence of conflicting interpretations of case data, so they do not take a position of choosing an interpretation that merely confirms their preexisting conceptions. Hence, the instructor needs to "shoot the arrows that may turn the group's attention to fruitful areas for dialogue" around competing theories and interpretations (Eeds & Peterson, 1994, p. 23). Edelsky (1994) and others indicate that the alternative to approaches that promote "one right answer" are not approaches that accept "any answer." Using cases for democratic instruction requires the instructor to promote and demonstrate a careful study of ideas, an acceptance of differing opinions, and methods for evaluating alternative actions and conclusions.

The benefits and problems we describe are common to case-based teaching whether the cases are written, videotaped, or presented with multimedia. We do know from our studies of how our multimedia cases affect our teaching and students' learning that several strengths of our cases also present our biggest challenges. We describe some of these challenges next.

There is the issue of comprehensiveness. Our cases represent entire units of instruction and are, therefore, filled with multiple, overlapping instructional episodes. We know the rich sources of information embedded in our cases provide a wide range of stimuli for discussion and invite in-depth study of multiple topics. We know, too, this richness of available information leaves much for the instructor to manage. Even though instructors begin each class with specific content goals, they must be prepared to help students think more deeply about issues that are identified. The instructor must also be prepared to access relevant information within and across cases (accessing scenes on the videodiscs or artifacts in the associated materials) when such access would enrich the discussions. The instructor's role as mediator takes on a new dimension (to the one just described) when multimedia applications are involved. Taking advantage of the many sources of information, the instructor needs to enable students to draw connections across the range of available information and help students think about the implications of this information.

Although we believe whole-class discussions are important for building community for our students, we know it is also important to provide for different organizations to support students' learning. Flexible applications of our multimedia allow for whole-class, small-group, and independent learning. For whole-class instruction, we take advantage of videodisc technology to project clear, sharp video images. We use our computer software to access scenes quickly with the random-access and frame-accurate search capabilities of videodiscs. This process allows us to support our discussions by revisiting appropriate scenes to clarify interpretations and to generate new issues. As noted, these whole-class discussions are effective for inviting participation.

We provide additional formats to allow students to pursue their own questions and to provide for focused discussions around selected topics. We are sensitive to the findings of others who suggest that some students participate more fully during small-group discussions and that such arrangements may produce deeper, personal understandings (Gall, 1984; 1987; Gall & Gall, 1976, 1990; Gall & Gillett, 1980).

When students are divided into small groups, they have access to the videodiscs or the cases on CD-Rom that can be accessed in computer labs. Additionally, we encourage students to study the CD-Rom materials so they can independently develop interpretations (Alvarez, 1996) before they share and extend their interpretations with their peers. Finally, students write cases about their own teaching in a practicum. These are shared with their peers during small-group discussions. All of these arrangements are designed to encourage inquiry.

We provide hypermedia to students so they can rearrange information to address different but related issues. Hypermedia provide flexible access to information. Such flexibility suggests the kinds of responses needed in multidimensional educational situations (Fitzgerald & Semrau, 1996; Spiro, Feltovich, Jacobson, & Coulson, 1991). Students explore case content in what Kaplan (1964) describes as a "logic of inquiry and the reconstructed logic in use afterward." They examine information, revisit ideas to support decisions, reconstruct connections to derive conclusions, and apply concepts to novel situations. We want students to make such connections as they make sense of case content and construct new knowledge (Kinzer & Risko, 1999). Our ultimate goal is to help preservice teachers apply newly learned information to respond to unpredictable situations.

CONCLUSIONS

The deliberate use of multimedia to enhance case-based instruction supports democratic teaching and learning principles by inviting preservice teachers to think critically about multiple sources of information and divergent viewpoints. We also want students to appreciate the value of collaboration to produce knowledge and reasons for applying what they are learning to solve problems they will face in their own teaching. These cases unleash the power of democratic learning communities in college classes. They help us display the contributions of each member for developing deep understandings of the content we are examining. They enable future teachers to envision how they can create similar democratically organized learning environments for children—environments that value critical thinking, collaborative learning, personal reflection, and respect for diverse perspectives.

REFERENCES

Alvarez, M. C. (1996). A community of thinkers: Literacy environments with interactive technology. In K. Camperell, B. L. Hayes, & R. Telfer (Eds.), *Literacy: The information highway to success* (pp. 17–29). Logan, UT: Utah State Press.

Alvermann, D. E., O'Brien, D. G., & Dillon, D. R. (1990). What teachers do when they say they're having discussions of content area reading assignments: A qualitative analysis. *Reading Research Quarterly, 25,* 296–322.

Applebee, A. N., Langer, J. A., & Mullins, I. V. S. (1988). *The nation's report reads best?* (Report No: 17–R-01). Princeton, NJ: Educational Testing Service.

Bransford, J. D., Kinzer, C., Risko, V., Rowe, D., & Vye, N. (1989). Designing invitations to thinking: Some initial thoughts. In S. McCormick & J. Zutell (Eds.), *Cognitive and social perspectives for literacy research and instruction* (pp. 35–54). Chicago, IL: National Reading Conference.

Bransford, J. D., Sherwood, R., & Hasselbring, T. (1988). The video revolution and its effects on development: Some initial thoughts. In G. Foremann & P. Pufall (Eds.), *Constructivism in the computer age* (pp. 173–201). Hillsdale, NJ: Lawrence Erlbaum Associates.

Bransford, J. D., Vye, N., Kinzer, C., & Risko, V. J. (1990). Teaching thinking and content knowledge: Toward an integrated approach. In B. G. Jones & L. Idol (Eds.), *Dimensions of thinking and cognitive instruction* (pp. 381–413). Hillsdale, NJ: Lawrence Erlbaum Associates.

Cazden, C. (1988). *Classroom discourse: The language of teaching and learning.* Portsmouth, NH: Heinemann.

Christensen, C. R. (1987). Teaching with cases at the Harvard Business School. In C. R. Christensen (Ed.), *Teaching and the case method* (pp. 16–49). Boston, MA: Harvard Business School.

Cognition and Technology Group (CTG) at Vanderbilt (1990). Anchored instruction and its relationship to situated cognition. *Education Researcher, 19,* 2–10.

Commeyras, M. (1993). Promoting critical thinking through dialogical-thinking reading lessons. *The Reading Teacher, 46,* 486–493.

Connelly, F. M., & Clandinin, D. J. (1990). Stories of experience and narrative inquiry. *Educational Researcher, 19*(4), 2–14.

Darling-Hammond, L. (1996). The right to learn and the advancement of teaching: Research, policy, and practice for democratic education. *Educational Research, 25,* 5–17.

Delpit, L. (1995). *Other people's children: Cultural conflicts in the classrooms.* New York: The New Press.

Edelsky, C. (1994). Education for democracy. *Language Arts, 71*(4), 252–257.

Eeds, M., & Peterson, R. (1994). Teachers as readers: Learning to talk about literature. *Journal of Children's Literature, 20*(1), 23–27.

Eeds, M., & Wells, D. (1989). Grand conversations: An explanation of meaning construction in literature study groups. *Research in the teaching of English, 23*(1), 4–29.

Egan, K. (1989, February). Memory, imagination, and learning: Connected by the story. *Phi Delta Kappa,* 455–459.

Ennis, R. H. (1987). A taxonomy of critical thinking dispositions and abilities. In J. B. Baron & R. J. Sternberg (Eds.), *Teaching for thinking* (pp. 9–26) New York: Freeman.

Fitzgerald, G. E., & Semrau, L. P. (1996, April). *Enhancing teacher problem solving skills in behavioral disorders through multimedia case studies.* Paper presented at the annual meeting of American Educational Research Association, New York.

Fox, D. (1994). What is literature? Two preservice teachers' conceptions of literature and of the teaching of literature. In C. K. Kinzer & D. J. Leu (Eds.), *Forty-third yearbook of the National Reading Conference* (pp. 394–406). Chicago: National Reading Conference.

Gall, J. P., & Gall, M. D. (1990). Outcomes of the discussion method. In W. W. Wilen (Ed), *Teaching and learning through discussion* (pp. 25–44). Springfield, IL: Thomas.

Gall, M. (1984). Synthesis of research on teachers' questioning. *Educational Leadership, 42*(3), 40–47.

Gall, M. D. (1987). Discussion methods. In M. J. Dunkin (Ed), *The international encyclopedia of teaching and teacher education* (pp. 232–237). Oxford, UK: Pergamon.

Gall, M.D., & Gall, J.P. (1976). The discussion method. In N. L. Gage (Ed.), *The psychology of teaching methods* (pp. 166–216). Chicago: University of Chicago.

Gall, M.D., & Gillett, M. (1980). The discussion method in classroom teaching. *Theory Into Practice, 19,* 98–103.

Gavelek, J. R. (1986). The social context of literacy and schooling: A development perspective. In T. E Raphael (Ed.), *The contexts of school-based literacy* (pp. 3–26). New York: Random House.

Grassman, P. L. (1992). Teaching and learning with cases: Unanswered questions. In J. S. Shulman (Ed.), *Case methods in teacher education* (pp. 222–239). New York: Teacher's College Press.

Greene, M. (1984). *Education, freedom, and possibility.* Inaugural lecture as William F. Russell Professor in the Foundations of Education, Teachers College, Columbia University, New York.

Hartman, D. K., & Allison, J. (1996). Promoting inquiry-oriented discussions using multiple texts. In L. B. Gambrell, & J. F. Almasi (Eds.), *Lively discussions!* Newark, DE: International Reading Association.

Hiebert, J., Carpenter, T. P., Fennema, E., Fuson, K., Human, P., Murray, H., Olivier, A., & Wearne, D. (1996). Problem solving as a basis for reform in curriculum and instruction: The case of mathematics. *Educational Researcher, 25,* 12–21.

Hynds, S. (1994). *Making connections: Language and learning in the classroom.* Norwood, MA: Christopher Gordon.

Johnson-Laird, P. N. (1985). Deductive reasoning ability. In R. J. Sternberg (Ed.), *Human abilities: An information-processing approach.* (pp. 177–199). New York: Freeman.

Kaplan, A. (1964). *The conduct of inquiry.* San Francisco: Chandler.

Kinzer, C. K., & Risko, V. J. (1998). Multimedia and enhanced learning: Influenced K–12 by transforming preservice classrooms. In D. Reinking, M. McKenna, L. Labbo, & R. Kieffer (Eds.), *Handbook of literacy and technology: Transformations in a post-typographic world* (pp. 185–202). Hillsdale, NJ: Lawrence Erlbaum Associates.

Kinzer, C. K., Risko, V. J., Meltzer, L., Bigenho, F., Carson, J., Degler, L., & Granier, D. (1993, April). *Designing videodisc-based case methodology for the reform of reading education courses: The classroom as a case.* Paper presented at the annual meeting of American Educational Research Association, Atlanta, GA.

Kleinfield, J. (1995). Our hero comes of age: What students learn from case writing in student teaching. In J. A. Colbert, P. Desberg, & K. Trimble (Eds.), *The case of education* (pp. 79–97). Boston: Allyn & Bacon.

Knowles, J. G., & Holt-Reynolds, D. (1991). Shaping pedagogies through personal histories in preservice teacher education. *Teachers College Record, 93*(1), 87–113.

Leal, D. (1992). The nature of talk about three types of text during peer group discussions. *Journal of Reading Behavior, 24*(3), 313–338.

Learned, E. P. (1987). Reflections of a case method teacher. In C. R. Christensen (Ed.), *Teaching and the case method* (pp. 9–15). Boston, MA: Harvard Business School.

McLarty, K., Goodman, J., Risko, V., Kinzer, C. K., Vye, N., Rowe, D., & Carson, J. (1990). Implementing anchored instruction: Guiding principles for curriculum development. In J. Zutell & S. McCormick (Eds.), *Literacy theory and research: Analysis from multiple paradigms* (pp. 109–120). Annual Yearbook of the National Reading Conference.

McMahon, S. (1992). *A group of five students as they participate in their student-led book club.* Unpublished doctoral dissertation, Michigan State University, East Lansing, MI.

Merseth, K. (1991). *The case for cases in teacher education.* Washington, DC: American Association of Colleges of Teacher Education and American Association of Higher Education.

National Commission on Excellence in Education (1983). *A nation at risk: The imperative for educational reform.* Washington, DC: National Science Board Commission.

Noori, K. (1995, Spring). Understanding others through stories. *Childhood Education,* 134–136.

O'Flahavan, J. F. (1989). *An exploration of the effects of participants' structure upon literacy development in reading group discussion.* Unpublished doctoral dissertation, University of Illinois, Urbana-Champaign.

Peterson, R., & Eeds, M. (1990). *Grand conversations: Literature study group in action.* New York: Scholastic.

Risko, V. J. (1991). Videodisc-based case methodology: A design for enhancing preservice teachers' problem-solving abilities. In B.L. Hayes & K. Camperell (Eds.), *Literacy international, national, state, and local. Eleventh yearbook of American Reading Forum* (Vol. 11, pp. 121–137). Logan, UT: Utah State University Press.

Risko, V. J. (1992). Developing problem-solving environments to prepare teachers for instruction of diverse learners. In B. Hayes & K. Camperell (Eds.), *Developing lifelong readers: Policies, procedures, and programs*. Logan, UT: Utah State Press.

Risko, V. J. (1995). Using videodisc-based cases to promote preservice teachers' problem solving and mental model building. In W. M. Linek & E. G. Sturtevant (Eds.), *Generations of literacy*. Seventeenth Yearbook of The College Reading Association (pp.173–187). Harrisonburg, VA: College Reading Association.

Risko, V. J. (1996). Creating a community of thinkers within a preservice literacy education methods course. In K. Camperell, B. L. Hayes, & R. Telfer (Eds.), *Literacy: The information highway to success* (pp. 3–15). Logan, UT: Utah State Press.

Risko, V. J., & Kinzer, C. K. (1999). *Multimedia cases in reading education*. Boston: McGraw-Hill.

Risko, V. J., McAllister, D., Peter, J., & Bigenho, F. (1994). Using technology in support of preservice teachers' generative learning. In E.G. Sturtevant & W. M. Linek (Eds.), *Pathways for literacy: Learners teach and teachers learn*. Pittsburg, KS: College Reading Association.

Risko, V. J., Peter, J, & McAllister, D. (1996). Conceptual changes: Preservice teacher' pathways to providing literacy transaction. In E. Sturtevant & W. Linek (Eds.), Eighteenth Yearbook of the College Reading Association. *Literacy grows* (pp. 103–119). Pittsburg, KS: College Reading Association.

Risko, V. J., Yount, D., & McAllister, D. (1992). Preparing preservice teachers for remedial instruction: Teaching problem solving and use of content and pedagogical knowledge. In N. Padak, T.V. Rasinski, & J. Logan (Eds.), *Inquiries in literacy learning and instruction* (pp. 179–189). Pittsburg, KS: College Reading Association.

Shulman, J. H. (1995). Tender feelings, hidden thoughts: Confronting bias, innocence, and racism through case discussion. In J. A. Colbert, P. Desberg, & K. Trimble (Eds.), *The case of education*. (pp.137–158). Boston: Allyn & Bacon.

Shulman, L. S. (1995). Just in case: Reflections on learning from experience. In J. A. Colbert, P. Desberg, & K. Trimble (Eds.), *The case of education* (pp. 197–217). Boston: Allyn & Bacon.

Silverman, R., & Welty, W. M. (1995). Teaching without a net: Using cases in teacher education. In J.A. Colbert, P. Desberg, & K. Trimble (Eds.), *The case of education* (pp. 159–171). Boston: Allyn & Bacon.

Slavin, R. E. (1990). *Cooperative learning: Theory, research and practice*. Englewood Cliffs, NJ: Prentice Hall.

Spiro, R., Feltovich, P., Jacobson, M., & Coulson, R. (1991). Knowledge representation, content specification, and the development of skill in situation-specific knowledge assembly: Some constructivist issues as they relate to cognitive flexibility theory and hypertext. *Educational Technology, 31*(9), 22–25.

Tharp, R. G., & Gallimore, R. (1988). *Rousing minds to life: Teaching and learning in social contexts*. New York: Cambridge University Press.

Vygotsky, L. S. (1978). *Mind in society: The development of higher psychological processes*. Cambridge, MA: Harvard University Press.

Welty, W. (1989, July/August). Discussion method teaching. *Change*, 41–49.

5

More and Less Acceptable Case Analyses: A Pragmatist Approach

Amy McAninch
University of Missouri–Kansas City

Editors' note: We save issues of evaluation for the end of the volume, when we might justifiably have addressed them at the outset. Does case-method teaching make a difference in how teachers behave and in what their students learn? Teacher educators often ask such questions as they consider adopting case methods. Amy McAninch suggests we must think more carefully about our expectations for cases. When we ask the right evaluation questions, and ask them early on, evaluation can have the effect of "pulling" teachers and teacher educators to behave efficaciously. McAninch puts the evaluation focus where it belongs: not on case methods versus traditional methods, but on how to determine if case methods promote democratic behavior in classrooms.

THE CASE

When Charles Langdell advanced the case method at Harvard Law School in the 19th century, assessment of students' case analyses was straightforward and uncomplicated. Case analyses, according to Langdell's philosophy of law, should adhere to precedent. In teacher education, however, it is currently averred that the knowledge base of teaching affords few, if any, precedents (Merseth, 1991). Clark and Lampert (1986) contend that knowledge for teaching is "tentative," and "transient" rather than static. Harrington (1995) asserts that in teaching there are "alternative solutions rather than 'correct answers'" (p. 203) and that these solutions are "competing, often equally valid" (p. 204). This new conception of knowledge for teaching is frequently cited as a rationale for case-based instruction aimed at the improvement of reflection, decision making, or problem solving (see, e.g., Merseth, 1991, 1996). Within this new conception of teacher knowledge, however, what makes one decision better than another? How are equally valid solutions to be assessed? Regardless of the nature of teacher knowledge, democratic teacher preparation requires well explicated, public, and justified evaluation standards.

One approach to this assessment problem is the construction of rubrics, which delineate specific instructional goals and a scale of performance standards for the purposes of evaluation. The growing literature on rubrics stems from the development of alternative assessment practices. Alternative assessments require an evaluator to exercise judgment in grading, unlike multiple choice or other types of standardized tests that can be machine scored (Herman, Aschbacher, & Winters, 1992). These assessment tasks provide students with "opportunities to *demonstrate* their understanding and to thoughtfully *apply* knowledge, skills, and habits of mind in a variety of contexts" (Marzano, Pickering, & McTighe, 1993, p. 13). Thus, the problem of assessing students' case analyses is part of the more general task of developing evaluation techniques for the alternative assessment of students' performance tasks.

Since teaching for democracy is the theme of this book, this chapter focuses on the development of rubrics for the purpose of assessing the degree to which democratic dispositions and understandings are manifested in case analyses. The objective is to construct rubrics that will explicitly delineate the qualities that differentiate more democratic from less democratic case analyses. Following an introduction to rubrics and their elements, assessment criteria are derived from theoretical sources, particularly one of Dewey's essays on democracy, and other philosophical writings. From these works, specific dimensions of learning outcomes, including definitions, examples, and nonexamples, are drawn. In the last half of this chapter, I use these assessment elements to assemble three different rubrics. Using one of the rubrics, I then assess a sample case analysis, written by a former student. The construction of a rubric is an interpretive task that requires considerable judgment on the part of an evaluator.

WHAT IS A RUBRIC?

The assessment of a task performance, such as a student's case analysis, requires a judgment by the evaluator as to how well the analysis meets instructional goals. Rubrics are one way of facilitating this task, whether the purpose of the evaluation is the provision of feedback for improvement (formative evaluation) or to see if standards were attained for the purposes of endorsement or promotion (summative evaluation). Rubrics vary in format, but they share the common characteristic of making evaluation criteria and standards public. Herman, Aschbacher, and Winters (1992) contend that rubrics should include four elements.

First, rubrics communicate instructional goals and their dimensions. For example, if English Usage is an outcome or goal for assessment, punctuation may be listed as a dimension. In the field of teacher education, the goal of cognitive growth was broken down into three dimensions: connectedness, flexibility, and perceived meaningfulness (Lundeberg & Fawver, 1994). Similarly, teacher reflection has been conceptualized in a wide variety of ways. Harrington, Quinn-Leering, with Hodson (1996) suggest that its dimensions, borrowing from Dewey, include open-mindedness and wholeheartedness, among others. According to Herman, Aschbacher, and Winters (1992), dimensions can be derived from curriculum guidelines, standards advanced by curriculum specialists such as the National Council for the Social Studies, educational theory, as well as other sources.

Herman, Aschbacher, and Winters (1992) advise evaluators to focus on those aspects of student performance that "reflect your highest priority instructional goals and represent teachable and observable aspects of performance" (p. 57). Thus, if punctuation is a dimension, then the teacher/assessor ought to have strategies for helping students attain greater achievement in punctuation and give it emphasis in instruction.

A second element in a rubric is the provision of examples, definitions, and/or descriptions of each dimension. These descriptors communicate the meaning of each dimension for students and for evaluators. Herman, Aschbacher, and Winters (1992) assert that for assessment purposes, each of these dimensions should be explicitly defined and accompanied by examples. The provision of nonexamples can also contribute to the clarity of dimensions.

A third element is a scale of values that demarcate different levels of performance on a particular outcome. Herman, Aschbacher, and Winters (1992) describe three different types of rating scales: checklists, numerical ratings, and qualitative ratings. They suggest that the type of ratings scale adopted for a particular assessment should depend on the purposes of the assessment:

> If your purpose is to *describe* what students can do, perhaps for parent conferences … you may be able to use the simplest rating scale of all, the checklist. If you need more information than simply whether or not a student is engaged in specific aspects of a task, you will need a more fully developed rating scale. When you want to know the *extent* to which dimensions were observed or the quality of performance, you need more elaborate scales. (p. 64)

Checklists require the evaluator to report on the attainment of dimensions in a "yes/no" manner, whereas qualitative ratings demand inference. For example, a qualitative rating scale might include labels such as "below expectations," "acceptable," and "well done." Marzano, Pickering, and McTighe (1993) suggest that one label or point on the scale represent satisfactory performance. In their rubrics, which are all based on a scale ranging from 1 (high) to 4 (low), a rating of 3 represents satisfactory performance. For grading purposes, these labels could be assigned a corresponding grade or point system. For example, a student could receive one point for each dimension he or she was below expectations, two points for each dimension performed "acceptably," and so on. These points could then be summed and attached to a grading scale, such as a total of 7 to 9 points would equal an "A." A fourth type of rating scale, an ipsative scale, is discussed near the conclusion of this chapter.

Finally, the evaluation of a performance must be based on a conception of what constitutes excellent performance for that particular learning outcome. One of the greatest virtues of a rubric is that it communicates standards of excellence, making them accessible to students and serving as a referent throughout a course (see Herman, Aschbacher, & Winters, 1992). Rubrics provide "performance targets" (Marzano, Pickering, & McTighe, 1993, p. 29). Too often, standards of excellence are tacit or implicit, rather than explicit and shared.

Given this brief introduction to rubrics, the next task is to derive learning outcomes and their dimensions from educational theory. An essay by Dewey (1939/1993) is the primary source of learning outcomes related to democracy.

DEMOCRATIC THEORY AS A SOURCE
OF INSTRUCTIONAL GOALS

Dewey's (1939/1993) essay on democracy is a particularly useful source for deriving dimensions, or the specific learning outcomes from which to develop rubrics for assessing case analyses. This essay is a particularly succinct argument that provides a compelling conception of democratic dispositions and values. His work is supplemented by the work of other pragmatists, including Bode (1924, 1927) and Griffin (1941). The work of the philosopher Dennis (1935) provides insight into undemocratic learning outcomes, suggesting nonexamples of democratic understandings and dispositions.

Dewey (1939/1993) asserts that "democracy is a *personal* way of individual life; that it signifies the possession and continual use of certain attitudes, forming personal character and determining desire and purpose in all the relations of life" (p. 241). He suggests that it can be characterized by a "working faith" in three principles summarized next.

The first tenet is that the citizens of a democracy are moral equals. Dewey (1939/1993) writes, "The democratic faith in human equality is belief that every human being, independent of the quantity or range of his personal endowment, has the right to equal opportunity with every other person for development of whatever gifts he has" and to lead his or her own life "free from coercion and imposition by others" (p. 242). This right transcends "race, color, sex, birth and family, of material or cultural wealth." (p. 242). Stereotyping and prejudice, for example, are undemocratic because they violate this faith.

The second tenet of democracy, according to Dewey, is that human beings are capable of intelligent judgment and action "if proper conditions are furnished" (p. 242). He asserts that reflection, the method of intelligence, is central to a democracy where good citizens participate in the reconstruction of values and decide for themselves what to believe. Where inquiry is closed off or where indoctrination takes place, democracy is eroded. Democracy implies a faith in the intelligence of individuals to thoughtfully foresee the consequences of alternatives for themselves and others, which Dewey (1910/1985) links to the concept of freedom: "Genuine freedom, in short, is intellectual; it rests in the trained *power of thought*, in ability to 'turn things over,' to look at matters deliberately, to judge whether the amount and kind of evidence requisite for decision is at hand, and if not, to tell where and how to seek such evidence…. To cultivate unhindered, unreflective external activity is to foster enslavement, for it leaves the person at the mercy of appetite, sense, and circumstance" (p. 232). In addition, where the social consequences of alternative courses of action are not considered, democracy is weakened. Griffin (1941) warns, "Cranks and spies may not be as dangerous to our democracy as is the careless attitude of many of us when we say, 'That's not my funeral,' or 'what do I care?' or 'That's your hard luck'" (p. 26). Griffin asserts that in a democracy, social sensitivity is necessary in any judgment of what to do.

Finally, Dewey (1939/1993) describes the third principle of democratic faith: the ability of individuals to work together on a day-to-day basis to settle conflicts and solve problems. Dewey observes, "Democracy is the belief that even when needs and ends or consequences are different for each individual, the habit of amicable cooperation … is itself a priceless addition to life." (p. 243). Citizens governed by a democratic attitude do not fear disagreement and conflict, but rather see in conflict the possibility for cooperation and enrichment of experience. What is undemocratic is suppression, force, and coercion.

From this brief discussion, dimensions of a learning outcome, "democratic dispositions," can begin to be derived to serve as a basis for judging students' case analyses. Democracy is strengthened by the day-to-day working faith in the commitment to moral equality and the capacity of individuals to construct their own purposes, and to cooperative efforts to resolve disagreements.

These dimensions are further clarified by examining a totalitarian model of school and society. Karier (1986) believes that the work of American theorist Lawrence Dennis is an exemplar of fascist educational thought. In the 1930s and 1940s, Dennis argued that schools should serve the interests of the dominant elite, those who do the thinking for the masses. In this view, the school should transmit the myths of the dominant elite through indoctrination and propaganda (Dennis, 1935). Further, this model of school and society assumes that individuals are incapable of self-rule and that inquiry is superfluous to the task of developing a stable collectivity. Social stability, when not accomplished through indoctrination, can be achieved through force. Thus, distinctly undemocratic faiths include the idea that an elite should rule the masses, that reason and inquiry are pointless, and that conflict should be resolved through force.

If the manifestation of democratic dispositions is an instructional outcome for assessment, the more these tenets are manifested in students' case analyses, the more satisfactory the performance. Evidence of undemocratic dispositions would result in a low ranking. This conception of democracy suggests another instructional goal for inclusion in the rubric; namely, reflective thinking.

REFLECTION IN A DEMOCRACY

This view of democracy means that an emphasis has to be placed on the thinking processes that will support intelligent choosing within a context of democratic values. In *How We Think* (1910/1985), Dewey forwards a conception of reflective thought that he believed was the best process for that task: *"active, persistent, and careful consideration of any belief or supposed form of knowledge in the light of the grounds that support it, and the further conclusions to which it tends"* (p. 185). Democracy requires a deep and careful assessment of the consequences of alternatives, rather than a superficial or half-hearted one. Intelligent decision making rests on the insightful and thorough assessment of what is likely to happen as a consequence of any particular decision, and a willingness to bring reflective thought to bear on problems. It also requires a capacity to assess the grounds for claims and a care for reasons. The pragmatists sought growth in reflective thought as the cornerstone of the curriculum, and gave emphasis to metacognition.

Of course, there are types of thinking opposed to reflective habits. One example is uncritical dependence on authority or experts for claiming to know what to think. This type of thinking is distinct from the judicious use of expert knowledge. Dewey notes that over-dependency on authority acts as a barrier to reflective thought; Belenky, Clinchy, Goldberger, and Tarule (1986) more fully elaborate the epistemological understandings that accompany this tendency. They describe this type of thinker as a *received knower*, because he or she claims to know exclusively from outside authorities and has little ability to think independently. Because democracy depends on citizens choosing for themselves based on reason (as opposed to receiving ready-made doctrine), this epistemological orientation does not support democratic culture.

A second type of authoritarian thinking is manifested by the individual who claims to know what is true from firsthand experience or gut instinct to the exclusion of other sources of evidence or better reasoning. Belenky et al. (1986) call this perspective *subjective knowing*. Subjective knowers rely on their unreflective firsthand experience to tell them what to do or believe, and repudiate claims to other sources of evidence (books, studies, etc.). They rely on their intuition in problem solving and repudiate science as threatening to their way of knowing. This is a highly subjective and individualistic worldview, one that hinders the assessment of assertions on the basis of reflective thinking. Belenky et al.(1986) points out that this type of orientation is as authoritarian as received knowing, but that the authority has shifted to an internal source. Individuals who are subjective in their outlook cannot assess arguments or engage in the type of reflective thinking Dewey prescribes; their minds resist the experimental attitude he sought.

In developing assessments with a view to democracy, these intellectual habits as they are manifested in performances are rated low because they are authoritarian in nature and opposed to the reflective habits Dewey and others associated with democratic life. The care for reasons and the thoughtful analysis of the consequences of various courses of action are rated high as they are manifested in case analyses.

MASTERY: THE DEVELOPMENT OF UNDERSTANDING

A third goal derived from these ideas about democracy is a conception of learning emphasizing the development of meaning and understanding, rather than rote or mechanistic learning. In *Democracy and Education*, Dewey (1916) forwards a definition of education as the reconstruction of experience "which adds to the meaning of experience, and which increases ability to direct the course of subsequent experience" (p. 76). To learn is to see connections and relationships between previous understandings and new information. Bode (1924), in a similar vein, suggests that learning consists of attaching 'meanings' to our environment and that conduct hinges on these meanings: "This dependence of conduct on "meaning" is familiar enough. To burn one's fingers, to get scratched by the cat, or to quench one's thirst at the drinking fountain, is to discover new meanings, which are then used for the guidance of conduct" (p. 5). Thus, educative experience also signifies greater power over subsequent experience, to anticipate outcomes with greater accuracy.

Subject matter mastery is associated with this idea of insight and control. Mastery in this sense is not the mechanistic ability to recite, but the ability to anticipate consequences and shape outcomes through an understanding of general principles. Broudy (1961) provides some insight into this conception: "Accordingly, we say that a physician has a higher level of mastery than the nurse. His theoretical context is so well developed that the novel, the peculiarities of the individual case, baffle him only until he can fit them into this theoretical framework. Because he may fear the effects of a narcotic on the digestive system of the patient, he may vary its amount or eliminate it altogether … Such adaptiveness based on theory is not expected from the nurse" (p. 84). This is why the analysis of cases as an assessment task can be so powerful: it tests mastery in this much more complex sense.

One last point about mastery is the role of concepts in understanding. Concepts are the standard meanings with which individuals think. Dewey (1910, 1985) observes "All judgment, all reflective inference, presupposes some lack of understanding, a partial absence of meaning. We reflect in order that we may get hold of the full and adequate significance of what happens. Nevertheless, *something* must be already understood, the mind must be in possession of some meaning which it has mastered, or else thinking is impossible" (p. 273). The acquisition of concepts is a necessary precondition to reflective thought because "increase of the store of meanings makes us conscious of new problems, while only through translation of the new perplexities into what is already familiar and plain do we understand or solve these problems" (p. 274).

When used as criteria for the assessment of case analyses, the accurate use of concepts, the ability to make connections among concepts, and the adaptive use of principles will be rated as above expectations, and the absence of these qualities will be rated low.

On the basis of this analysis, a rubric in the form of a table can be constructed (see Table 5.1). The three rows represent the three learning outcomes derived from the preceding discussion and the three columns represent different levels of performance, labeled "below expectations," "acceptable," and "well done." Within each cell are descriptors for each goal and level of performance. This rubric provides fairly elaborate feedback regarding the students' performance along each dimension. It would be possible to divide the rating scale into even finer gradations, perhaps differentiating five or six levels of performance. Such decisions, again, depend on the specific purpose of the assessment, a point that Herman, Aschbacher, and Winters (1992) repeat frequently.

In examining this rubric, two issues warrant further discussion. First, it is important to return to the question of whether these dimensions are teachable. Herman, Aschbacher, and Winters (1992) make the point that teachers ought to have interventions to improve student performance along the dimensions selected for assessment. It is not fair to assess for an understanding or skill that a teacher has no means of improving. Reviewing this rubric, one should ask if there are interventions to improve democratic dispositions, for example. That efficacious interventions are available to strengthen all the outcomes will be assumed for the sake of this analysis.

Second, and perhaps more complex, is the observation that simply because particular dimensions can be logically derived from theory does not necessarily imply a straightforward translation into educational goals. For example, reminiscent of some of the debates in the Depression-era journal, *The Social Frontier*[1], some philosophers might object to the idea of systematically attempting to strengthen and assess democratic values. Such an instructional goal, they might argue, is undemocratic in itself because it constitutes shaping. They might favor a rubric that contains only the "reflection" and "mastery" outcomes as more democratic. Again, although this issue is an important one, for the purposes of this chapter, I assume that the inclusion of "democratic dispositions" as a learning outcome is itself democratic. In the next section, I use the rubric represented in Table 5.1 to assess a student case analysis.

---

[1]*The Social Frontier: A Journal of Educational Criticism and Reconstruction*. New York: The Social Frontier, Inc., 1934–1939.

TABLE 5.1

Rubric for Summative Evaluation of Case Analyses

	Below Expectations	*Acceptable*	*Well Done*
Mastery	Addresses topic, but mischaracterizes the problem posed in the case or doesn't describe the issue posed. No use or misuse of concepts and principles	Addresses topic and characterizes the problem, but not elaborately or with precision. Uses concepts, but with errors. Little flexibility or adaptability in use of concepts.	Accurate and detailed description of problem. Flexible and adaptive use of concepts and principles.
Reflection	No or few reasons offered for analysis, little concern for facts of the case or their accuracy. Consequences of alternative courses of action not described or weakly anticipated.	Some reasons offered, but not compelling or convincing. Concerns for consequences of alternative actions evident, but these are only moderately elaborated.	Reasons offered which are compelling and insightful. Anticipates consequences with insight and creativity. Elaborate analysis.
Democratic Dispositions	No or little social sensitivity, e.g., uses stereotyping or generalizations about groups. Manifests a self-interested view: "What's in it for me?"	Concern for equity issues and respecting individuals, but not elaborated. Attempts to understand perspectives of others, but lacking insight.	Manifests concern for equity and analyzes case with a view toward respecting persons. Seeks to understand positions of others and generally succeeds. Manifests concern for knowledge and facts, and quality of thinking done.

USING A RUBRIC: AN EXAMPLE
OF A STUDENT'S CASE ANALYSIS

To illustrate how this rubric might guide judgment, a student's case analysis is provided next. The case analysis was written for an 8-week graduate course that I taught entitled "Political and Ethical Structure in Education." One of the books for the course was Feinberg and Soltis's *School and Society* (1992), which introduces three sociological theories: functionalism, conflict theory, and interpretivism. The text includes a selection of cases for analysis. The students were assigned to interpret one of the cases, "Workforce School" (pp. 125–126), from a functionalist perspective, making ample use of the concepts and theoretical principles in their analysis. Functionalism is associated with the sociologists Parsons and Merton, among others, and emphasizes the functional role social processes and institutions play in maintaining equilibrium in a social system. The integration of individuals into society through the transmission of social norms is, according to functionalist theory, a key role for the school.

"Workforce School" describes an inner city school that had long suffered a high dropout rate and violence in the surrounding area. A new principal is hired who develops a community-based work-study program for the students. The crime in the neighborhood wanes, the dropout rate falls, but students in the school who had intended to go to college are penalized in their applications to selective colleges by the reputation of the school as vocationally oriented. The case ends with the following question: Did the principal, Mr. Gomez, do the right thing in developing the work–study program? What follows is the case response of one student, Linda Jones, who volunteered her work for inclusion in this chapter:

Workforce School: Case Study Analysis by Linda Jones

In this case study, a dysfunctional school changes its approach to a more vocational school in order to serve the social and community needs of its students. Faced with low morale, the deterioration of an inner-city school, a population of culturally and economically deprived students, and a high drop out rate, Elmo High took drastic steps to reach out to the community and school population in an attempt to once again play a key role in the development and education of the citizens that it served.

Regarding its success after implementing this experimental curriculum, I believe a functionalist might agree that this school is striving to serve the society. By offering a program that educates children to serve a role, even a vocational one, within our society, a functionalist could argue that the need for role differentiation is served within the given educational system at Elmo High. Since functionalists believe that universally compulsory education is closely related to the requirements of an industrial society, I believe that they would at first support the efforts of Elmo High. The school has stepped forward to assume its responsibility to teach necessary skills and attitudes toward work and achievement that are necessary for our society.

It could be argued that the schools' goals fit with the functionalist concepts of *universalism,* or *uniform treatment of individuals* at Elmo High; *achievement*, hands-on work–study programs; and *independence*, by nurturing responsible actions.

Yet another functionalist goal for education, meritocracy, which suggests that the distribution of social rewards should be based upon merit, and not on gender, race, or social class, is not adhered to at Elmo High. By making such sweeping curriculum changes at Elmo High, entire populations of children have been cast into a world of limited choices. In this way, Mr. Gomez's changes, while providing opportunities for some students, have not provided opportunities for all. Individual merit is no longer a goal when there is a cciling on attainment. A student who is deprived of an opportunity to proceed with their education simply because he or she is living in the surrounding community and attending Elmo High, has not been judged based upon merit, but instead upon class.

With regard to the functionalist educational goal of specificity, which should allow for exceptions to be made for the individual, the functionalist would argue that Elmo High needs to make changes in its curriculum so that individuals could choose to complete enough credits to attend college. By not making a specific exception for students who need to go beyond the prescribed curriculum, the functionalist norm of specificity is being violated. I feel that the norm of specificity must be observed in order to allow for *meritocracy*. How can we provide opportunities for children to succeed based upon their own merit if we oblige them to settle for educational programs that close doors to their potential?

In summary, although Elmo High is striving to serve the vocational needs of the surrounding community, fostering role differentiation, while implementing educational norms of independence, achievement, and universalism, the norm of specificity and the goal of meritocracy are limited. I believe the functionalist would have to admit that Elmo High's policies ultimately threaten social solidarity by creating a group of people who are locked out of higher levels of education, not because of their lack of merit, but because of ascribed characteristics.

Returning now to Table 5.1, this rubric facilitates the assessment of each outcome in turn. Across the mastery domain, we can look at each dimension of mastery and how well Linda performed on it. Clearly, Linda provides an accurate and succinct description of the problem in the opening paragraph of her analysis. She uses the concepts from the functionalist perspective throughout her paper and elaborates two of them in particular, meritocracy and specificity. She defines these ideas accurately and aptly in her analysis. By elaborately showing how the principal's actions did not serve either meritocracy or specificity, her analysis reflects adaptive use of concepts. Thus, on this outcome, she earns a rating of "well done."

On the outcome of reflection, Linda's work clearly manifests a concern for grounding her conclusions, carefully offering reasons for her assertions. A good example of basing her conclusions on reasons is in paragraph 4, in which she states that Mr. Gomez's changes do not forward meritocracy because the students are deprived of opportunity based on class. She also anticipates the consequences of Mr. Gomez's actions creatively in the final paragraph in which she concludes that he may well threaten social solidarity in the long run by blocking opportunities to a particular group. Thus, on this outcome, a rating of "well done" also is apt.

Finally, on the outcome "democratic dispositions," Linda expresses concern for the inequity of the situation at Elmo High and notes in paragraph 4 of her analysis that some students have a ceiling placed on their attainment. To the extent that she recognizes this violation of the principle that all citizens of a democracy have the right to develop themselves to the fullest regardless of race, sex, social class origin, and so on, she is manifesting a democratic attitude. She does not address the perspectives of those who might favor Mr. Gomez's position, such as the individuals living in the crime-ridden neighborhood surrounding the school. On this particular dimension, this chapter might warrant an "acceptable" rating, yet she expresses the concern for equity quite well. Perhaps the "well done" rating is justified, with feedback on the need to improve the multiple perspectives dimension.

Table 5.1 represents a rubric that contains analytic scoring criteria: it provides separate ratings for each learning outcome. The rubric in Table 5.2 is designed to provide a global or holistic score (see Herman, Aschbacher, & Winters, 1992, pp. 70–71). The holistic score could be assigned numbers or labels, as in Table 5.1. The rubric in Table 5.2 is loosely based on a format included in Herman, Aschbacher, and Winters (1992, pp. 56–57). It has been adapted to the instructional outcomes advanced in this chapter.

TABLE 5.2

Score	Description of Performance
0	No attempt
1	Addresses topic, but mischaracterizes the problem posed in the case or doesn't describe the issue posed. No use or misuse of concepts and principles. No or few reasons offered for analysis, little concern for facts of the case or their accuracy. Consequences of alternative courses of action not described or weakly anticipated. No or little social sensitivity, e.g., uses stereotyping or generalizations about groups. Manifests a self-interested view (What's in it for me?)
2	Addresses topic and characterizes the problem, but not elaborately or with precision. Uses concepts, but with errors. Little flexibility or adaptability in use of concepts. Some reasons offered, but not compelling or convincing. Concerns for consequences of alternative actions evident, but these are only moderately elaborated. Concern for equity issues and respecting individuals, but not elaborated. Attempts to understand perspectives of others, but lacking insight.
3	Accurate and detailed description of problem. Flexible and adaptive use of concepts and principles. Reasons offered which are compelling and insightful. Anticipates consequences with insight and creativity. Analysis well elaborated. Manifests concerns for equity and analyzes case with a view toward respecting persons. Seeks to understand positions of others and generally succeeds. Manifests concern for knowledge and facts and the quality of thinking done. The rubric could be expanded to include more finely differentiated levels of performance. While the global score does not provide as much specific feedback as the analytic score, it may be appropriate for certain types of case analysis or case assignments.

Sort 1 Mastery

	No use or misuse of concepts, does not address problem or mischaracterizes problem	Accurate use of concepts, but not elaborate, addresses problem but not well detailed	Accurately and elaborately connects concepts to each other and to each other, adjusts principles to case
Incomplete sentences, poor organization	Rate as 1	Rate as 1	Rate as 1
Complete sentences and logical organization, but errors	Rate as 1	Rate as 2	Refer to Sort 2
Succinct word choice, varies sentence structure, effective organization	Rate as 1	Refer to Sort 2	Refer to Sort 2

(a)

Sort 2 Reflection

	No or few reasons offered for analysis, little concern for accuracy of facts, alternative courses of action not described or weakly anticipated	Some reasons offered, but not well developed or compelling. Concerns for alternative actions evidence, but not elaborate	Reasons offered which are compelling and insightful. Anticipates consequences with creativity and insight. Elaborate analysis.
No or little social sensitivity, may be stereotyping or generalizing about groups. Little concern for perspectives of others.	Rate as 2	Rate as 2	Rate as 3
Concern for equity issues and respecting individuals, but not elaborated. Attempts to understand perspectives of other, but lacks insight.	Rate as 2	Rate as 3	Rate as 4
Manifests concern for equity and analyzes case with a view toward respecting persons. Seeks to understand positions of others and generally succeeds.	Rate as 2	Rate as 3	Rate as 4

(b)

FIG. 5.1. (a) Sort 1: Mastery; (b) Sort 2: Reflection.

In Fig. 5.1, a very different format for a rubric is presented. This rubric guides the evaluator in the assignment of a numerical score through the elaboration of levels of performance along both the rows and columns of a series of tables. Levels of performance for one outcome are described across the columns, and for a different outcome down the rows. For this reason, this type of rubric requires the assessment of an even number of learning outcomes. Writing quality as an outcome was added to the three instructional goals elaborated in this chapter. If the rubric depicted in Fig. 5.1 was used to assess Linda's case analysis, for example, the evaluator would first turn to the first table, Sort 1, and no doubt find that her paper warranted a score higher than 2, given the quality of writing and the ample and apt use of concepts and principles in her paper. Moving on to the next table, Sort 2, the evaluator could move to the far right column with respect to reflection, but what about the "democratic dispositions" aspect? Here, because of the way the sort has been designed, whether or not the "democratic dispositions" manifested were acceptable or exceeded expectations, the paper would be rated as a 4.

One interesting feature of this rubric is that it is not symmetrical. That is, the scores are arranged such that weakness in reflective thinking, even if democratic dispositions are manifested well, is not going to earn a student more than a score of 2. On the other hand, excellence in reflection and weakness in democratic dispositions earns a student a score of 3. This weighting system illustrates the flexibility of rubrics to emphasize the evaluator's priorities.

Finally, Table 5.3 presents an ipsative scale, which forces a ranking of dimensions from most well done to least well done relative to each other. This scale forces an evaluator to select the learning outcome on which the student was the strongest and the weakest, even if the student's performance was above expectations on all the outcomes. The purpose of the scale is to provide formative evaluation for improved performance.

This ipsative ranking supplements the rubrics in Tables 5.1 and 5.2, and Fig. 5.1. In the case of Linda's case analysis, the ranking process is probably easiest by starting with what was done least well. In Linda's case, the weakest dimension is proba-

TABLE 5.3
Ipsative Rating

The following six dimensions are to be ranked (1 = most well done, 6 = least well done) according to the student's relative performance on the following dimensions.

Rank	Dimensions
_____	Use of concepts
_____	Description of problem
_____	Provision of reasons
_____	Anticipation of consequences
_____	Concern for equity
_____	Concern for perspectives of others

bly "concern for perspectives of others." By assigning that a 6, the ranking process would proceed to the next weakest aspect of the case analysis. Perhaps it would be the "description of the problem," because Linda's description was accurate and succinct, yet it might have also been described using the functionalist concepts. This dimension might be ranked fifth. If we rank her use of concepts as first, and her provision of reasons as second, then perhaps her concern for equity and anticipation of consequences can be ranked 3rd and 4th, although it is close. As I have noted, ipsative scales are difficult when there is little variation in performance among dimensions, but they have the potential of conveying helpful information that supplements the other rubrics.

CONCLUSION

In this chapter, I addressed the question of what makes one case analysis more acceptable than another, given the goal of promoting democratic dispositions. One possible set of answers is encoded in the rubrics presented in this chapter. Rubrics themselves reflect democratic values. They manifest respect for persons by making evaluation criteria explicit and by elaborating standards of excellence as goals for all students. Further, the construction of rubrics, ideally, is a collaborative process taking into account the perspectives of all the stakeholders in the evaluation process. It is also a reflective act, requiring evaluators to consider alternatives, examine consequences, and reexamine the choices made. Finally, rubrics are designed to assess the type of thinking and learning Dewey described as essential to democracy. This type of learning involves the development of understanding, rather than simply rote memorization. As rubrics are embedded in instruction, they actually contribute to the process of learning that Dewey called the reconstruction of experience.

REFERENCES

Belenky, M. F., Clinchy, B. M., Goldberger, N. R., & Tarule, J. M. (1986). *Women's ways of knowing.* New York: Basic Books.

Bode, B. H. (1924). *Fundamentals of education.* New York: Macmillan.

Bode, B. H. (1927). *Modern educational theories.* New York: Macmillan.

Broudy, H. (1961). Mastery. In B. O. Smith & R. Ennis (Eds.), *Language and concepts in education* (pp.72–85). Chicago: Rand McNally.

Clark, C. M., & Lampert, M. (1986). The study of teacher thinking: Implications for teacher education. *Journal of Teacher Education, 37*(5), 27–31.

Dennis, L. (1935). Indoctrination: The task before the American school. *The Social Frontier, 1*(4), 11–15.

Dewey, J. (1916). *Democracy and education.* New York: Macmillan.

Dewey, J. (1985). How we think. In J. A. Boydston (Ed.), *How we think and selected essays: 1910–1911. John Dewey: The middle works, 1899–1924. (*Vol. 6, pp. 277–356). Carbondale, IL: Southern Illinois University Press. (Original work published 1910)

Dewey, J. (1993). Creative democracy: The task before us. In D. Morris & I. Shapiro (Eds.), *John Dewey: The political writings* (pp. 240–245). Indianapolis, IN: Hackett. (Original work published 1939)

Feinberg, W., & Soltis, J. (1992). *School and society* (2nd ed.). New York: Teachers College Press.

Griffin, A. F. (1941). *What do you mean Be Good?* Columbus, OH: J. W. Irwin.

Harrington, H. (1995). Fostering reasoned decisions: Case-based pedagogy and the professional development of teachers. *Teaching and Teacher Education, 11*(3), 203–214.

Harrington, H., Quinn-Leering, K., with Hodson, L. (1996). Written case analysis and critical reflection. *Teaching and Teacher Education, 12* (1), 25–37.

Herman, J. L., Aschbacher, P. R., & Winters, L. (1992). *A practical guide to alternative assessment.* Alexandria, VA: Association for Supervision and Curriculum Development.

Karier, C. (1986). *The individual, society, and education.* (2nd ed.). Chicago: University of Illinois Press.

Lundeberg, M. A., & Fawver, J. E. (1994). Thinking like a teacher: Encouraging cognitive growth in case analysis. *Journal of Teacher Education, 45* (4), 289–297.

Marzano, R. J., Pickering, D., & McTighe, J. (1993). *Assessing student outcomes.* Alexandria, VA: Association for Supervision and Curriculum Development.

Merseth, K. K. (1991). *The case for cases in teacher education.* Washington, DC: American Association of Colleges of Teacher Education.

Merseth, K. K. (1996). Cases and case methods in teacher education. In J. Sikula, T. Buttery, & E. Guyton (Eds.), *Handbook of research on teacher education* (2nd ed., pp. 722–744). New York: Macmillan.

II

CASES

6

Leslie Turner: A Teacher Under Stress

Edward R. Ducharme
Mary K. Ducharme
Drake University

Editors' note: Leslie Turner enters her first year of teaching in a small, midwestern town with a commitment to help students "live" American history, not simply to acquire facts and read the standard interpretations of the past. She slowly makes friends at home and work, but like so many other teachers, she feels essentially alone. Not until Leslie turns the community into a learning laboratory where inquiry is the norm and no historical events are out of bounds does she realize the true excitement of teaching. Students eagerly explore the Holocaust, World War II draft resistance, Farther Coughlin's radio diatribes, and more, all with the intent of making connections from historical events to life in their own community. When angry parents complain about the invasiveness of student investigations, Leslie begins to understand just how closely the curriculum and community values can be linked. When she works with a colleague to recast and reteach the unit another year, Leslie must face the classic dilemma of many socially active teachers—that of deciding what is legitimate compromise and what constitutes "selling out" one's beliefs.

THE CASE

The Community

Moretown is one of four small communities in a midwestern, rural state. Its population is 3,500. Two of the four towns are essentially bedroom communities for

Urbanville, the only large city in the region; 10 years ago they were farming areas. The commuters from these towns work at such places as a large electronics plant, a regional hospital, the state university, banking and insurance organizations, and a variety of businesses. The other two towns are primarily farming communities; the individuals in these towns generally have no more than a high school education, although some of the farmers graduated from the state agricultural college. Residents of Moretown and the three other towns are 91% White; the remaining 9% are composed of recent immigrants from Latin America who work on farms and a small number of African Americans with roots dating back to the 1860s. Forty percent of the people are Catholic; the remainder who identify themselves as belonging to any formal religious group are scattered among various Protestant denominations; there is a small born-again Christian community that maintains its own school; 2% of the population is Jewish.

The residents of the communities have traditionally voted Republican by a 2-to-1 margin. There are occasional clashes in the communities between the newcomers and the old-timers; the clashes typically deal with such matters as possible sites for a new elementary school, books in the school library, raising of school levies. However, other than an occasional dispute, general harmony exists among the towns.

The School and the Students

Prairie View High School, the senior high school, serves Moretown and the three other rural towns and enrolls 1,100 students. Built in 1987, it remains the subject of occasional controversy. Old-timers recall when each town had its own high school, and everybody knew everybody. In the past several years, Prairie View students garnered a number of regional and state-wide honors in academics. The athletic teams are intensely competitive with those of the schools in Prairie View's division. Although these developments ameliorated some of the dissatisfaction over the loss of the towns' high schools, some community members still lament the loss and wistfully recall the days when "everybody got to play."

The population changes engendered by the growing commuter characteristics had some effects on the school curricula. The percentage of graduates going on to higher education rose from 23% to 47%, a change largely resulting from the presence of the children of the newcomers. Some parents pushed for a more college-oriented curriculum. This produced occasional confrontations between some long-term residents and the newcomers. The issue, in part, is whether or not the school should prepare students for life in Moretown and the surrounding communities or for a life that includes going away to school.

The students fall into the late-20th-century pattern of dividing into brains, jocks, and geeks, with an occasional crossover. Unrest among the students is minimal; there appears to be a tolerance for everybody else, as long as individuals do not try to be too integrative in their social activities. Prairie View has had no racial incidents.

The Teachers

Seventy percent of the faculty at Prairie View are from the local area; only 2% are minority. Most of the teachers attended the regional college that 40 years ago was a state teachers college. They tend toward a traditional teaching style of lecture and recitation. They have been slow to adapt to the recent technological additions to the school. A year ago, the electronics company in Urbanville donated computers for all the classrooms. Those utilizing the computers and the attendant World Wide Web access are mostly the 10 or so recent hires in the school. Skepticism toward the technology runs high among the veterans who, in the main, resisted the voluntary staff development program offered last semester.

A pleasant ambiance exists in the school. Students view the teachers as helpful, kind, and intelligent. A few of the more technologically talented students complain about some of the veteran teachers who refuse to use technology, but they find solace in the presence and support of the newer teachers. The teachers take a casual attitude toward the use of technology. Most conclude that, with the range of interests among the faculty, the students will acquire the necessary skills prior to graduation.

Leslie Turner

Leslie Turner is a first-year social studies teacher, a graduate last June from the state university. She grew up in another state; her parents are university professors and social activists. She herself has been active since early high school days on social issues. A magna cum laude graduate in history, she sees her job as that of raising the academic potential of the students and awakening their social conscience. She believes that the study of history must go beyond the facts and the standard interpretation, that students should develop critical skills in considering historical events. They should be able to "do" history. From her first day in the school, she makes use of technology in her teaching.

Leslie's original career plans were to go on to graduate school and pursue a PhD in American history. During her junior year in college, she attended a conference that stressed the need for teachers of quality, and she decided to give teaching a try. She quickly enrolled in as many precertification courses as she could, took summer school courses, and student-taught during the second semester of her senior year. She applied for positions in several communities but heard nothing. In mid-July, while she was at home wondering what she should do, she received a phone call from the principal at Prairie View High School, one of the schools to which she had applied. He explained that an older teacher had suddenly decided to retire and asked her if she would like to come in for an interview. She agreed and had her interview with the school principal in mid-August. A few days later, she received an offer for the position. She accepted, quickly moved into a small apartment in Moretown, and eagerly awaited the opening of school.

The teacher whom she replaced was a veteran social studies teacher at Prairie View High School, a longtime resident of the community who had seen the teaching of social studies primarily as a vehicle for indoctrinating students in the "rightness of the American way of life," as he so often expressed his view during his 30 years of teaching. He had earlier taught in one of the town high schools; many in the town saw him as a link between the old and new ways.

Prior to the opening of school, the district had a day-long workshop in which an outside consultant talked about new ways of assessing student performance. Inasmuch as Leslie knew very little about the old ways of assessing students, she didn't find the session very helpful. The rest of her induction to the school system was a half-day of activities consisting of filling out necessary papers for payment and insurance. In other words, she had no introduction to the world of work she was about to enter. She knew virtually nothing about the communities from which the students came. There were three other new teachers starting their careers; no one made any attempt to bring the first-year teachers together nor was there any mention of mentoring. The other three new teachers all had grown up and gone to school in the region. The principal did introduce each new teacher and indicate how happy he was to have them here, and how good they were going to be.

The Incidents

School begins, and, although Leslie suffers some of the travail of most beginning teachers, she does rather well during the opening months of the school year. The students like her, and she likes most of them. She feels a bit lonely, but she stays in touch with her parents and slowly makes a few friends in the school and in the condo association where she is living. The months fly by, and it soon is the second semester. The busy activities of teaching, the planning and revising—these and related activities keep her so occupied that she has little opportunity to develop anything beyond casual relationships with the other teachers. For their part, the other teachers are cordial and friendly, but they, too, are preoccupied with their own lives and work. Beyond a couple of relationships, she is left much to herself.

The school has alternate Wednesday afternoon staff development activities. Leslie initially thought these might be useful to her, but she quickly discovers that the meetings turn into information giving by the principal or other, to her, mindless activity. No one visits her classes; occasionally the social studies department chairperson asks her how things are going. Leslie, on two occasions, dropped by the chairperson's office and talked with her briefly about obtaining a video for her classes. The chair was pleasant but clearly not of a mind to have long conversations.

Among her several classes, Leslie teaches a twelfth-grade American history section with 23 students, about half of whom plan to attend college. During the first 7 months of the year, Leslie and the students established good working relationships. The students are cooperative, do their homework, participate in class, and get along well with one another. Despite these positive conditions, Leslie believes that, although they are nice kids, they need to be shaken up a bit in their beliefs. When Leslie brings current events to the fore in the class, students appear bored and restless. What's happening in Washington and in the state's capitol does not appear to interest them. Their indifference frustrates Leslie; she wants them to examine in more detail the meaning of democracy and the roles citizens should play. Her social activism habits emerge; she decides to change her curriculum by focusing on issues she believes will both interest the students and cause them to raise questions. After one of the staff development sessions, she walks out of the meeting with Mr. Barenson, an experienced social studies teacher, and tells him a little bit about her slowly forming plans to bring some exciting materials to the class and try to get the students more involved in thinking about history and its implications for contemporary life. He listens intently, senses her excitement, talks a little bit about the conservative side of some members of the community, and then says, "Be careful Leslie; your excitement may carry you a bit far." Leslie nods and says that she doesn't think what she's planning will cause any problems. As she walks to her car, she reflects that the three or four sentence conversation with Mr. Barenson and a couple of brief conversations with the department chairperson have been the extent of "curriculum discussion" she has had since arriving at Prairie View High School. In one of her preservice courses, the professor had talked about how lonely teaching can sometimes be, how often veteran teachers are little inclined to talk with new teachers in any detail beyond basic conversation. She had not thought it would become as isolated a situation as it apparently had become.

Leslie, however, is determined to change the status of her course with the twelfth-grade American history class. Thus, as part of the curriculum for this class during the last 2 months of the academic year, Leslie decides to focus on prejudice in America in the first half of the 20th century. She spends all of her spring break in planning the course for the rest of the semester. Because of where she and the class are in the course, which is based on a chronological approach to history, she decides to focus on the 1930s and 1940s, the period of study where the class "should" be if it is to finish the semester by reviewing the 1970s. She obtains books, films, periodicals, Internet sites, and other materials detailing American reactions to the Nazi treatment of Jews in the 1930s and 1940s; controversial papers about the role of the Catholic Church in the Holocaust, Franklin Roosevelt's positions on these matters, and the American Nazi Party; the internment of Japanese Americans in the 1940s; Ku Klux Klan activities in the 1930s and 1940s, even to the extent of demonstrating the existence of a local 1940s chapter in this Midwestern state; and tapes of Father Coughlin's radio talks in the 1940s. She makes extensive use of the World Wide Web and develops book marks with important pages for student use.

Leslie introduces the materials and the implicit ideas in them. At first puzzled by the change in the curriculum, the students soon become very excited; they eagerly ask questions, engage in discussion, and ask one another about their families. Leslie and the students, using traditional textbooks and the Web, develop copies of the original documents about the period. They explore the limits of knowledge acquisition on some of the issues as a consequence of the Freedom of Information Act. They discover that the Web contains "nonhistory" as well. One student finds a page dedicated to those who claim the Holocaust was a hoax. The students are learning how writers can use material to fit their preconceptions, distort the past, and confuse readers.

The students go home and talk about what they are reading and studying, raising questions with their parents about what their grandparents did during the decades under study. Some come to class with old letters and journals; one student has a complete collection of photos of her ancestors. Two students want to work together, using United States draft board records, to develop a paper on enlistments by members of various local ethnic groups in the armed forces; another student is interested in determining the number of conscientious objectors from the area in World War II. Another has written to one of the major networks to try to obtain transcripts of some of Father Coughlin's radio talks. All appears to be going well. Leslie is ecstatic. In her enthusiasm, she fails to notice four or five students who, while they are participating, appear tentative about the materials.

The scene shifts forward 3 weeks. Suddenly, much is not going well. Excited students have been exploring things that upset some of the parents. One student has examined documents and records about the internment of Japanese Americans in the Midwest during World War II and learned that at least one local person—a relative—served as a guard for the camps; another discovered a membership list of a regional KKK group from the 1920s. One of the African American students in the class learns that, although most members of the community were sympathetic to the plight of slaves and were generally Abolitionists, one family had held slaves. The lone Jewish student in the class learns that several communities in the state had practiced unwritten discrimination against Jews owning property. Leslie is excited with the discoveries of these and other students, but some parents are displeased. They do not like the idea of digging into the negative sides of the communities' histories. One parent sends a note to Leslie in which she says, "That is all in the past and best forgotten. I don't want my kids learning bad things about their family and getting cynical about this great country." Several sets of parents get together and conclude that they must do something about this young teacher and her weird ideas about what is appropriate for high school students to study.

As a consequence of the parental furor over what their children are studying and doing, the questions they are raising, what is perceived by some as "snooping" into the beliefs and practices of ancestors, this group becomes a volunteer committee of parents from the political right and mostly from the farming communities that meets with the superintendent of schools and persuades him to look into Leslie Turner's curriculum. Hearing of the controversy, other parents, mostly from the commuter towns and a few from the farming towns, who favor Leslie's curriculum, enter the matter. The superintendent asks the principal to hold a meeting with the concerned parents from both sides. A week later, during the twelfth-grade American history class, Leslie receives a note asking her to come to the principal's office after school.

Thus does Leslie end up sitting in the principal's office with the principal and some parents from both sides of the issues. The questions and comments on the agenda from the right are: "What has this stuff got to do with American history and when are you going to start teaching my kids some good things about American history?", "Why should my kids learn unpleasant things about this community, things that got resolved a long time ago?", and "My family has been in this community for 100 years; we're loyal Americans and don't want anybody raking us or our ancestors over the coals." The questions and comments from the parents on the left on the agenda are: "What's the matter with this curriculum?", "Why shouldn't the schools teach about the weaker aspects of American history?", and "It's about time this school got away from lectures and facts. Kids need to learn to think for themselves."

Leslie is dumbfounded; she had no warning about the topic of this meeting; she had heard no word of criticism from any parents until this meeting. She remembers that Mr. Barenson, when he saw some of the handouts that Leslie was giving the students, had cautioned her about the conservative side of many of the residents of the community. She recalled his words: "Be careful, Leslie; your excitement may carry you a bit far." But she had never thought she would end up in the principal's office.

The meeting goes on for about an hour and a half. There is considerable animosity between the two groups of parents. Leslie sits perplexed. The principal allows all parents to have their say on the matter. He tells them that, although Leslie has altered the curriculum somewhat, the students are still learning American history. This statement does little to calm the parents who feel negatively; one comments, "Yeah, but what history!" Given a few moments at the end of the meeting, Leslie tries to explain her curriculum and her reasons for using the approach she has used. "I did this to help the students begin to think about how complex the world is; I want them to be able to function effectively in the 21st century. The world is changing. They're not always going to live in Moretown, and even if some of them do, Moretown is changing, too." Her remarks provoke resentment in several of the parents who don't like the curriculum: "Well, I don't know about anybody else's kids, but mine are staying right here in Moretown when they get out of high school." "Maybe things are changing in other places, but Moretown is going to stay the same." And on it goes. Those who like the curriculum are full of praise: "It's about time someone helped these kids think about tomorrow." "My son actually is curious about history now." And so on.

Finally, the meeting ends as an uneasy truce evolves. The principal makes a couple of comments including one that Leslie should have contacted parents when she was planning a controversial curriculum. Leslie wonders silently how she was supposed to know it was controversial, but she agrees to shorten the unit; both sides of parents agree, some reluctantly, that their children were learning some good things from the curriculum. The weeks go by and, as always happens, the semester closes. Leslie is exhausted. She had remained tentative during the last few weeks; for the first time, she questioned her approach, her values. She wonders, "Was I right to try to teach so many things that would cause students and parents so much concern? How was I to know?"

Questions for Part 1

- What are the curriculum issues in this matter?
- What are possible answers to Leslie's last two questions?
- What are the academic, developmental, and social rationales for what Leslie is teaching?
- Should Leslie have taught what she did?
- What is the role of the principal? Do you think his behavior appropriate?
- What principles of learning apply to this situation?
- How do you think you would have acted differently? Why?
- Considerable controversy exists in America about the teaching of religion in public schools. Do you think Leslie, in her examples of the Pope and Father Coughlin, is violating any strictures about religion and the public schools? Why or why not?

THE SECOND YEAR

Leslie had eagerly begun her summer break, a break that included a visit to the university from which she had graduated and some discussions with Professor Marion Mandarin, her former social studies methods instructor. Although the professor sympathized with Leslie, she was not particularly helpful. At the end of her second meeting with Professor Mandarin, the professor suggested that perhaps Leslie should get a " … few years teaching under your belt before you take on such a curriculum." Because Leslie was not very eager to get into controversy again, she thought that might be a good idea. She decided she was simply going to teach the "standard" social studies curriculum. She returned to Moretown in late July and began to prepare for the opening of school.

In early August, five incoming seniors, who were going to be in her American history class, come to see her. They heard about some of the exciting things that the last group did and say that they wanted to study, as one of them put it, "Exciting stuff like they did, not the same old book junk." Leslie quickly becomes excited; just as quickly she puts aside the unpleasant memory of meeting with the principal and the parents, the pain at having to close the controversial portion of the curriculum down sooner than she had wanted to. After an hour or so, the kids leave. Leslie promises them that she will give some thought to their request and meet with them before school starts.

As soon as the students leave, she calls Mr. Barenson, the veteran social studies teacher who had told her, "Be careful Leslie; your excitement may carry you a bit far." She briefly describes what happened and asks if they can meet and talk about the situation. She says she needs someone to help her think through what she should do. She knows she wants to respond to the students' request, but she also knows she does not want to end up in the principal's office again with a bunch of parents.

A week later, Leslie and Mr. Barenson have lunch together. Each brings the school district social studies guide to lunch. It is not a very helpful document. It ends with the statement: "The goal of the social studies curriculum in Prairie View High School is to provide students with curricular experiences so that they will have both an understanding of the richness of the nation's past and the wherewithal to be effective citizens in a democracy."

Mr. Barenson and Leslie have a good conversation at lunch. They spend part of their time discussing teaching in general terms. Mr. Barenson quickly establishes that she should call him "Gene" and not "Mr. Barenson." This distinction gets them off in a good frame of mind. Gene then reminisces a bit about his own career, telling Leslie how he had gotten into hot water a number of years ago during the Watergate controversy when he asked students to interview their parents about how they felt about President Nixon's role in the matter. He laughs and says that it had been a good learning experience for him. Leslie asks him what he learned, and Gene responds that he learned that he should be more careful about what he focused on in class, that he should have known more about community mores and norms before he began innovating in the curriculum. Leslie feels somewhat relieved at hearing that this respected teacher had similar problems early in his career, but she is still worried about the coming semester and how she will be able to teach "controversial" topics without being controversial.

Gene indicates how he had been aware of Leslie's difficulties last spring, but that he had chosen not to talk with her beyond his simple warning, believing that it was the right and role of each teacher to work out his or her difficulties. But he then says that this attitude or belief of his should not be construed to mean that he is not willing to listen, talk, and help.

Some general conversation follows about the nature of teaching in America in the 1990s, the growing conservatism on the part of general public, regional and national pressures to improve test scores, and other such matters. At this point, Leslie refers to the district social studies guide and reads aloud the statement that "The goal of the social studies curriculum in Prairie View High School is to provide students with curricular experiences so that they will have both an understanding of the richness of the nation's past and the wherewithal to be effective citizens in a democracy." She asks plaintively, "How do I do both of those things—provide stuff on the nation's past and help students become effective citizens—without getting into trouble? How do I respond to these students who want to explore controversial issues?"

Gene and Leslie spend the next hour discussing these matters. They agree to meet again and do so on two successive Monday afternoons. Over time they work out a way in which Leslie can both teach about American history and involve the students in asking questions and exploring issues through extended readings, work on the Internet, and studying current newspapers for parallels. They decide to work closely together in the teaching of American history. Most important, they agree that they will host a couple of citizens' nights at school to which they will invite all the parents in each of their American history classes and talk with them about the curriculum. They will ask the parents for their suggestions about what contemporary issues they would like to see their sons and daughters exploring in their schooling.

Leslie meets with the students, as she had promised. She tells them of the plan. They listen intently and appear a bit deflated because they interpret the curriculum Leslie is now talking about as less exciting. She reassures them that things will be exciting and important. She feels a little bit as though she is trying to convince herself.

School opens and things go extraordinarily well. The students in both Gene's and Leslie's classes enjoy looking at the early history of America through the various perspectives that the teachers help them set. Gene and Leslie spend time developing lessons and activities using the World Wide Web. The students are interested to learn that all was not as pure in the origins of the country as they had learned in earlier grades. Gene, using his long experience and considerable historical knowledge, is able to provide a leavening presence to some of the things that Leslie proposes to teach. For example, when the matter of the contradictions between some of Thomas Jefferson's written views and his actual life comes up, Gene provides counterbalancing materials that teach the students the complexity of history.

More than 30 parents come to their first evening session and are excited about being asked for their thoughts on the curriculum. Their suggestions turn out to be a bit pale: teach them to respect their government; teach them to be good citizens; don't turn them into troublemakers; prepare them for college; don't turn them against their communities. However, Leslie and Gene have prepared handouts on several key items they are studying; after they distribute them, the meeting becomes much more animated. One of the handouts features the various points of view of the Loyalists and the Revolutionists prior to and during the Revolutionary War; they show how family members sometimes were against family members. One parent comments about how he remembers his dad saying how that was the way things were in his family during the Vietnam War. Several parents ask for copies of some of the things Leslie and Gene are providing the students. It is clear from the nature of the request that interest in the materials has stimulated the action, not a desire to pry and control. Gene and Leslie leave the meeting happy. Leslie's crisis of the past year, at least for the time being, seems a long time ago.

Questions for Part 2

- Do you think Leslie yields too much in her agreement with Gene?
- Is it possible to teach "controversial" topics without being controversial?
- What would you have done in Leslie's situation? Why?
- What do you think students are learning about the democratic process as they watch and participate in the classes of Gene and Leslie?

- Maxine Greene (1995) wrote that classrooms " ... ought to resound with the voices of articulate young people in dialogues always incomplete because there is always more to be discovered and more to be said" (p. 43). In what ways is Leslie Turner's teaching, with its inclusion of alternative interpretations of history, supporting the idea that students should learn that " ... there is always more to be discovered and more to be said"?

TEACHING NOTES

The case of Leslie Turner offers students and teachers opportunities to consider a variety of issues including teaching about democracy, foundation issues, curriculum, pedagogy, and professional development. Leslie probably studied these issues in her teacher preparation program; now she must wrestle with them in all the complexities of her own teaching situation. But the dilemma is not Leslie's alone; other teachers, the principal, parents, and students also have both their own perspectives about what has taken place and their own roles to play. An initial approach to this case, then, is to unravel the threads of the case, so the case study participants can consider the various actors in the case and their perspectives, major issues that must be resolved, information that is needed, and potential courses of action. The case is useful for more in-depth study of some of the issues in the case.

In the first part of this section, we pose some overarching questions and suggest some activities and questions to explore the case as a whole. In the second party, we consider key issues in more depth, suggest resources that might be helpful in studying the issues, and propose activities for in-depth exploration of the issue.

Using the Case

We recommend using this case with either advanced undergraduate or graduate preservice students, either just before or after student teaching, or with masters level students with experience in teaching.

We suggest the first activity should be with small groups after students have read the case carefully. In our own use, we have given the case as part of a reading assignment outside of class. Once the students are in class, after reading the case, we divide them into groups.

Exploring the Case in Small Groups

If the group studying the case is larger than seven or eight people, individuals will probably profit from the case by first analyzing it in small groups. In small groups, discuss the case, using the following questions as a guide:

- What are the facts of this case?
- What has happened?

- What is the story from Leslie's perspective?
- What does she perceive to be the issue(s)?
- What is the story from the parents' perspectives? What do they perceive to be the issues? From students' perspectives? The principal's perspective? Are there other perspectives that should be taken into account?
- What do you consider the central issues of the case? In your group, discuss them, and list them in order of importance.
- What are the issues that relate to living, learning, and teaching in a democracy?

Issues Inherent in the Case

In this case, Leslie Turner encounters many questions beginning teachers often face:

- How do I decide what to teach? Does material have to fit both a curriculum demand and an interest and developmental level of students?
- How do I balance my own personal beliefs and values with those of the community? How does a new teacher learn abut the community beliefs and values?
- How do I balance meeting student needs and preferences with parent concerns and expectations?
- Should the curriculum reinforce prevailing student thinking and community norms or challenge them?
- What should I do?
- What do I need to learn?
- Where can I get help?
- What do I need to know about a community in order to teach effectively in it?
- What must I know about the developmental levels of the students as I select ideas and materials for study and discussion?

Education Standards and Democracy

Often teachers teach materials, concepts, and facts simply because they are in the text or they have "always" been part of the curriculum. Most of the disciplines that teachers teach in secondary schools have either state or national standards for what the curriculum should contain, particularly with respect to broad goals and outcomes. The Leslie Turner case raises issues related to the controversies in 1996–1997 with the proposed standards for history. The authors of *National Standards for History in the Schools* state that "Students may acquire the habit of seeing matters through another's eyes and come to realize that by studying others, they can also better understand themselves. Historical understanding ... does not require approval or forgiveness for the tragedies either of one's own society or others'; nor does it negate the importance of critically examining alternative value systems and their effects in supporting or denying basic human rights and aspirations of all peoples (p. 1)." Further, "These learnings directly contribute to the education of the *public citizen*, but they contribute to nurturing the *private individual* as well. Historical memory is the key to self-identity, to seeing one's place in the stream of time, and one's connectedness to all of mankind.... Denied knowledge of one's roots and of one's place in the great stream of human history, the individual is deprived of the fullest sense of self and of that sense of shared community on which one's fullest personal development as well as responsible citizenship depends (p. 42)."

The instructor can distribute a copy of the quotations from the *National Standards* document and raise questions with the students. Leslie's curriculum additions during her first year of teaching might well have forced the students to look into their own roots and begin to ask the larger questions of life in a complex democracy. Students might consider the following questions:

- Do you agree with the perspectives in the quotations from the *National Standards* document?
- Would you support the directions of Leslie's endeavors?
- Why or why not?
- Writing of the goals in a New York State report on curriculum, Neil Postman (1995) notes: "There are many other goals along these lines with which no one could disagree. But there is one, as we say, conspicuous by its absence, at least to me. I refer to the goal of 'acquiring and/or deepening a love of one's country.' One would have thought that among forty-one goals designed for students going to school in America, and going to school free of charge, and pretty close to as long as they wish, at least one of them would concern promoting an affection, even if a muted one, for their country" (p. 130). Should love of country be a goal of public education? Why or why not? Do you think Leslie's curricular innovations will or will not promote love of country?

Role Playing

We developed various scenarios for role playing including the following:

- A playing out of the meeting in the principal's office in which students play the various parts. The role-playing event requires that the students strive to get into the minds of the different participants and try to understand what makes them behave the way they do and forces them to attempt to articulate views clearly and persuasively.
- An imagined sequence between Leslie and the social studies department chair halfway during her second year of teaching. As students prepare to assume one of the two roles they should consider: What issues should the chair raise with Leslie? What kinds of questions might Leslie have of the chair?

• A meeting between Professor Mandarin and Leslie during the winter vacation after the successful autumn. Students will recall that Professor Mandarin advised Leslie to wait for a period of time before she tackled such controversial material, yet here she is visiting him and telling him of success. Perhaps the professor can play the professor.

• A social event of the students in which they talk about their class. Students often talk of school events outside of the company of adults. Those role playing should attempt to think through what the students are experiencing. They got what they asked for in slightly altered conditions. Will they think that Leslie has sanitized the material and that they are not getting what the other students told them they had experienced?

• A midautumn meeting between Gene and Leslie.

Student Writing

Students should do a journal entry in which they (a) write a futures scenario about Leslie; (b) speculate on the long-term effects of Leslie's teaching on her students; (c) relate what occurs in the case to what they know about human development; (d) reflect on how they might have acted in parallel situations; and (e) ask themselves how they think they would have reacted to something similar in their own secondary school days.

Enacting Democracy

We noted in the introductory remarks that famous Americans from Thomas Jefferson through William Jefferson Clinton have argued for the need for this nation to have an educated citizenry, one that will know how to live with others and be a contributing force in the greater society.

To explore the application of the material of this case to that observation, the class can break into small groups and consider the following questions:

• Why do you think students studying Leslie's material will or will not be helped to become members of an educated citizenry, one that will know how to live with others and be a contributing force in the greater society?

• How has Leslie supported or not supported students' rights in schooling? Has she demonstrated "democracy in action" as she attempted to teach about life in a democracy? Do you think she had an obligation to ensure that students would also find and study some positive events as well as the negative, disturbing ones?

• To what degree should Leslie have or not have involved community in her curriculum changes? What rights do citizens have in these matters? Education is a mater of local concern and control. In this democracy, what level of control over curriculum should the community have? What obligations do teachers have to involve the community in key curricular decisions?

• What do you think are the students' likely learnings about democracy when they learn of how the superintendent and principal have handled Leslie's situation? Consider: The superintendent and principal discussed, however briefly, the classroom situation and the community reaction without consulting Leslie; the superintendent handed the matter over to the principal; the principal called a meeting of community members and Leslie without informing her. How do these actions reflect the values of participatory democracy, or do you believe that the situations merely reflects how things should happen in an organization? What would be your reaction if something similar occurred to you in your first year of teaching, or your fifteenth year of teaching?

Human Development

Educators study human growth and development as they pass through their preparation programs. Often, however, they may or may not attend to principles of human growth and development of the students whom they teach when they prepare materials for students to study that are of particular interest to them. They sometimes are unaware of how developmentally unsettled they themselves may be to confront and deal with the issues student reactions may raise in them. Students should consider the following questions either in large or small groups:

• From your experience and knowledge, how prepared developmentally are twelfth-grade students to encounter the type of material that Leslie is giving them? Leslie is asking them to study and write about events and ideas that may call into question long-held community values and beliefs. The list of things she invites the students to explore include those questioning the role of religious leaders, politicians, government in general, concepts of equality. Some students may have quite settled views about one or two of these matters; for instance, they may hold very positive views of those in leadership positions in religious groups. Will the questioning of seeming absolutes be helpful or harmful to them? No "magic" age exists when all students are ready to confront such material, but one can surmise that different students may be ready at different ages.

• How prepared developmentally do you believe that Leslie is to deal with the complex materials and their possible reactions? Think about yourself and how you will be able or unable to deal with the complexities of adolescent emotions, parental and community values and norms, and administrative decisions affecting you.

• In your experience and knowledge, do communities have levels of development that make it easy or hard to accept certain things being taught? Think back to the community in which you were reared. Was there ever an incident or event that startled the community? Sometimes things occur in communities that produce an "anywhere but here" reaction.

• Living in a democracy is a complex concept for learners of almost any age to grasp fully. Think about yourself and the degree to which you were able to think through such complexities when you were the age of Leslie's students. Do you think you would have been able to relate such matters to everyday life? Why or why not?

• Where or to what sources could Leslie go to find material that would help her with developmental issues?

Final Activity

Students should write what they have learned about pedagogy, learning, and democratic principles from their experiences with Leslie Turner, either in a formal paper or in a journal entry.

REFERENCES

Greene, M. (1995). *Releasing the imagination.* San Francisco: Jossey-Bass.
National Center for the Study of History in the Schools. (n.d). *National Standards for History in the Schools.* Los Angeles, CA: National Center for the Study of History in the Schools, University of California, Los Angeles.
Postman, N. (1995). *The end of education: Redefining the value of education.* New York: Knopf.

7

A Case of Cruel
and All-Too-Usual
Punishment

Betty Hallenbeck

Editors' note: Hallenbeck's case raises issues of fairness, caring, professionalism, and colleagueship. If children are to emerge from their schooling with positive feelings about the society in which they live, they should go through school receiving fair and just treatment. Hallenbeck presents a situation in which the administration of a school, and at least some of the faculty, accept beatings as a normal occurrence in schooling, even when the students receiving the beatings have obvious mental or physical problems affecting their behaviors. Ms. Palmer faces the classic dilemma of a teacher caught in a situation clearly in conflict with her own values and beliefs. What is Ms. Palmer to do if she continues to find employment in schools with codes of conduct and punishment alien to her beliefs? What are the responsibilities of individuals like Ms. Palmer as they attempt to teach the young in fair and equitable ways?

THE CASE

It's Over

It's hard to describe how I felt as I put the last of my students' good-bye cards into the copy-paper box along with a few other personal items. Although I was sad at how things turned out and angry at a system that victimized children, I was mostly just relieved the year was over. My first year of teaching had finally ended. It had been disastrous. Summer vacation couldn't last long enough.

I didn't stop to say good-bye to anybody on my way out. As I drove away, I imagined the teachers and administrators giving a collective sigh of relief. They were as glad to see me go as I was to leave.

On my way home, I stopped for a walk in a small park that was one of my favorite places. I sat on a sunny rock recollecting my first year as a teacher, trying to remember when things began to unravel.

The New Job, the School, and the County

The job was my first teaching position, and I was incredibly excited about it. I was teaching fourth grade in the morning and special education resource classes in the afternoon. This was my ideal job; it allowed me to use my skills in both general and special education.

The school, Oak Forest Elementary, is one of four schools in the Emory School District. Oak Forest had the unusual configuration of fourth through seventh grades. The district also ran a primary school, an eighth- and ninth-grade middle school, and a high school for Grades 10 through 12. All of the schools were located together, thus simplifying the logistics of busing, cross-school collaboration, and sharing services such as speech/language pathology and specialty area teaching.

Emory County is a rural farming community that is developing into a bedroom community for people working in nearby Kingston, a small city with a major university and a range of industries. Although good for the county, the new growth strained the school system and other social service agencies. Previously, all the students came from similar backgrounds. Now the rural children from homes without running water found themselves in classes with children who lived in upscale developments, had television sets and stereos in their bedrooms, and owned all the Nintendo® games. Teachers struggled to meet the needs of these two diverse groups of students.

Almost all of Emory's teachers and administrators were native to the area. Born and reared in Emory County or one of the adjacent, equally rural counties, they had known each other for most of their lives and spent many nonworking hours together at church or in community activities. Most of the teachers had taught parents, cousins, and older siblings of some of their current students.

I was one of few exceptions to Emory's unstated policy of hiring individuals who had grown up in the area. The district hired me because no locals had graduated with degrees in special education in the past few years. I felt every bit the outsider when I was at work. Although my colleagues were always outwardly friendly to me, I sensed that they talked about me behind my back and snickered at this stranger to their small community.

Once, when I walked into the faculty room, the conversation stopped suddenly. I had heard only broken phrases like "thinks she can love them into behaving" and "toughen up soon or she won't make it," before the talking ceased. I kept my cool and acted like this didn't matter, but I was hurt and angry at being a topic of public discussion. I had no idea that I would soon become the talk of the entire school district, branded as "that liberal troublemaker" for my ideas on classroom discipline.

The Beginning of the End

The day that Derek fell apart during his special education reading class was the beginning of the end for me. I could tell Derek was about to lose control but felt powerless. I tried the few management techniques that came to mind: stating the consequences for his behavior, praising him for the things he did right, attending to students who were behaving well. The few tricks I learned during student teaching were useless now. Nothing seemed to help. Then it happened.

"Five minutes until recess," I reminded my students, trying to sound casual.

"No fair," hollered Derek. "I can't be done in 5 minutes!"

"Derek," I responded gently, "You've had as much time to do your assignment as everyone else. You chose not to use your time well."

Derek glared defiantly at me. "You made me lose recess. I hate you and you're ugly."

As the knot in my stomach tightened, I tried to keep my voice steady. "Derek, I know you're angry about losing recess. You've had enough time to do your work and you knew the consequences if you chose not to." Derek muttered something that I was glad I couldn't hear clearly and returned to his assignment. I thought that I had avoided disaster and marveled at my luck.

"Okay," I said to the class, "If your work is done you may turn it in and head out for recess. Thank you for working so hard today."

After my remarks, students began their usual chaos of scraping chairs, chatting, and locating playground equipment. Suddenly one sound drowned out the rest of the mayhem: a low groan from Derek grew to a wailing that sounded like a wounded animal. He was standing by his desk making the most terrifying sound I had ever heard. When his anguished cry finally faded, he jerked a globe off the desk next to his and flung it through the air. The next few seconds of silence felt like an eternity. Carol (my instructional assistant), the students, and I were transfixed by what had happened. Derek stood frozen, anger and defiance glinting in his eyes.

When I could speak again, I motioned for Carol to remove the other students as quickly as possible. I scrawled a note for Carol to take to Mr. Morris, the assistant principal: "Please come to my classroom and remove Derek Beach."

As Carol and the other students left, I felt nervous being alone in the classroom with Derek. I had no idea of what to say to Derek now. I was counting on Mr. Morris to arrive soon. I could never have predicted what would happen when he walked through my classroom door.

Royal Morris is a large man with a weathered face. He is strong and might have been intimidating if he weren't so courteous. Royal had always been soft-spoken and polite when talking with me. He was a southern gentleman—holding the door for me, standing whenever a woman entered the room, subtly touching his hat brim to acknowledge me in the local market. I thought of him as a gentle giant, sort of a large teddy bear. I assumed that Royal would be as amiable and calm with my students as he had always been with me. I couldn't have been more wrong.

"BOY!" barked Royal, as he slammed through the door, John Wayne style. "You are in a world of trouble now, boy!" Royal bellowed as he jerked Derek by the arm and pulled the boy off his feet toward the door.

Royal turned to me and with a startling transformation said softly, "Ms. Palmer, I'd be pleased if you would kindly accompany us to the office." I followed mutely several steps behind as this massive man hauled Derek down the path between the portable unit and the main school building. I noticed that Royal looked like a toddler dragging a stuffed animal or small doll behind him, with no regard for the damage he was doing.

Once in Royal's office, I began explaining what had happened. "Mr. Morris, " I said shakily, "Derek was.... "

"No need for you to explain a thing, Ms. Palmer," Royal interrupted. "The boy here has done wrong and he knows what we think of that around here, don't you, son?"

I was struck by the menacing edge to Royal's voice. He sounded as if he were enjoying this. A shudder ran through me as I realized that this powerful man liked dominating this boy. I suddenly worried about where all of this was going.

"You don't need to be troubled any more by this, Ma'am," Royal added, "Except, of course, you'll do the witnessing."

"Witnessing?" I asked, still in the dark about the process I had inadvertently started.

"Yes, Ma'am. It's standard for the teacher to witness the paddling."

"Paddling?" I could not hide the astonishment in my voice. I had to help Derek out of this. "Mr. Morris, Derek has made some bad choices, but I don't think...."

"Don't worry, Ma'am, we know how to handle this. In fact, Derek is used to it, aren't you?"

"I really don't want him to be paddled," I was almost pleading now. As the words came out, I realized I had made a serious mistake. Royal glared at me as if I had broken a secret code. "You will be the witness here," proclaimed Royal, using the same intimidating tone with me that he had previously reserved for Derek.

My anger won out over my fear and I tried one more time. "Mr. Morris, let's all just talk about this calmly. I'm sure we can come to a resolution that will satisfy all of us."

"No offense, Ma'am, but the only ones of us who need satisfying here are perfectly satisfied. Derek, drop your pants and grab hold of my desk." With these words, Royal grabbed a wooden paddle from its place of honor on the wall next to his desk. The paddle was as big as an old-fashioned cast-iron frying pan and appeared nearly as heavy. Through the handle was a small, leather strap used for hanging it up. I will never forget the sound of that paddle hitting Derek's naked buttocks. I had never heard anything like it before, nor have I since. Each slap of the paddle drove Derek into the edge of the desk. He made no sound, bit his bottom lip, and stared glass-eyed at the wall in front of him. It seemed like Royal would never stop beating him. Derek's bottom was bright red now and I knew he would have bruises where he had been slammed into the desk. Finally, Royal said, "That ought to about do it until next time. Pull 'em up, boy." With this, he hung the paddle back up and said, "You're done now, too, Ms. Palmer." Although I hated being dismissed this way, I walked out, shaking with rage.

I muddled through the rest of the day in a sort of a fog. I still couldn't comprehend what I had seen. The events of the day had violated the values learned during my professional training and my own deeply held beliefs. I felt angry and hopeless and saddened by it all.

I'm Not Alone

That night I called Mary Lou, a good friend from my master's degree program, who had taken a job at the high school next to Oak Forest Elementary. She agreed to meet me for supper and to hear the details of my horrible day.

After I had told Mary Lou the details of Derek's punishment at the hands of our assistant principal, she answered with similar horror stories from her own experience. Like me, Mary Lou preferred to manage student behavior within her classroom. On a few occasions, however, she had sent students to the office. When they returned, she reported that they were crying and often had welts on the backs of their hands or bruises on their upper arms. One student came back bleeding from a cut near his eye. She didn't know exactly what had gone on, but she quickly stopped relying on administrators to help with behavior management problems.

It felt good to talk about my experiences. Knowing that Mary Lou and I were wrestling with the same management problems and difficulties with the administration offered some comfort. We both felt better knowing that another person shared our problems. After talking a few more minutes, however, we both believed that individuals in our school district were abusing students through the practice of corporal punishment. Since neither of us knew of a written policy statement outlining the administration's response to student misbehavior, we knew it would be difficult to prove what was happening. In our hearts, though, we knew that this community condoned and perhaps even celebrated corporal punishment. Many community members held strong religion-based beliefs in "Spare the rod, spoil the child." Paddling a child was, as they explained to me, a way of doing the child a favor by helping him or her achieve some greater religious goal. Soon we would discover the depth of some people's feelings on this subject.

Pushed Too Far

LaVerne taught in the fourth-grade classroom next to mine. We were as different as night and day in teaching styles and personalities. LaVerne ran her room like a drill sergeant. Students spoke only when spoken to. They answered, "Yes Ma'am" when she talked to them. She took pride in the fact that her students were terrified of her. "Honey," she would counsel me, "Worst thing to do is be nice to 'em. Scare the hell out of 'em and you might be able to teach 'em something."

I regularly heard her screaming at students, humiliating them in front of their peers. On several occasions, I heard her throw something across the classroom toward a student who had offended her. Her favorite "behavioral instructional methods," as she called them, included making students hold a book at arm's length for extended amounts of time and forcing students to do push-ups at her feet. I found one of her "teaching tricks" truly abhorrent: LaVerne would draw a small circle on the chalkboard at the front of her classroom. She would then instruct the misbehaving student to touch his or her nose to the board inside the circle. She would leave students standing like that, in front of the whole class, for hours.

LaVerne and her inexorable management methods were another area about which I felt helpless. She had taught in the district for years and was held in high regard as a teacher; parents and teachers alike sang her praises. It seemed impossible that I could change such firmly entrenched attitudes and behaviors. So, against my better judgment, I left LaVerne to her own devices. I focused on using consistent and positive management approaches in my classroom, even though, each time I walked by and saw a student standing with his or her nose pressed to LaVerne's board, I winced.

An Accident

One day, my students returned from physical education buzzing about an accident that occurred in the gymnasium. Derek fell when using the trampoline. The kids excitedly told me the details of Derek's mishap. "He hit like a ton of bricks, Ms. Palmer," they reported. "He was hurt bad, I think." According to my students, Mr. Conley, the PE teacher, yelled at Derek to quit crying and to grow up. I finally quieted their comments and returned to teaching the rules of capitalization.

After the students' report of Derek's accident, I was surprised to see him later that morning standing in a familiar spot, nose against LaVerne's chalkboard. A few minutes earlier, I had heard LaVerne ranting at him. "Derek," she beseeched, "suck it up and act like a man. Quit your sniveling right now!" Her voice, and the content of her message, grated on me like fingernails on a chalkboard, but I was learning to keep teaching no matter what she did or said.

As I passed her room, I briefly glanced at Derek. His shoulders were shaking and his face looked very pale. Normally able to be stoic in the face of nearly any punishment, he didn't look right at all. Despite my concern, I forced myself to walk by and return to my students.

At the end of English, as my students filed out to lunch and I prepared to transform into a special education teacher for the afternoon, I saw that Derek was still at the chalkboard. I stuck my head a bit further through the door and was alarmed by his appearance. His shirt was soaked in sweat; he was shaking and ashen. I knew something was terribly wrong. LaVerne, seeing me in her doorway, tried to dismiss me: "He's just being a baby. He'll be fine. I'll have him out to special ed. right on time, don't you worry." This time I couldn't walk away.

"LaVerne, I think something is really wrong with him," I began.

"He wants you to think that. The boy is playing you for a fool," she answered.

"Still, I'd feel better if I could talk with him for a minute," I kept trying to soften her up a bit.

"Honey, it's up to you. You want to waste your lunch break with a crybaby, I can't stop you, " LaVerne said as she left the room without looking back.

I gently led Derek down the hall to the office. I was apprehensive and unsure of what to do. Trying to sound authoritative, I told Darlene, the secretary, that Derek needed to see the nurse. "You're in luck. She's right in the infirmary. Go on in." Darlene said without looking up from her *Woman's Day* magazine.

Connie, the school nurse, was one of a handful of people in the district whom I liked and respected. I knew many occasions on which she had gone out on a limb for students; I trusted her to help Derek. She looked at Derek and her face registered alarm immediately. "When did this happen?" she asked. "A long time ago, in PE," answered a weak and shaken Derek. "We need to take you to the hospital right now," she told him. Leaving me to call his parents, Connie drove Derek the 20 miles to the nearest hospital. She called in about an hour later and asked to speak to me.

"Leah," she said, "Derek has dislocated his shoulder and has broken his wrist and forearm. He is in surgery right now. He was in shock by the time we reached the hospital."

On hearing the news, I burst into tears, overwhelmed by everything that had happened in past few weeks. "Leah, " Connie said in a near whisper, "You did exactly the right thing. You're the only one who helped him. It's not your fault."

As I hung up, I knew she was wrong. It was my fault. As long as I said nothing, I was contributing to this school district's regular pattern of brutality against children. By overlooking the district's practices, I had been contributing to this problem. "No more," I thought to myself. "I won't keep quiet about this any more!"

Data Collection Denied

The night of Derek's surgery, I again shared dinner with Mary Lou. We agreed that we would work together to improve the quality of life for kids in Emory School District. We decided to begin by getting copies of each of the school's policies on discipline and behavior management. Acting on that decision pushed us from the frying pan directly into the fire.

The next morning I arrived at school early, energized by our plan and excited to be working in agreement with my own beliefs, rather than against them. I was surprised to see the principal, Mr. Swenson, in his office. Normally at this hour, he was sharing coffee and cigarettes with a large group of people in the staff room. I knocked on his door and was asked to come on in.

"Ronald," I began confidently, filled with a new sense of purpose, "I'm a bit confused by the behavior management policies here. It would help me a lot if you could give me a copy of them so that I will know what to expect when I send a student to the office."

"Sorry, Leah," he answered, with a forced smile on his lips. "No can do. Those policies are for administrative use only. We don't want them circulating around. There are lots of folks around who might not understand them the way we professionals do."

"Oh, sure. I understand that, " I persisted. "Could I just take a look at them here in your office, for my own information? It would really help me to be a more effective teacher."

"Sorry, again," he said, evading me further. "Like I said, administrative use only. Myself, Royal, the school board, the superintendent. We're the only ones that get to see the actual policy. Are you having trouble managing your students, Leah? We expect our teachers to have strong management skills, you know."

Ronald was turning this around to make it appear as if the problem were all mine. He was tricky, and I had to work hard to out maneuver him.

"No, no, not at all." I gave it right back to him. "But, as you know, an important part of managing student behavior is being sure children know in advance what the consequences of their behavior will be. I can't tell them that if I don't know myself. I was certain that, in your role as mentor, you would want to help me be a more effective manager."

Ronald's response stopped me cold. "Oh, I will help you plenty," he said in an icy cold voice. "I will personally be in your classroom at least once a day to make sure that your instructional and management skills are up to snuff. We believe in supporting our new teachers here, and to do that, I plan to observe you as often as possible. I think that answers your question, Ms. Palmer."

"Well," I stammered, backing out of his office, "that would certainly be helpful. I'll look forward to your feedback."

I called Mary Lou as soon as I could find a semiprivate phone. Her queries had been answered even more harshly than my own. Her principal had told her not to stir up trouble. "Drop it, Mary Lou, or you will be sorry," were his exact words. We hung up discouraged and frightened. It was difficult to concentrate on my teaching that day, but not as hard as it would be in the days that followed.

Mr. Swenson was true to his word. At least once each day, he was in my classroom watching me teach and looking for the slightest infraction of any policy, however esoteric. Once he put a note in my file because I kept rubber cement in my desk, rather than in a locked storage area. Other teachers had trays of rubber cement around for students to use and received no censure for it. He called me into his office weekly to discuss the fact that my students were "totally out of control" and that I was teaching "opinion rather than fact." Mr. Swenson denounced all aspects of my professional behavior: curriculum, instruction, classroom management, report cards, individualized educational plans, even my bulletin boards.

Things were bad for me, but much worse for Mary Lou. Her teaching and management were under intense scrutiny as well, but her principal went one step beyond what Mr. Swenson did: When the new grading period began, he assigned her 15 extra students, most of whom had serious behavior problems and who were chronically truant. At times, she had nearly 30 high school special education students crammed into her tiny, hot classroom. In short, he had mixed the ingredients for an explosion and, from a safe distance, pushed the detonator button himself.

Things went on like this for the remainder of the year. Mary Lou and I were assigned every imaginable extra responsibility. We were given marginal performance ratings. We were under observation at all times. Our lives were made miserable in ways that we found difficult to document and that we were powerless to stop.

At one point, desperate for anything that might help us, we met with the local education association representative. He was polite but not encouraging. We didn't realize until it was too late that this man was a golfing buddy of both of our principals. Immediately following our meeting with him, our principals turned up the heat. They made it clear that trying to get outside help would only make matters worse.

Like prisoners serving out sentences, Mary Lou and I suffered silently through the rest of that school year. It affected us quite differently. I began to run compulsively. I lost nearly 15 pounds, ran mile after mile in a futile attempt to run from my misery, and eventually damaged both of my knees so badly that I needed surgery. Mary Lou developed insomnia and depression. She looked like a totally different woman. Once energetic and radiant, she had developed dark circles under her eyes. In time, she required antidepressant medication and was very nearly hospitalized after mentioning her suicidal thoughts to a counselor.

Now it was finally over. I sat on that rock until the sun dipped behind the mountains, the air took on a chill, and a shiver ran through me. I thought of the children of Emory County and the pain they would endure. It seemed that I should be crying, but I had no tears left. I walked slowly back to my car and drove away from the nightmare, knowing that it would haunt me forever.

ANALYSIS

Critical Problems and Dilemmas

This case illustrates several challenging issues. Perhaps the most significant question this case raises is the role of public schools and the extent to which local values and beliefs should control them. This case forces consideration of the tremendous variation among cultures in the nation and that the climate of public schools may vary in response to local subcultures. Given local religious beliefs and cultural norms, is it wrong for Emory County schools to use corporal punishment to manage children's behavior? Regardless of whether Emory County was wrong in its disciplinary measures, Leah found the district's use of corporal punishment intolerable. This conflict in values forces questioning the rights and responsibilities of individual teachers regarding the larger school district's treatment of students.

Other questions raised in this case include:

- How did Leah's values clash with those of the other school district employees regarding discipline and the treatment of children?
- How should teachers and administrators discuss controversial topics? What can be done to solve emotionally charged problems such as this one?
- How and why do some administrators and other teachers intimidate teachers like Leah and Mary Lou when they challenge the system?
- To what extent must teacher preparation institutions prepare future teachers to serve as agents of change within the complex system of public schooling?
- What is the administrators' responsibility in regard to laws and policies regarding the discipline of a student with a disability? What were Leah's and Mary Lou's responsibility and options in this case, given his disregard to those laws and policies?
- What knowledge did Leah and Mary Lou lack regarding the legality of corporal punishment? What was their responsibility to report child abuse to outside authorities? Was the paddling child abuse?

Opposing Views on Discipline and Children

Leah's beliefs regarding discipline conflict with those of other school district employees, specifically the principal and other teachers. This case is unusual in that the prevailing beliefs regarding discipline are so deeply entrenched in the local culture. Although neither Leah nor Mary Lou knew it when they took their positions, the attitude that corporal punishment is both necessary and desirable is a primary facet of the dominant religion in Emory County. Defenders of the paddling procedure would often tell Leah that paddling a child was, in fact, a way of doing the child a favor by helping him or her achieve some greater religious goal.

Leah abhorred the local approach to discipline and considered it a graphic example of the culture's demeaning attitude toward children. Most Emory County residents honored the adage that "Children should be seen and not heard." Unfortunately, it took Leah several months to realize the extent to which Emory County locals supported corporal punishment. In the early months of her employment, as she encountered people who advocated paddling, spanking, and similar disciplinary methods, Leah assumed that these people were in the minority. By the time she realized she was one of very few professionals in her school district who objected to paddling children, she had already offended most of her coworkers.

Discussion of Controversial Topics

A principal's approach to disagreement often may determine how teachers handle controversy. Some principals build time into faculty meetings to discuss any issues that are bothering the staff. Others, in places like Emory County where it is forbidden to dissent from the majority opinion, feel no need for such time.

The education profession and its primary institutions, public schools, do not have a system for resolving professional disagreement. Perhaps even more importantly, they lack a strongly agreed-on body of professional knowledge and concomitant set of best practice recommendations. Thus, strong factions within the profession can propel their ideas into practice without being subject to the scrutiny of their peers. It also allows microcultures, such as that found in Emory County, to exist for long periods of time without having to justify themselves or critically examine their own beliefs.

In Emory County, very few professionals were hired who did not already subscribe to the local belief that children must be kept in their place by forcible and physical means, if necessary. Consequently, the administrators had almost no experience working with people who did not share their values. When Leah and Mary Lou came along, the administrator's response was to intimidate them. This method of handling conflict is quite consistent with the way these professionals handled children who did not act as expected.

Governing by Intimidation. An especially baffling element of this case is the principals' use of intimidation to control Leah and Mary Lou. The speed with which these two men became defensive and the fierceness with which they protected their policies and procedures are a bit unexpected. Unfortunately, their response is not unique among principals, other school administrators, and managers in different professions. It takes a singularly strong principal to allow teachers or parents to scrutinize his or her policies. To allow such an open discussion of one's administrative decisions raises the possibility that the way in which one operates a school might change. Neither principal in this case was willing to consider any sort of change in his approach to discipline.

Neither man was able to separate questions about or criticism of his professional decisions from questions about or criticism of him as a person. Both men took criticism of their policies very personally. The fact that the criticisms came from women likely added insult to injury. The two principals may have felt less threatened or intimidated if the teachers who questioned their policies were male.

Preparing Teachers to Be Systems Change Agents. Leah's teacher preparation program was a strong one with a national reputation for excellence. She began her teaching career with the skills necessary to deliver instruction and manage student behavior effectively. Although Leah was prepared for the aspects of her job that involved directly providing instruction to students, she, like many beginning teachers, was woefully unprepared for the full range of responsibilities she faced as a teacher. She had received no instruction in working with parents, discussing controversial issues with administrators, or responding to other teachers who disapproved of her methods.

Leah had no idea of how she could begin to act as an agent of change in such an insulated system. She was so naive that she began her teaching career with the belief that most educators shared similar views about children and that any disagreements would be minor and easily resolved. It did not occur to her that professionals who had chosen education as their field would argue that corporal punishment was a key component in an effective school.

This case illustrates the importance of discussing the culture of teaching with preservice teachers. Before taking full-time employment as teachers, teacher education students must understand the organization of schools, the processes that drive and hinder change in those schools, and their own role in the larger culture of a public school.

Disregard for Special Education Laws and Policies. Throughout this case, the teachers and administrators blatantly disregard the laws and policies concerning the education of students with disabilities. Derek, a student with a disability, had an Individualized Educational Program (IEP) mandated by the Individuals with Disabilities Education Act (IDEA). Because Derek had a learning disability that made it difficult for him to comprehend oral instructions, and because most of his behavior problems resulted from not correctly following teacher directions, his disciplinary procedures were directly related to his disability. Any unusual disciplinary procedures to be used with Derek should have been explicitly described on his IEP, subjected to committee approval, and signed by his parents. Best practice suggests that Derek's IEP committee reconvene and review his entire education plan in light of his frequent disciplinary problems. Neither of these steps occurred, and Derek did not receive the protection he was due under IDEA.

This blatant violation of the law was typical of Emory County's approach to students with disabilities. LaVerne's behavior suggests that, unless a student had a highly visible disability, such as Down Syndrome or blindness, teachers refused to afford that student his or her rights as guaranteed in IDEA. Teachers and administrators believed that students with mild or moderate disabilities, such as learning disabilities or behavioral disorders, did not deserve any special protection or treatment. In fact, some teachers asserted that these students were just "acting handicapped" so that they could get away with doing less work.

Obligation to Report Child Abuse. Most people would probably agree that hitting a child's naked buttocks with a large wooden paddle and thereby forcing the student to smash into the corner of a desk constitutes child abuse. Many people would consider abusive other behaviors in the case, such as yelling at children or forcing a child to stand with his or her nose against the chalkboard. Leah and Mary Lou clearly saw all of these behaviors as abusive and degrading, yet they did not know what their obligations were concerning this situation. They had both been taught to report cases of suspected child abuse *by parents* to the proper authorities within their school building. They did not know whom to call when school officials were doing the abusing. They did not realize that they were legally obligated to contact child protective services. Although they discussed this option, neither believed that it would be helpful because the people in charge of that agency were parents of children in Oak Forest school who condoned the disciplinary procedures there.

Explanation of Characters' Behavior

Four primary forces drive Leah's behavior in this case: her desire to protect children from abuse; her ignorance of the options available to her as she pursued this goal; her position as an outsider in a close-knit community that appears impervious to outside influence; and the fact that she is a first-year teacher.

Desire to Protect Students From Abuse. The abuse Leah witnessed during her employment by Emory County horrified her. The principle that children's behavior is shaped most effectively by positive, consistent consequences was at the core of her professional training. Leah believed in delivering frequent positive reinforcers contingent on students' displaying appropriate behavior. During her teacher preparation program, she read the writings of Kazdin, Baer, Hall, and other applied behavior analysts. She fully adopted the behavior analytic approach to changing student behavior and assumed that other professionals would use such an approach or one compatible with behaviorist theories. Throughout her teacher training program, all of her professors and the cooperating teachers with whom she had worked operated from this perspective. Leah did not expect to encounter professionals with beliefs completely at odds with a behaviorist approach.

Ignorance of Options for Responding to the Situation. Leah's first response after seeing Royal paddle Derek was to handle all behavior problems within her own classroom. She felt that this was a small, insignificant step that would not lead to notable changes in a degrading system of school-wide management. Being a new teacher, however, Leah had no knowledge of other options that she could pursue to change things in her school district. Following a recruitment meeting for the National Education Association, she did speak with the local representative, but that action worsened her situation.

Leah did not know her legal obligations when witnessing child abuse, nor did she have skills to work toward consensus in a divisive situation such as this. Her teacher preparation program had prepared her for her instructional and management responsibilities only. She had received no training in working with others whose views differed from her own.

Position as an Outsider.   Leah was perceived as an outsider by the community. The other teachers, administrators, and parents were wary of her even before she began questioning the party line that corporal punishment was a great thing. Once she became open in her criticisms of the district's policies, she was seen as dangerous by many members of the community.

First-Year Teacher.   A final driving force behind Leah's behavior was her status as a first-year teacher. Most first-year teachers struggle mightily to fulfill their basic responsibilities as teachers. Beginning teachers are usually consumed by the basic tasks that face them: planning for instruction, teaching, managing behavior, keeping grades, talking with parents, serving on committees, and attending to the innumerable details inherent in running a classroom. New teachers are working so hard to do their jobs and learn how their schools work that they have little time for trying to modify policies and procedures in their schools. If Leah had been an experienced teacher, even one with 2 or 3 years of experience, she would have had more energy for working toward change in her school. As it was, she simply could not keep up with her classroom and act as an agent for change.

Royal, Ronald, and LaVerne

It is very easy to cast Royal, Ronald, and LaVerne as the villains in this case. In fact, that is how Leah perceived these people throughout the year. What is more challenging is to understand their motivations in a more meaningful and open-minded way. These three people grew up and lived in a culture that stressed the importance of children being submissive to adults. They all attended a fundamentalist church and took quite seriously the notion that if one spares the rod, one spoils the child. Royal, Ronald, LaVerne, and most of the others in Emory County sincerely believed that they were doing what was best for their children. In fact, they would argue that to refuse to physically discipline children was to sentence them to eternity in Hell. Most people, if they truly believed that allowing children to misbehave would result in their eternal damnation, would probably opt for paddling as a preventative measure.

Although it is possible to understand Royal, Ronald, and LaVerne's attitudes about paddling, it is more difficult to explain their animosity toward Leah and Mary Lou. If they had been confident in their own beliefs, one might have expected Royal, Ronald, and Mary Lou to defend their beliefs without becoming vicious about them. Clearly, this did not happen. These people became extremely defensive and hostile toward Leah. This suggests that her beliefs posed a threat to Royal and his peers. They may have feared that some outside agency, such as the police or child protective services, would be brought in to examine their practices, and that they would be forced to change the way they disciplined children.

What If...?

It is interesting to speculate on different decisions that the main participants in this case might have made and the possible consequences of these decisions. Leah might have been a much more assertive advocate for the children of Emory County. For example, she might have contacted the police and child protective services to report the abuse happening at Oak Forest Elementary. The positive outcome of this decision would have been feeling that she had responded in a way that was ethically and morally necessary to an intolerable situation. In addition, it is possible that the abuse might have stopped or been reduced following investigation by outside agencies. On the other hand, reporting the corporal punishment to outside agencies could have had disastrous consequences as well. At a minimum, it would have caused administrators to make Leah's life even more miserable. It is not impossible that she would have been fired and/or harassed at home in response to such actions.

Another option available to Leah, and one that she seriously considered, was to quit her job. Quitting would have allowed Leah to avoid contact with very hostile people, given her the knowledge that she was not actively contributing to the abuse of children, and improved her mental and physical health. Quitting the job would have produced several undesirable results as well. First, Leah needed the money from her job. In addition, she was afraid that she would ruin her chances of getting a teaching job anywhere in the area if she quit. Finally, quitting would have made her feel more like she had abandoned the kids of Emory County.

A third option open to Leah, but one for which she was not adequately prepared, was to attempt to enlist parents in her effort to change the system of discipline in her school. A small but significant number of parents, particularly among the new members of the community, might have argued for more moderate disciplinary procedures to be used with their children. Parents could have forced the principals to change in ways that Leah and Mary Lou could not. Inducing parents to help lobby for different management processes would likely have produced some changes in the school district's approach to discipline. It would also have begun to dispel the myth that every single person in Emory County supported corporal punishment. Finally, such actions could have encouraged more parents to become actively involved in the schools and to monitor their children's education more carefully.

It is also interesting to speculate on the different ways that Royal and Ronald might have behaved. For example, what would have happened if Royal and Ronald had entertained open discussion about their disciplinary procedures? They could have shared their policies with Leah, discussed their beliefs with her openly, and allowed discussion at faculty meetings about their approach to discipline. These actions could have been beneficial in several ways. First, this approach would remove the necessity of intimidating Leah, keeping close tabs on her, and acting in a defensive manner. Watching Leah so closely was time consuming for Royal and Ronald. If they had been open rather than defensive about their beliefs, they would not have been obligated to keep Leah under such close scrutiny. In addition, an open discussion of disciplinary procedures might have led teachers to publicly validate Royal and Ronald's actions. A wide-spread, open endorsement of corporal punishment would have left Leah unable to argue strongly for different disciplinary approaches. If they had allowed discussion of their policies, Royal and Ronald might have achieved the same outcomes (Leah leaving and their policies staying in place) but would not have had to work so hard in the interim.

Final Thoughts

This case delineates several important issues for teacher education programs, public school teachers, administrators, parents, and students: the role of teachers as agents of change within the complex system of public schools, the use of corporal punishment to manage student behavior, and the ways in which school employees resolve professional disagreements. This case illustrates one type of school environment in which American children are forced to exist each day. The case sets the stage for discussion about the role of public schools in modern American society. It forces consideration of the extent to which local values should determine the climate of public schools, as well as the obligation of society to develop schools that treat children in a fair and ethical manner. Finally, this case deals with the rights and responsibilities of teachers, the ways in which teacher preparation institutions can best prepare teachers to fulfill those responsibilities, and the obstacles faced by teachers trying to act as agents of change in public schools.

8

A Delicate Dilemma: Religion in the Classroom

Eugenie Potter
University of Pittsburgh

Editors' note: Potter introduces Susan Walters, a first-year teacher, who by virtue of her naiveté and honesty, raises unexpected questions about her own religious beliefs from the students in her class. Walters finds herself caught in the dilemma of religion and its complexities as a result of being open with her students. The case bears on the fundamental issues of individuals' rights to privacy, free assembly in public settings, and levels of discourse about religion in public schools. Susan Walters believes that she is following the implications of her teacher preparation program, but ponders the degree to which she can succeed. She turns to her former professor for help, thereby raising for case readers the issue of legal responsibilities of teacher preparation programs to provide students with appropriate knowledge and skill to deal with the complexities this inexperienced teacher must face.

THE CASE

In the years since the *Engel v. Vitale* case (1962) forbade the recitation of prayer in public school classrooms, educators developed increasing sensitivity to the volatile issues of religion and religious observance. This sensitivity led to misunderstanding about what is and is not allowable to say and do concerning religion in classrooms and on school grounds. Numerous court cases subsequent to Engel (cf.

111

Abington v. Schempp, Wallace v. Jaffree, Smith v. Mobile, Mozert v. Hawkins) clarified allowable statements and practices; a coalition of organizations published guidelines conforming to court rulings (Haynes & Thomas, 1994). Nonetheless, educators continue to be confused about religious issues. Most opt to build a higher wall than is legally necessary between religion and the school. For example, teachers have forbidden students to bow their heads in silent prayer before lunch in the mistaken belief that such a practice is illegal, although the "freedom of exercise" clause in the First Amendment clearly protects this practice. Teachers have not allowed students to talk about family religious practices in class, even when such a contribution to discussion might be highly relevant to the course material. Again, these teachers confuse the "establishment" and the "freedom of exercise" clauses (see case analysis for an explanation of the differences and tensions between these two clauses), thus unnecessarily banning from their classrooms an important facet of at least some of the students' lives, as well as a rich part of history, culture, and democratic belief.

Not all teachers and administrators labor under such confusion. Thanks to revised curriculum standards, such as California's Framework for the Social Studies Curriculum, the study of religion as an academic subject has returned to the public school classroom in some states. This in itself can pose other kinds of problems, however, as the following case illustrates.

Susan Walters felt tired but happy. Her first day as a *real teacher* was going well; she was looking forward to her last period teaching social studies. It was a dream job, she felt, having none of the problems her professors in the teacher certification program had warned of. She was in a large, well-run, rural/suburban high school. Her students came from mostly middle-class backgrounds reflecting the transitional mix of the area: smaller towns, farms becoming developed subdivisions with lots of green space, areas of light industry, and a few pockets of lower income families—mostly older people and retirees.

The principal and other teachers had welcomed Sue cordially, although with some reserve. Sue attributed the diffidence to the cautious conservatism she had been used to in her farm youth, as well as to the fact that she had taken over all the assignments of a recently promoted, very popular male teacher. Moreover, her assignments were in areas that, in this school, men had always taught or coached: social studies, computers, and women's volleyball.

Although Sue knew it was her ability to fill the last assignment that had actually landed her the job, this assignment worried her most. She had been a star forward throughout her high school and undergraduate years and had voluntarily coached an inner-city team during those same years. Thanks to Affirmative Action and increased funding under Title IX rules, women's sports had increased rapidly in number and visibility at both college and high school levels. In fact, the high school where she now was a faculty member had long fielded a regional and occasionally a state-championship team, sending many young women to college with full athletic scholarships. An Affirmative Action hire herself, Sue wanted to continue these traditions. This year's team had greeted her somewhat warily, not sure that she could adequately replace their beloved former coach.

Her high degree of competence in the new computer and information technology had been a plus; the school had only recently acquired Internet access and most of the teachers did not yet know how to use it. In her two computer classes of the day, Sue had won over the students immediately by showing them how to use e-mail. She had warned them of the school's severe sanctions against sending "flame" notes and harassing or obscene material, but otherwise had let them delight in sending each other the usual teenage teasing insults. Study hall had also gone without problems, and she had been spared hall and cafeteria duty on her first day. So now she looked forward to her first truly academic class. She wished it were not the last period of the day.

As the students trooped into the room, Sue smiled at them and at her own memory of herself as a tenth-grader—outwardly assured and inwardly unsure, wanting to succeed but not wanting to be too far ahead of her classmates, above all wanting to hold on to the popularity she had enjoyed in middle school. The students before her now were not very different, she noted. Their clothes and mannerisms were carefully careless. The boys pushed each other around a little when they passed the desks of the pretty girls. The girls preened themselves and checked their hair and makeup in little mirrors. All but a few avoided looking at Sue until she called them to order.

Sue stood and walked to the front of her desk. "Hello, everyone. Thank you for coming today." One of her college professors said that at the beginning of every class, and Sue liked both the implied courtesy and the freedom of choice. Her students, however, looked at her, then at each other in some surprise. Sue blushed a little, realizing they had no choice about being in class, but immediately resolved to continue the practice as a way of modeling both behavior and an attitude toward learning.

"I'm new here, so I don't know any of you or your families yet, but I hope that changes soon," Sue continued. "In the meantime I'm going to hand out what I call 'our United Nations cards.' These have your name on them, just like delegates to the UN. I'll also send around tape so you can tape the cards to the front of your desks." As she made this announcement, Sue noticed several students toward the back of the room exchange looks between themselves. "I wonder what that's about," she thought. She then launched into her carefully prepared introduction to the course. She explained the importance of knowing about one's society and the cultures of the world. She described the increasing global interconnectedness, both economically and politically. She talked about the growing diversity in the United States, although the faces before her reflected little of that diversity, she realized suddenly. She handed out a list of topics she planned to cover that term, and told the students that they should be prepared in the next class to choose one of the topics for a research report. Feeling suddenly buoyed and confident that her careful preparation had paid off, she paused and asked, "Are there any questions so far?"

The students dropped their eyes and shuffled their feet, reluctant to be first to speak. Then one girl slowly raised her hand. "Yes, Melissa," Sue said, glad that she need only glance at the card on the student's desk and not have to search through a seating chart. "This really does confirm their individual worth and dignity," she thought.

"What about tests, Mrs. Walters?" Melissa asked. "Will you be giving us quizzes and stuff?"

"I will be giving you tests, of course," Sue replied, "if only to prepare you for the kinds of questions you'll see on the SATs next year. But I don't like to rely on rote memorization; I really want you to learn this material because it has some personal meaning for you. I want you to be able to see yourselves in this material. And I want you to be able to question the way things are in society so that you will be able to go out and change things as adults!"

Melissa and the other students stared at her uneasily, unwilling to think so far ahead to adulthood with all its responsibilities. Sue smiled encouragingly, "That's why it's so important for you to pick a topic that's important to you. You'll learn more that way than if I just gave you textbook pages to study for tests that you'd forget right away. This way you might hang onto it, even just in the back of your minds. And you'll be able to use it in your discussions in college." The students looked at her doubtfully and Sue decided to try for safer territory. "Who else has a question?" One of the boys at the back of the room raised a hand. "Yes, Mark."

The boy rose from his seat, prompting titters from his classmates. Discomfited, he eased slowly back into his chair. Sue recalled another teacher's comments about a small group of students from a nearby Christian day school entering the high school that year. "Mark must be one of them," Sue thought. "They were probably taught to rise when the teacher enters the room, too. That kind of courtesy went out ages ago, so they must feel pretty awkward with the casualness of the public school students. I'll have to make a special effort to make them feel at home."

Mark looked to a couple of his classmates for support. They were the same group that had exchanged looks when she had explained the United Nations cards. Mark cleared his throat, then spoke in the cracking voice of adolescence, but with a little extra tremor at the edges. "Mrs. Walters, are you really serious about questioning stuff, and trying to change things?"

"Of course, I am," she replied in astonishment. "You don't really think the world is as good as it could be, do you?"

"No, ma'am," Mark said emphatically, "and it's part of my mission to make it better. But what I really meant was, what would you do to us if we questioned you and what you're doing?" His fair face was tense with the daring of his question. His companions reflected his anxiety, and the other students hushed at the changed atmosphere in the room.

Sue took a deep breath. She had always prided herself on her openness and had even been reproved mildly by her supervising teacher during her student teaching for allowing the kids to express whatever they thought. But she believed that democracy meant just that, and that it was her duty as a teacher to respect and encourage all varieties of views. That sometimes meant taking risks, she knew, and listening to opinions at sharp odds with her own beliefs. "That's a very helpful question actually, Mark," she began slowly. "What I want to establish in this classroom is a sense of intellectual safety. That means that, if you think there is something I'm missing, or that we could be doing things differently and better, you are free, and more important, safe, in expressing that view. It doesn't mean I, or I should really say, we will agree with you, but it does mean that I won't impose sanctions—punishment—on you for being honest. After all, that's part of what freedom of speech is about." She paused, pleased that she had been afforded the opportunity so early in the term to establish the kind of free, open atmosphere of intellectual inquiry she had so enjoyed in her college classes. "Now what would you like to suggest for improvement, Mark?"

Mark stared at his desk for a moment as if in debate with himself, then he raised his eyes in a level gaze full of intelligence and determination. "The most important topic of all is missing from your list, Mrs. Walters."

Sue laughed lightly and said, "Well, first of all, let's all get one thing clear, I'm Miss Walters, or Ms. Walters, but certainly not Mrs." The students grinned back at her, squirming a little with relief at her evident good humor. "And what do you think the most important topic is, Mark?"

"Religion," Mark shot back. Then he continued more slowly in great earnest, "You talked about how important it is for us to have an understanding of diversity and a tolerance for all cultures, but one of the most important parts of almost any culture is religion, but you don't even have it on your list."

"That's true, Mark, but there's a reason. We're in a public school, which means that there has to be a strict separation between church and state. So I can't include that as a topic because it's impossible to teach about religion without actually teaching religious doctrine. Besides, I know there is a comparative religions class that you can take without credit, if you are really interested in that."

"It's not the same!" Mark said vehemently. "That class treats religion as something separate from everyday life—we can't even get credit for taking it! Besides, you said we should choose something that is important to us, that has personal meaning to us. Well, religion is very important to me!" He slumped back into his chair as his companions smiled and nodded their approval. The rest of the class waited expectantly.

"Uh, oh," thought Sue, "Now what?" As she stood casting about in her mind for a reply, she could feel her earlier confidence and buoyancy slipping away. Before she could respond, however, Mark suddenly sat up in his seat. "Anyway, it's not true!" he said.

"What isn't true, Mark?"

"It isn't true that you can't teach about religion in the public school. The Supreme Court said it was OK. That's what my dad told me."

At that moment the bell rang and the students moved noisily out of the room. Only Mark and his companions lingered, conferring together at the back of the room. They seemed to reach a resolution and slowly walked up to Sue. "Mrs. Walters," Mark began. One of the girls hissed, "Miss!" "Oh! I mean, Miss Walters, I didn't mean to cause trouble, but it's just that people are always talking about respecting other people's rights and opinions, but if the subject is religion, then that doesn't seem to count. And for us religion is important! It's just as important to us as race and gender are to other people. Is it fair that those things count and religion doesn't?"

Sue was impressed. Here was a boy who had taken her at her word, who had the courage on the very first day of class to question the tight society of the classroom, and who believed passionately about something in contrast to the apparent insouciance of most of his classmates. He could go far under her tutelage, she thought, but religion! "I suppose it really isn't fair," she replied slowly, "but I have to ask someone else about this. I do remember something about Supreme Court decisions, but it was a long time ago that I studied that. Can we talk about it again? Maybe in the next class?"

"Yes, ma'am," said Mark. "That would be fine. And Miss Walters," he continued, "we know you're new here, so we wanted to invite you to come to our church on Sunday to start meeting folks. That is, if it's OK with your religion. What religion are you, Miss Walters?"

Mark and his companions stood, holding their breath slightly, waiting for her reply. Sue gulped inwardly. A couple of years before she had left the church of her childhood, but had not yet resolved her own religious feelings. This conflict of beliefs was one she had been determined to keep to her private life, now here she was being asked by an eager student, and she was uncertain of an appropriate response. "Well," she said finally, "I don't have a specific church right now. I guess you could say I'm a seeker."

"Wonderful!" Mark cried. A radiant smile flooded his face and his companions beamed. "Our church can help you seek! And you could also come to our club meetings here at school on Thursday afternoons."

"Club meetings?" asked Sue.

"Yes!" One of the girls now spoke up. "We belong to the Students for Christ Club and Mr. Bradley is our faculty sponsor. Sometimes other teachers come to the meetings, too, to pray and study the Bible. It's a wonderful way to get away from all the prejudice toward us at this school."

"But, but surely you don't meet here at the school, do you?" Sue asked in bewilderment. "Why, yes," said another student. "It's a legitimate student club, and one of the reasons our parents were willing to let us come to this school." Mark, who appeared to be the unspoken leader, glanced out the window and said, "Come on, guys, we're going to miss our bus. 'Bye, Miss Walters. See you in class!" "And in church!" sang another as they ran, laughing happily, out the door.

Sue sat down slowly at her desk. "How should I handle all this?" she wondered. "Who can I ask?" She did remember vaguely something about Supreme Court decisions, but didn't they forbid prayer in the school? But this wasn't about prayer. Would she be on safe ground if she allowed Mark and others to research a topic in religion in her class? Could students actually have a Bible study club in school? And what about her own religious beliefs? That subject sure wasn't going to go away now that Mark and his companions saw her as a potential convert.

As she sat pondering her dilemmas, Sue began to recall the time her professor had made a special presentation on religion in her Social Foundations of Education class. At the time, Sue had been impatient with the Foundations course, thinking it a waste of time in view of her own previous studies in politics, history, and sociology. And she had been eager to get into the more exciting methods courses that would really prepare her for teaching. This professor had not actually lectured, but had asked the class a lot of questions that led them to see their own misconceptions and assumptions. Sue realized with a start that this was actually the way that she herself wanted to teach.

Sue had missed this particular class, enduring a long bout of flu. When she returned to school, one of her classmates gave her a copy of a set of guidelines, published by a professional organization, that the professor handed out. The professor said that the material wouldn't be on their final exam, but admonished them to tuck the guidelines into their portfolios for reference at some future time. Beset by the work of catching up in all her classes, and aware that the material would not be tested, Sue had simply filed the paper and notes without giving them more than a glance. Now she dived for the folders in the bottom drawer of her desk. Finding the one for Social Foundations, she skimmed the pages, noting with surprise some materials she could use in her social studies course. Then she found it: "Including Study About Religions in the Social Studies Curriculum: A Position Statement and Guidelines," published by the National Council for the Social Studies (1981).

At the top of the sheet, her classmate had scribbled a note: "Prof says can always e-mail her if need help." An e-mail address followed. Her heart bounding, Sue almost ran to the computer lab. Calling up the Internet access, she entered the professor's e-mail address and began: "Dear Professor Potter, You probably don't remember me, but I was in your Social Foundations class about 3 years ago when you gave a presentation about religion. You said then that we could contact you if we needed help with a problem relating to this subject. Well, here I am. I hope your offer is still good. Here's what happened today—my first day of "real teaching .... ''

ANALYSIS

This case contains three main issues related to the religion clauses of the First Amendment: teaching about religion in public school classes, religion-related student clubs, and students' and teachers' personal religious beliefs. The first two issues relate to the "establishment clause" ("Congress shall make no law respecting an establishment of religion.... "), and the third relates to the "free exercise" clause (" ... or prohibiting the free exercise thereof ... "), as well as to the establishment clause.

The subtexts in this case have a potential bearing on the central issues. These subtexts concern Affirmative Action, definitions and assumptions about cultural diversity, hidden biases, and pedagogical philosophy and approach. Although the subtexts are interwoven in the case, I will, for analytical purposes, separate them and point out the relevant passages.

Affirmative Action

Affirmative Action Federal legislation passed in 1972 and generally referred to as "Title IX" provides for a broad sweep of actions to redress historical injustices to women and racial/ethnic minorities. Sue Walters obtained her job through Affirmative Action favoring placing women in positions traditionally held by men: coaching, technology, and in many cases, certain academic areas. Although Affirmative Action rectifies injustices based on what sociologists term "ascribed characteristics"—those over which an individual has no control, such as race or gender—the law does not address "achieved characteristics"—those over which an individual has control or choice, such as religion. Indeed, any public entity, such as a school board, would be in violation of both clauses of the First Amendment if it encouraged hiring and promotion decisions based on religious belief.

Cultural Diversity

Toward the end of the case, when Mark and his companions approach Ms. Walters after class, Mark says, "It's just that people are always talking about other people's rights and opinions, but if the subject is religion, then that doesn't seem to count. And for us religion is important! It's just as important to us as race and gender are to other people. Is it fair that those things count and religion doesn't?" Here Mark presents Sue Walters directly with one of the persistent omissions in multicultural study.

Cultural diversity is conventionally defined in terms of race, class, and gender. Yet, as Mark points out earlier in the case, " ... one of the most important parts of almost any culture is religion, but you don't even have it on your list." Part of this omission in multicultural studies owes to widespread perplexity and reluctance on the part of school personnel to tread the potentially volatile and litigious ground of church–state relations. Another part of the omission, however, can be attributed to defining multiculturalism, as with Affirmative Action, on the basis of ascribed characteristics, and ignoring achieved ones, even though "class" straddles the border between these two types. Yet, increasingly in the United States, as in many other countries, religion defines cultural differences, what both philosophers and sociologists call "Weltanschauung"—one's world view based on fundamental beliefs about the nature of reality and behavior, especially moral behavior. Thus, Mark's cry of frustration could signal additional confrontations in this classroom as he and his companions try to work out the different values placed on certain cultural attributes and not on others.

Hidden Biases

Quite a number of hidden biases are present in this case: Sue's assumptions about the quality of life in inner-city schools, the teachers' and team members' reservations about a woman's ability to replace a man in certain positions, the students' own gender biases reflected in their behavior toward each other, the students' bias toward conformity expressed in their tittering at Mark's first rising to respond to the teacher, and Sue's scorn as a student herself toward the "usefulness" of her Social Foundations course. There are two other hidden biases, however, to be addressed specifically.

First, Sue has a decidedly liberal point of view that is manifest in a number of ways, such as her general openness, her use of the United Nations as a model, her own questioning of religious doctrine, and her assumptions about the conservatism of her new community. Although political bias is part of a person's Weltanschauung, it is often an unexamined attribute that can lead teachers like Sue to assume that hers is really the right way. In *The Morality of Pluralism* (1993), Kekes explores the liberal dilemma of being open to all points of view, even to those that require closedness toward pluralism. The point to be made is not that teachers should be without political bias, but rather that they must, first, be alive to their own points of view, and second, be continuously reflective about how their biases shape their words and actions. Sue may not be able to avoid future conflicts between her views and those held by others, but she may be able to handle the conflicts better if she understands their basis.

The second hidden bias deserving special note relates to the first and concerns a growing prejudice against various forms of fundamentalism. An area of potential disagreement exists between Sue and some of her students, as well as their parents. As the term progresses, Sue may find that Mark and his companions belong to a Christian fundamentalist church. She may also find that they subscribe to certain millenialist beliefs about apocalyptic implications of global entities, such as the United Nations, the Trilateral Commission, the World Bank, and others, as well as ideas of a "global village" and a "new world order." Others, including Survivalists, hold such beliefs but do not necessarily subscribe to the religious dimension.

Sue may find this attitude preposterous and be tempted to marginalize her students and their families as "fringe elements." Although Mark agreed with Sue that the world is not as good as it could be, and that he had "a mission to make it better," both he and Sue were speaking essentially the same language. Although their words are alike, they are speaking from two different universes of discourse, neither of which can be said to be True, although both might believe that Truth is on their respective sides. In dealing with such diversity of beliefs, Sue may find significant challenges to her liberal beliefs and her conception of democracy.

Pedagogical Philosophy and Approach

Sue's approach to teaching is what Fenstermacher and Soltis (1992) labeled "liberationist"; she combines a requirement that students take seriously the content of her social studies class with a self-imposed requirement that she treat the students respectfully as inquirers and not as empty vessels. She also belongs to the school of educational philosophy, most often associated with John Dewey, variously called pragmatism, experimentalism, or progressivism. She believes that learning begins best with the personal interests of her students, and she encourages them to find that meaning in the course content. She has little belief in the efficacy of rote memorization. Finally, she believes strongly in free intellectual inquiry and a commitment to social change.

Teachers wear pedagogical manner and style almost naturally, for they derive from Weltanschauung, although they also develop through study and reflection. Sue may find, however, that her approach discomfits students more accustomed to an authoritarian (Fenstermacher's "executive") or a nurturing (Fenstermacher's "therapist") style. Moreover, her insistence on free, open inquiry may trouble unquestioned beliefs held by her students and their families. Sue's admiration for Mark's intelligence and courage, for example, could lead her to take him under her wing. Indeed, she thinks that he could go far under her tutelage, but is taken aback by his passion for religion. If Mark responds to Sue's admiration and her pedagogical approach, he might question the tenets of his belief system. While some might applaud such questioning, if she is to be true to her own ideals, Sue must realize the intellectual and moral dilemmas that face her. If she comes to see religion as an important aspect of cultural diversity, she must ask what right she has to disturb religious belief. If, through her approach to teaching, she does disquiet those beliefs, she must ask where her responsibility lies in guiding students through difficult passages in their lives. If she is to maintain her commitment to open inquiry, she must continuously consider the consequences of her pedagogy, acknowledging her role in changing the small society of her classroom.

Analysis of the Three Central Issues

Congress shall make no law respecting an establishment of religion, or prohibiting the free exercise thereof, or abridging the freedom of speech, or of the press, or the right of the people peaceably to assemble, and to petition the Government for a redress of grievances.

Many call the First Amendment to the U. S. Constitution "The Great Amendment" because it encompasses the nation's most cherished—and most problematic—rights and freedoms: religion, speech, press, assembly, justice. These concepts were so new and difficult that the framers of the Constitution left these and other guaranteed freedoms out of the original document to assure ratification by those states where, for example, established religion or prior restraint on the press was still part of the political culture. The first Congress added the first ten amendments to the Constitution, commonly called the Bill of Rights. The First Amendment was originally the third proposed, following two that dealt with structural, rather than philosophical, issues, which the States did not ratify.

At this point, I review briefly the actual changes that the first Congress debated in phrasing the religion clauses of what was to become the First Amendment, for these changes reflect differences in philosophy and viewpoint about what was at stake.

James Madison, whose constitutional expertise was largely responsible for the form and content of the final adopted document, introduced some proposed amendments to the Constitution into the first session of Congress in 1789. On June 9, 1789, he suggested, "The civil rights of none shall be abridged on account of religious belief or worship, nor shall any national religion be established, nor shall the full and equal rights of conscience be in any manner, or on any pretext, infringed...." Other members of Congress suggested changes or other propositions and the debate was engaged. By the middle of August there was concern that, however the amendment was worded, some would see it as an attempt to abolish religion altogether. Madison clarified his intent, saying that Congress should not establish a religion, and enforce the legal observation of it by law, nor compel men to worship God in any manner contrary to their conscience. He also observed that certain of the states had, in their own Constitutions, made laws infringing the rights of conscience, and perhaps even establishing a national religion; he opposed both. On August 20, the House passed the amendment that read in part, "Congress shall make no law establishing religion, or to prevent the free exercise thereof, or to infringe the rights of conscience."

The matter went to the Senate, which disagreed with the word "religion," and suggested instead, "One Religious Sect or Society in preference to others." After additional discussion, the Senate deleted the phrase concerning rights of conscience. Several days later, as the debate proceeded, another proposal suggested, "Congress shall make no law establishing articles of faith or a mode of worship, or prohibiting the free exercise of religion...." On September 24, 1789, the two chambers agreed on the final wording of the amendment.

Disagreeing from the outset about just what latitude the right to religious freedom would encompass, the framers of the Constitution, along with their other colleagues in Congress, finally settled on two clauses that have since been interpreted in the widest possible way. It is clear from the debates that, for the first *clause—Congress shall make no law respecting an establishment of religion—*the

Congressional representatives had in mind the long and troubled history of established religions in Europe and then in the American colonies. Even though some states, such as Virginia, had already passed laws disestablishing religion by the time the Constitution was written, it was not until 1833 that the last state, Massachusetts, severed its ties between civil and religious authority. Thus the writers of the First Amendment lived in a period when 8 of the original 13 states still had an established religion, and Congress was reluctant to allow the possibility that, through an Act of Congress, any one of these religions might eventually emerge as the established religion for all of the states. Moreover, forms of state-imposed dogma or orthodoxy were anathema to the Enlightenment rationalism that shaped the thinking of this early Constitutional period.

The second clause of the First Amendment—*nor prohibiting the free exercise thereof*—was tied intimately to the first clause in that its ancestry is to be found in countless examples of religious discrimination through the ages. In contrast to the first clause which dealt with a central, state-supported religion, the second clause, encompassed the right of individual conscience and made clear that, in matters of religion, Congress could never dictate what an individual could or could not believe. These clauses, when first adopted, applied only to the national government. Not until the ratification of the Fourteenth Amendment was the primacy of the U. S. Constitution certified. These Amendments concerning the rights of former slaves clarified and set limits on the scope of states' powers encompassed by the earlier Tenth Amendment: *Powers not delegated to the United States by the Constitution, nor prohibited to it by the States, are reserved to the States, respectively, or to the people.* That had been the umbrella under which several states still held to policies and practices, such as established religion, prohibited to the federal government.

The mere passage of laws, of course, does not mean that people immediately conform to the new principles or the philosophy that informed them. Indeed, the history of the United States since ratification of the Bill of Rights in 1791 is replete with incidents of religious intolerance and, worse, violence toward adherents of unpopular beliefs. Jews, Roman Catholics, Baptists, Quakers, Mormons, Muslims, all have endured terrible acts in the name of religion. Nearly all religions practiced today can claim periods of discrimination in the United States toward their belief systems. The First Amendment, however, does not safeguard individuals or groups against discriminatory actions by others, but only safeguards against actions by governmental entities and their extensions, such as educational institutions.

In the 20th century, numerous court cases have tested the religion clauses of the First Amendment. In one of the first such cases, *Everson v. Board. of Education* (330 U. S. 1, 1947), the Supreme Court, surprisingly enough, upheld transport of parochial school children on public school buses because the Court deemed having the children educated constituted a "public good." Yet in this same case the Court spoke strongly in favor of Thomas Jefferson's concept of a "wall of separation" between church and state, saying unequivocally, "Neither a state nor the Federal Government can, openly or secretly, participate in the affairs of any religious organizations or groups and vice versa" (quoted in Haynes 1990, p. 54). Jefferson's concept has since been invoked both in and outside of courts as a (sometimes misunderstood) general principle to guide decisions about a range of incidents involving religion in public places.

Of the cases heard by the Supreme Court since Everson, perhaps the two most frequently relied on by school personnel in questions about religion are *Engel v. Vitale* (370 U. S. 421, 1962) and *Abington v. Schempp* (374 U. S. 203, 1963). In the Engel case, the Court ruled that the New York State Regents violated the Constitution by devising a "nondenominational" prayer to be recited each morning, saying, "It is neither sacrilegious nor anti-religious to say that each separate government in this country should stay out of the business of writing or sanctioning official prayers and leave that purely religious function to the people themselves and to those the people choose to look to for religious guidance." In the Schempp case, the Court held that the Abington Township School District similarly violated the establishment clause by requiring the reading of a Biblical passage as part of each day's opening exercises. These cases were followed by others—*Stone v. Graham* (449 U. S. 39, 1980); *Wallace v. Jaffree* (472 U. S. 38, 1985), and *Lee v. Weisman* (499 U. S. 918, 1990)—that firmly denied to public schools any role in promulgating any religion or religious practices. The effect of these cases was to create a climate in which school personnel often became overzealous in prohibiting any discussion of religion or display of religious symbols by students. Thus in the actual enactment of the establishment prohibition, teachers, principals, and other school personnel often infringe on the protections of the second clause: free exercise.

Judges and other scholars have long recognized the tensions between these two clauses, so it is not surprising that lay persons find both spirit and letter of the law confusing. Nor is the confusion helped by the general use of the expression, "separation of church and state." Indeed, this expression perhaps accounts for much of the confusion because by invoking it, school personnel and members of the community seem to believe that there must be no consideration or treatment of religion in public schools. The Supreme Court also ruled favorably in two cases that allow "equal access" by religion-based clubs in secular educational institutions. The first case, *Widmar v. Vincent* (454 U. S. 263, 1981), concerned the rights of students in public colleges and universities to form religion-based clubs that meet in the institutions' facilities. The Court held that the institutions need not support the goals of any student or other group that made use of the institutions' traditional policy of open, public forums, but that, so long as the institutions permitted other nonreligion-based groups to meet, they must also permit the religion-based groups equal access. In addition to drawing on arguments about the establishment and free exercise clauses, the Court relied on the free speech and free assembly clauses of the First Amendment.

The U. S. Congress took up the central questions of this case as they might apply to elementary and secondary public schools by passing the "Equal Access Act" (20 U.S.C. 4071–74) in 1984. The Act specifically prohibited discriminatory treatment of students' religious speech, stating that any school district that permitted one or more noncurricular student groups to meet on or in its facilities must allow all such petitioning groups regardless of the content of their speech, provided that discipline and student well-being at such meetings would be assured. In the subsequent Mergens case—*Westside v. Mergens* (110 U. S. 2356, 1990)—the Supreme Court upheld the constitutionality of the Equal Access Act. In rendering the Mergens verdict, the Court made it clear that equal access did not mean endorsement, and that the previous decisions about school-mandated prayer and devotional exercises still stood.

One other case bears on the matter at hand, *Tinker v. Des Moines* (393 U. S. 503, 1969). In this case the Supreme Court ruled that controversial speech in and outside the classroom is permitted as long as school discipline can be maintained and the rights of others are safeguarded. The Court specifically stated that public school students and teachers do not leave their First Amendment rights at the schoolhouse gate.

Application to the Case

In her first day of teaching, Sue Walters faced the issue of teaching about religion in the public school. It would seem that the cases cited would forbid religious studies as part of the curriculum. Indeed, if the intent of such a curriculum were promulgation of belief, that study would be impermissible. In rendering the decision in *Abington v. Schempp*, however, the Supreme Court noted that, although a school may not impose doctrinal or devotional exercises (such as Bible reading) on students, the study of religion as an academic subject is permissible and even desirable. Associate Justice Tom Clark stated the matter succinctly:

> One's education is not complete without a study of comparative religion or the history of religion and its relationship to the advancement of civilization. The Bible is worthy of study for its literary and historic qualities. Study of the Bible or of religion, when teachers present it objectively as part of a secular program of education, may not be affected consistently with the First Amendment. *Abington v. Schempp* (374 U. S. 203, 1963; cited in Lowell, 1976)

When Mark challenged Sue to add a unit on religion to the social studies curriculum, he was well within a correct interpretation of the law. Sue, on the other hand, incorrectly used the separation of church and state argument, even though her logic about the difficulty of the task was correct. She said, "I can't include that as a topic because it's impossible to teach about religion without actually teaching religious doctrine." Although aspects of a religion can be studied "for its literary and historic qualities," as Justice Clark said, any truly qualitative understanding of a religion must explore its belief tenets. In this respect, doctrine is the central element of a religion.

Sue can overcome this difficulty through several measures. First, she must be able to render doctrines veridically, that is, she cannot give such a general or shallow interpretation of a faith system's central beliefs as to make them virtually meaningless to her students. I noted elsewhere (Potter, 1991) that this requires a vast and deep knowledge about religions that few teachers possess. In the (likely) absence of such knowledge, Sue must acknowledge her ignorance and draw on other resources, including both textual material and persons from the community. She must advise her resource persons against proselytizing for a specific religious view or advocating religious belief generally.

Second, she must be fair and balanced in her treatment of various religions, neither favoring nor slighting some belief systems in relation to others. Fairness requires that both Sue and her students think critically about the historical record and its interpretations, including the less commendable acts committed in the name of religion. But as Charles Haynes counsels: "Consideration of destructive or oppressive acts carried out in the name of a religious belief is not an opportunity to attack the integrity of the religion itself. All religious traditions can point to tragic chapters in their story and historical incidents where the ideals of the faith were not fully lived. This part of the record can be taught without condemning a particular religion or religion in general. Teaching that includes attacks on religion or on the theology or practice of any faith does not belong in a public school classroom" (Haynes, 1991, p. 4).

Third, she must avoid injecting her own beliefs into the discussions, both as a Constitutional matter and as a responsibility of being a model for her students. Her Constitutional obligation is to avoid advocacy. She has an ethical responsibility to not disturb the religious beliefs of her students.

Fourth, she must maintain in herself, and try to teach her students, a respect for differences. Mark's comment, "You talked about how important it is for us to have an understanding of diversity and a tolerance for all cultures ... " is important. If Sue teaches "mere toleration," whether for a religion, a race, a gender, a class, a culture, or any other category, she will have assumed a position, perhaps unwittingly, of superiority toward that which is tolerated. Instead, she must adopt a profound attitude of respect requiring the treating of each belief as she would wish her own beliefs to be treated. Respect extends to teaching method. Ordinarily, role-playing and enactments can be effective ways to communicate curricular concepts. In matters of religion, however, such activities risk violating or trivializing the sacred character that believers attribute to certain religious practices.

The "Equal Access Act" of 1984 (Colby, 1991) and the Court decision upholding its constitutionality demonstrate that student clubs, such the "Students for Christ Club," fall within legal constraints. By having a faculty sponsor, the school meets its obligations concerning disciplinary oversight and assurance of student well-being. These latter points provide an answer to objections about a school policy that could conceivably foster anti-social clubs, such as racist groups. In both the Mergens and Tinker cases, the Court made it clear that schools may prohibit disruptive groups or any that engage in illegal activities. Requiring a voluntary faculty sponsor is one measure schools can use to assure adult monitoring. Another is to require parental permission for students to belong to a noncurricular club. Such a requirement must be imposed on all noncurricular organizations, not only on those that school personnel might consider problematic.

The faculty sponsor's role in relation to the club, as well as other teachers' participation in club activities, merits analysis. The Equal Access Act specifically states:

1. The meeting is voluntary and student initiated;
2. There is no sponsorship of the meeting by the school, the government, or its agents or employees;
3. Employees or agents of the school or government are present at religious meetings only in a nonparticipatory capacity. (Section 4071, c)

Although the case does not specify what Mr. Bradley (the faculty sponsor) does, one of Sue's students says, "Sometimes other teachers come to the meetings, too, to pray and study the Bible." In so doing, the participating teachers and the school could be held in violation of the specific provisions of the Equal Access Act that derive their authority from the establishment clause of the First Amendment. The critical tension between the establishment clause and the free exercise clause becomes manifest. All teachers have the personal rights to free exercise of religious belief, but as employees in a public school they cannot put themselves in the position, in or on school facilities, of endorsing or promoting a particular belief.

The final issue in this case—students' and teachers' own religious beliefs—remains Constitutionally ambiguous. After class, Mark and a few of his classmates invite Sue to attend their church, then ask her what her religion is. Sue is going through a time of questioning and is also uncertain what an appropriate answer might be. She says, "I guess you could say I'm a seeker." That response elicits further invitations from the students, including an invitation to join the student club.

Sue has breathing space in the form of a weekend, time to think through the issues, and the opportunity to consult with her former Social Foundations professor. Not all, and probably not many, teachers confronted by similar difficulties have these luxuries. Although Sue could safely stand behind Jefferson's wall of separation and refuse to answer her students' direct query, such a response would be contrary to some of the basic pedagogical principles she enunciated in her classroom: openness, safety in free exercise, respect for rights and differences of others, and not least, the importance of topics her students consider central to their lives.

Fenstermacher observes that teachers convey as much through manner as through explicit didactics (Fenstermacher, 1986). If Sue is to retain the trust that her students seem willing to invest in her, she must come to grips sooner rather than later with their questions. She must demonstrate through her manner that their interest is worthy of consideration, and she must be honest in her reasons for either accepting or rejecting their invitation to join their club and their church. Haynes notes,

"Answering the question ... can be a good lesson in civic values. Students learn that people with deep convictions can teach and learn about the convictions of others in ways that are fair and balanced" (Haynes, 1991, p. 6).

Sue also has the responsibility to ensure that all students in the class are protected in their right to express, or not express, their own beliefs. For example, if Mark and his co-believers volunteer their religious views during an appropriate part of the curriculum, Sue must safeguard their right to do so. Again, the respect she accords such exercise will show the other students that their own views about other profoundly personal topics (not just religion) will receive similar acceptance. As the Supreme Court noted in the Tinker case, controversial speech in and outside the classroom is permitted as long as school discipline can be maintained and the rights of others are protected. In summary, then, public schools and school personnel may not engage in activities that can be construed as promoting or endorsing religion generally, or any particular religious belief. Such activities include devotional exercises, mandated scripture reading, and employee participation in school-site religious clubs except as monitors. The Equal Access Act, however, provides that such clubs must be permitted if the school sanctions any other noncurricular clubs, provided that orderliness and safety are ensured. The free exercise clause of the First Amendment permits both students and teachers to state publicly their religious beliefs, but prudence dictates that such statements by teachers be minimal and in an appropriate context.

On the subject of religion and public schooling, there are numerous resources available to school personnel and other interested persons. Some states recently adopted legislation providing for inclusion of religion as an academic topic in several high school courses. Perhaps the best known is the California framework set out in the State Board of Education's handbook, Moral and Civic Education and Teaching About Religion. The Center for Law and Religious Freedom and Americans United for the Separation of Church and State are two organizations that monitor court cases throughout the United States and publish briefing papers on legal decisions and legislation concerning religion and public life. The Freedom Forum First Amendment Center at Vanderbilt University offers a variety of materials that assist understanding of First Amendment issues and consequences. Among the Center faculty is Dr. Charles Haynes, himself a tireless resource in promoting the Three Rs of civic life in relation to religious issues: Rights, Responsibility, and Respect. Lastly, the World Wide Web is an increasingly rich resource for information about all aspects of religion and public life.

REFERENCES

Colby, K. W. (1991). *A guide to the Equal Access Act.* Annandale, VA: The Center for Law and Religious Freedom.

Fenstermacher, G. D. (1986). Philosophy of research on teaching: Three aspects. In M. C. Wittrock (Ed.), *Handbook of research on teaching* (3rd ed. pp. 45–48). New York: Macmillan.

Fenstermacher, G. D., & Soltis, J. F. (1992). *Approaches to teaching (2nd ed.)*. New York: Teachers College Press.

Haynes, C. C. (1990). *Religion in American history: What to teach and how*. Alexandria, VA: Association for Supervision and Curriculum Development.

Haynes, C. C. (1991). *A teacher's guide to study about religion in public schools*. New York: Houghton Mifflin Co.

Haynes, C. C., & Thomas, O (Eds.) (1994). *Finding common ground: A First Amendment guide to religion and public education*. Nashville, TN: The Freedom Forum First Amendment Center of Vanderbilt University.

Kekes, J. (1993). *The morality of pluralism*. Princeton, NJ: Princeton University Press.

Lowell, C. S. (Ed.). (1976). *Constitutional provisions on church–state relations—Federal and state*. Silver Spring, MD: Americans United Research Foundation.

National Council for Social Studies. (1981, March). Statement on the essentials of the social studies. *Social Education, 45:3*, 163.

Potter, E. (1991). Covenants, conscience and excommunication: Some reflections on religion and schooling in America. Philosophical studies in education. *Proceedings of the Annual Meeting of the Ohio Valley Philosophy of Education Society*. Terra Haute, IN: Indiana State University.

Wilson, J. F., & Drakeman, D. L.(Eds.). (1987). *Church and state in American history (2nd ed.)* Boston: Beacon Press.

9

Stripped of Dignity

Deborah Sharp Libby
Slippery Rock University

Editors' note: Libby writes of a situation that most teachers face, even if not in the extremes of strip searches; namely, invasive acts toward students resulting from the schools' desire to maintain order. Whether the community be rural, urban, or suburban, some students inevitably get entangled in the disciplinary practices of the school. New teachers are often befuddled and baffled by events that go against their basic beliefs. In this case, Jane Powers must come to grips with her reactions to events beyond her control.

THE CASE

The morning headline in the local newspaper read, "Five Youths Strip Searched at Local Junior High School." Everywhere I turned, it was the hot topic of discussion. A relatively quiet and calm community and school district were now in turmoil, at odds with each other on how to handle and react to the recent events. Most of the families in this semirural area are working class; a number are below the poverty line. The community is 70% White and 30% African American. That the five boys searched at the middle school were African American appeared to ignite feelings of mistrust and despair throughout the town.

The strip search occurred only days ago at the junior high school where I teach. Because of the school district's strict policy of confidentiality applicable to the conduct and protection of all minors in our school, the facts remain somewhat vague;

however, a number of the alleged facts became public through the newspaper and statements by the students, their parents, and administrators involved in the situation: five African American students were involved in the incident; each was suspected of possessing and using marijuana; the possibility exists that some crack cocaine was involved as well.

The search occurred after a student at the junior high went to the principal and reported he had seen one boy smoking crack cocaine and several others smoking marijuana. Another student apparently corroborated this story. In response to the allegations, the principal contacted the district superintendent; they decided to search for the drugs. The superintendent came to the building and he, the principal, and a male teacher began the search. First, without the five boys' consent, they searched their lockers. This search proved fruitless; they found no drugs or drug paraphernalia.

The administrators remained determined to find the drugs if drugs were to be found, so they continued their search. After further discussion, the principal, superintendent, and teacher decided to conduct a strip search. The five boys were called over the public announcement system and asked to come to the office. The principal, superintendent, and teacher then escorted them to the boys' locker room to strip search them. They did not allow the boys to call their parents until after they completed the searches, even though several verbally pleaded and protested. Apparently, they asked the boys to remove their shoes and socks, lift up their shirts, and unfasten their pants. In addition, they ordered several of the boys to drop their pants to their knees and pull their underwear up tight against their bodies. The boys were embarrassed and frustrated; several appealed to the principal, superintendent, and teacher, asking what was going on and pleading for them to stop this search. Each maintained his innocence.

After repeated appeals, the boys apparently began to vent their feelings, telling the administrators that situations like these made Black students not want to come to school. They believed that they were being treated unfairly. They stated that ordeals such as these make them feel stupid, humiliated, nervous, and ultimately afraid to return to school. Finally, the men completed the strip search. It revealed no drugs. The students' argument that the men's allegations and searching activity were both ridiculous and racially driven appeared valid.

Once the students contacted their parents, the tension mounted. The parents were enraged and quickly arrived at the school to collect their children and express their concerns. They, too, found this incident, and especially the administrators' actions, racially motivated and expressed their displeasure verbally and by contacting legal counsel and the National Association for the Advancement of Colored People (NAACP). The parents questioned whether the administrators had reasonable suspicion to strip search their children. To the parents and many others in the community, it seemed that the principal, superintendent, and teacher violated the students' constitutional rights. Many saw this search as an invasion of privacy, similar to assault and abuse, that could potentially lead to emotional trauma and eventual poisoning of students' minds about school and education. Others questioned why larger inner city school districts with much more serious drug problems run safe and effective schools without conducting strip searches. The parents clearly believed the strip searches were ethically and constitutionally unacceptable.

Yet, others in the community and the district administration strongly believed there was nothing wrong with the search. Furthermore, the district administration felt strongly that their actions were warranted and that they would have behaved in the same manner with any student regardless of skin color. They felt that they had "reasonable cause."They stated that they wanted to keep their school drug free and would take whatever actions necessary to ensure that it would be. They regarded the use and possession of drugs as a serious problem requiring their immediate and undivided attention and believed that maintaining a drug-free environment was part of their obligation to the district and community. They saw it as a moral and ethical situation; the school board backed their decision 100%. Our district, like many other districts, has had no formal policy concerning strip searching; district employees have had no cultural sensitivity training. Some in the community call both these conditions into question. Unfortunately, both these issues cast a dark shadow over our district.

Individuals of the school and community are struggling with the recent events. The faculty, staff, students, parents, and administration all have strong opinions about how the situation was handled; opinions range from complete horror over injustice to beliefs that the administrations' actions were warranted and that the district should enforce stricter policies in the future.

New to teaching, I worked diligently over the past 3 years to develop a solid rapport with the faculty and the students in my building; I also sought to develop good relationships with parents. I believe that a strong working rapport results in greater classroom harmony and ultimately a more productive learning environment. I continue to learn a great deal about school procedure and policy, about interacting with students and parents, and about my evolving role as a teacher. Given the recent events, I wonder about the decisions of the administrators in my district. Something simply does not seem right to me. I feel that the students' rights were grossly violated. I vaguely remember learning about a legal case in my education law course during my undergraduate preparation that dealt with search and seizure it described an assistant principal finding a student holding onto a calculator case that had a questionable looking bulge protruding from it. The assistant principal asked the boy to show him the object; the boy asked to be left alone. Finally, after repeated requests to see the object, the principal pried the calculator case out of the boy's hand, unzipped it, and found marijuana and other drug paraphernalia. The assistant principal called the authorities and the young boy was arrested. The boy was eventually convicted, but appealed the decision stating that the evidence against him was a result of an illegal search (In re William G., 221 Cal. Rptr. 118 [1985]).The Supreme Court of California agreed, basing its decision on the reasonable suspicion standard set forth in *New Jersey v. T.L.O.* (1985).

I wonder if there were other options that our administration could have pursued that would have alleviated the need for the strip search. If the courts found that this earlier instance was an illegal search when drugs and drug paraphernalia were found, what would they say in this case where nothing was found?

I simply cannot believe the events that transpired over the past several days. It all seems like a bad dream, but then I walk into my classroom and realize that the events are definitely a reality I must deal with. Now, it seems as though the days when my teaching life was carefree and calm are gone, and I truly wonder if my classroom, school district, or community will return to any sort of normalcy.

I may be taking this situation more to heart because I know the students; two are members of my fifth period class. I teach eighth-grade social studies in a middle school made up of the sixth through the eighth grades. My colleagues and I teach in a house team consisting of five core academic teachers responsible for teaching English, reading, science, social studies, and mathematics. In our building, students at each grade level are divided into five houses consisting of approximately 26 students each. Students in each of the five groups travel from class to class together. Each group sees the same group of teachers, the house team, which allows the teachers to plan thematically and collaboratively together. I like the idea of planning collaboratively with a small group of my colleagues. Another added benefit of the house team is that we have a daily common planning period to prepare instruction.

In view of the recent events, I thought our team meeting would be particularly helpful. Darius and Tyrone, two of the students involved in the search incident, were in my house, so my colleagues and I saw each of them in class daily or when they attended school. Since the strip search, the boys' attendance had become somewhat irregular. This week I really looked forward to our daily meetings. I thought it would be helpful to sit down with my colleagues and get their feedback on my teaching ideas and how to help the two students in our house work through the situation.

In the past, my teams' planning periods were at least somewhat helpful. Philosophically, we all seemed to agree that our main goal was to engage students in their own learning. We also shared a strong commitment to teaching thematically, because we believe that such teaching allows us to make the connections between the subject areas explicit; however, that's where our shared philosophy ended. In discipline and classroom management, we held different views that the recent events simply magnified. Several teachers supported a behavior modification program involving tokens and prizes; two others believed in ruling with an iron hand. I believed that these approaches focused on extrinsic rewards and were at odds with my own university training and personal philosophy. I embraced a system focusing on positive reinforcement and intrinsic motivation. I wanted my classroom to operate in a democratic fashion.

When our house team planning period discussions began to focus on the issue of the eighth-grade boys involved in the strip search incident and their behavior and performance in our classes, I was shocked at my colleagues' comments. Several had no concerns about the administrators' actions; the others were indifferent. I believed that the strip search was extreme and unjustifiable. I shared my opinions with my colleagues and voiced my belief that these boys should be given a great deal of support in our classrooms to help them feel safe to express their opinions and thoughts. My colleagues promptly dismissed these positions. They viewed me as a sympathetic soul needing a "reality check." It was obvious that none of them planned to do anything differently in their classes to help these boys deal with the issues that had occurred. This left me even more concerned about how to handle the brewing feelings of mistrust in my class.

It did not help that my house team was focusing on an interdisciplinary unit of study on the effects of the Revolutionary War on the United States. My social studies class discussions were about the events leading to the writing of the Constitution and the eventual development of the Bill of Rights. Recently, we were spending time discussing the Constitution, the Bill of Rights, the Founding Fathers' purpose for writing it, and its current meaning to United States' citizens.

Unfortunately, my students were becoming increasingly unruly during class discussions. Our discussion never stayed on track. It seemed as if every amendment in the Bill of Rights led a heated discussion concerning the recent strip search. Everyone seemed to have an opinion; many opinions represented opposing views, which resulted in arguments in class. Although my students needed to feel free to express their thoughts, I wanted them to do so in a kind and pleasant fashion. I also wanted them to stick to the point of our discussions. Instead, my class became a forum for rehashing the events of the last few days. Discussions became increasingly difficult to control. The students were angry, resentful, and argumentative. They interrupted their peers in midsentence. The volume of their voices grew; the intensity of our discussions escalated, becoming almost unbearable. I found it troubling that they could not share their views in a civil manner. It seemed as if the students were drawing clear lines down the floors of my classroom. I had never assigned seats in the classroom, yet now the students began physically positioning themselves near those sharing their own views, in a way taking seats they assigned to themselves. The students divided themselves into several distinct cliques representing the various viewpoints that the community and school held about the strip search.

About a week after the strip search, I found the tension in my fifth-period class more than I could bear. The class was particularly difficult under normal circumstances; the recent events in the district appeared to cause this particular group of students to become increasingly restless, agitated, and unruly. To complicate matters, Tyrone and Darius, two of the boys involved in the search, were in this class. Both came from working-class African American families. Both were somewhat below average in academic subjects and not always consistent about turning in assignments; however, they usually participated in class discussions. They were always somewhat mischievous; now they were angry, agitated, argumentative, and frustrated with the system and everyone associated with it. Their attitudes toward my class, their peers, teachers, and the school in general changed for the worse. They trusted no one, and suspected everyone—particularly White people—of being out to get them. This belief or fear applied to the teachers in our school, myself included, because the majority of us were Caucasian. Who could blame them? The boys began to miss more and more school. When they attended class, they refused to participate constructively. Seemingly hostile and bitter, they spent a great deal of time harassing me and the other students in class. They called out of turn; they were argumentative and challenging. It took little to provoke a heated discussion with these two boys, and the rest of my fifth-period class did not behave much better. In short, life was tough.

On the particular day I am about to describe, the class concentrated on the Bill of Rights, specifically Amendment #4, which dealt with search and seizure. I hardly had a choice. With the end of the school year near, we had to cover the material stipulated in the curriculum. Yet, the timing of this subject matter could not have been worse.

I decided to forge ahead with Amendment #4, but to try a new approach. There had to be a way to reach these students with a productive discussion, one that closely tied the larger world to the current events in our building. I decided to write the fourth amendment of the Bill of Rights on the board for the whole class to see:

Amendment #4
The right of the people to be secure in their persons, houses, papers and effects, against unreasonable searches and seizures, shall not be violated and no warrants shall be issued upon probable cause supported by oath or affirmation and particularly describing the place to be searched and the persons or things to be seized.

I opened class by asking the students to read the amendment and react to it in their journals. In their reactions, they were to write what they believed the Founding Fathers intended in the amendment and what the amendment meant to them. I was excited about their initial response to the activity as I walked around the room. They wrote feverishly. I noted that in their responses they addressed an array of thoughts and opinions. I was excited about the prospect that the discussion might be focused and profitable.

After the students wrote for about 15 minutes, I asked them to share their thoughts. The class discussion began smoothly as some suggested that the Bill of Rights had meaning, but that the meaning depended on who you were. Others believed the Bill of Rights was clear and universal—the American justice system treated everyone equally and fairly regardless of race, ethnic origin, or religion.

Unfortunately, civility went downhill in a hurry. Some students soon began dominating discussion as usual. They returned to their opinions about the strip search. However, this time they seemed more passionate about their opinions. Although this was the outcome I initially wanted, I was not prepared for their anger.

"Okay, guys, that's enough. Come on, I need your attention!" As I struggled for control, I found myself wondering if I could ever make a difference in these students' lives. Did they really want to learn? The students ignored my efforts to get their attention, and I was left at the front of the classroom wondering what to do next.

Three students—Tyrone, Darius, and Tim—engaged in a heated exchange. Tyrone and Darius almost screamed that they felt they had no rights in this school or community because they were Black, and that the White people could not deal with their Blackness. Tim, a White student, argued that they got what was coming to them. "Go live in the ghetto if you don't like it here!" he blurted out. Before I knew it, these verbal attacks turned physical and a fight broke out among the three boys. I raced across the room, but by the time I reached them, punches had been thrown and Tim had a bloody lip. Without any discussion, I immediately sent the boys to the principal's office. I had no idea what to say or do to make the situation better.

After school I phoned the students' parents. I tried to set up conferences with Tyrone's and Darius's parents, but they acted distant and seemed reluctant to come to school. I could tell they harbored negative feelings toward the school and its teachers. I called Tim's parents, but they said there was nothing to discuss. They thought Tyrone and Darius were the problem, and they expected extreme disciplinary measures to be taken with the two boys. I simply did not know what to do. I had a feeling that, no matter what happened, I had lost my class. I did not know how to get through the final 4 weeks of school. I wanted to quit. I was actually questioning whether I should remain in the field of education at all.

QUESTIONS, DISCUSSION, AND COMMENTARY

1a. What are the major pedagogical issues in the case? (What are the key issues/elements in this case?)

Pedagogical Issues

Classroom Discussion. Jane Powers set out to discuss Amendment #4 of the Bill of Rights. The subject matter—search and seizure—is very controversial given the strip search at the school. She decides, however, to forge ahead and discuss the Bill of Rights trying a new approach to promote a productive discussion. The main challenge that Jane experienced in past discussions is that the students tended to dominate discussions focusing on the strip search. These discussions resulted in mounting tension among students in the classroom. Unfortunately, this class is particularly difficult under normal circumstances and, due to the recent events, has become increasingly restless, agitated, and unruly.

Jane must think about strategies she can implement to channel students' energies. She continues to focus on discussion, but does not state why (the purpose) she chose to use discussion; she shows little consideration concerning how that discussion may take place and no thought about her specific role in helping the discussion maintain focus.

Jane first needs to think about the instructional purpose of this particular classroom discussion. More specifically, what outcome? Normally, teachers use discussions to achieve at least three important instructional outcomes (Arends, 1994): the teacher hopes to improve students' thinking in an effort to help them construct their own meaning about a specific concept; the teacher hopes to promote student involvement and engagement in the classroom; the teacher hopes to help the students develop, cultivate, and refine important communication skills and thinking processes.

1b. How do you think the students viewed the lesson on Amendment #4 dealing with search and seizure? Is there anything Jane Powers could have done to avoid the problems that arose during this lesson?

Classroom Discussion.   The students appeared engaged and involved in the discussion. They began the lesson deep in thought and involved in the task at hand. They shared their thoughts concerning the meaning of the Bill of Rights and began to discuss their opinions concerning the recent search and seizure, which is directly related to Amendment #4 of the Bill of Rights. Jane found she was unprepared to deal with the students' strong feelings on the issue.

Jane must realize that having a discussion requires a great deal of planning. In this case, it appears that she did no specific form of planning other than to generate a writing prompt to help focus students' thinking. Although this is a good beginning, it is not nearly enough. Classroom discussions—and other models of teaching as well—require teacher planning for what will occur before, during, and after the lesson. Planning for a discussion is difficult because students' responses are unknown, yet it is extremely important that a discussion be governed at the outset by some rules, even though the teacher plans to maintain flexibility. Teachers teach their students how to become effective participants during classroom discussion. It is not something that simply happens as the result of an interesting discussion prompt. Cazden (1988) points out that spoken language enables students to discuss what they know and form meaning from new knowledge as it is acquired. If teachers want students to learn and grow from a discussion, however, they must carefully plan for reasonable exchange among students.

Teachers facilitate or help nurture rich discussions in several ways. First, they must think about getting started. What must teachers do to prepare for the discussion? What is their purpose? How do they plan to introduce the lesson to their students? How will they capture students' interest and motivate them to become involved? To keep students focused, teachers can review the rules of classroom discussion, ask a question, present a puzzling situation, or describe a discussion issue. In this case, Jane begins by having the students write in their journals about the Founding Fathers' intentions and the meaning students ascribe to the Amendment. It is a good beginning, but she should explore other ways of building on this introduction. Reviewing the rules for classroom discussion might help.

Questions can engage students in a discussion. Questions can also play an important role throughout the discussion. They can help maintain the focus of the discussion, tactfully redirect those who start to digress, and encourage individuals who may be somewhat reserved to share their thoughts. Questions can also encourage others to listen carefully to the ideas and points of view of their peers.

The development of thought-provoking questions is critical. Teachers must consider a variety of questions that will promote higher level thinking. The questions must be interesting for the students and open-ended, allowing for sufficient input of students' ideas. In this particular case, the discussion focuses on the Fourth Amendment and the search that occurred in the school, but Jane poses only one question to the class. It is open-ended and allows students to infer the thinking of the Founding Fathers, yet this is the only question posed to the class throughout the whole lesson.

There are a number of additional verbal behaviors teachers demonstrate during a discussion. Teachers must find appropriate ways to respond to students' ideas and opinions. Jane should have been able to facilitate the discussion with prompts or verbal assists to encourage students to think about specific issues and make connections between and among current issues, assigned readings, and their own personal experiences.

Verbal assists and discussion prompts encourage involvement by requiring students to synthesize key ideas, clarify concepts, and bring closure to the discussion. Teachers may wish to encourage the students to reflect on other students' thoughts and opinions, to consider other ideas and perspectives, and to provide clarification. These actions help teachers provide a structure to support and channel student discussion in a productive fashion.

Teachers also should be prepared to share their own thoughts and ideas, being careful to avoid being seen as having all the answers. This type of participation allows teachers to model appropriate ways to become involved in a discussion. It also helps teachers demonstrate to students that they see themselves as part of the classroom learning community.

Jane Powers might also consider keeping some sort of record of class discussions. She or a student could record some of the students' ideas on the chalkboard, chart paper, or flip charts. Graphic organizers can help students see various view points, as well as hear them.

There are many ways to bring a discussion to closure. Some teachers choose to end a discussion by summarizing or expressing the meaning that the discussion held for them. Others have the students perform these functions. In some instances, teachers make connections to a larger or more inclusive concept. The main goal of a discussion's closure should be to encourage students to reflect on the discussion. In this particular case, Jane simply leaves the lesson hanging. Unfortunately, the main memory that the students will probably carry away from this lesson will be the one about who threw the hardest punch.

Classroom Management.   Many individuals consider classroom management to entail only students' behavioral conduct in the classroom. But classroom management is much more complex. It involves teacher preparation, planning and organization, maximizing student cooperation and engagement, and minimizing disruptive behavior. In this particular case, Jane must exercise better planning and demonstrate management techniques to gain and hold students' attention. Through preventive approaches, Jane could avoid many of the problems encountered, especially those associated with student misbehavior.

For example, Jane could have established rules and procedures for classroom discussion. Rules specify what the teacher expects students to do and how they will accomplish the task that was set. More specifically, she could provide students with clear guidelines for student talk, such as: Only one of you can speak at a time. Listen carefully to other individuals ideas. Raise your hand if you have a question or would like to share. Take turns and be patient. It is okay to disagree, but use your words, not your actions, to communicate your thoughts and feelings.

Another way to encourage desirable behaviors is to verbally praise. To discourage undesirable behaviors, let students know why they are unacceptable. These actions might allow Jane to become more involved in the discussion and to model for the students what is acceptable and unacceptable.

2. What is known about the backgrounds of the students who were involved in the strip search? What else would be helpful to know about these children?

Tyrone and Darius are eighth-grade boys who come from working-class families. They live in a semirural, working-class community where a number of individuals find themselves living below the poverty line. The community is 70% White and 30% African American. Both boys are somewhat below average students who are not always consistent about turning in assignments; however, they usually get involved in class discussions. The boys are somewhat mischievous, but they are also good natured. After the strip search, they become angry, agitated, argumentative. Their attitudes toward their peers, teachers, and the school in general changed for the worse. The boys think that the search was racially motivated.

The boys' parents are also angry and have contacted legal counsel and the NAACP. They question whether the administrators had reasonable cause to strip search their children. They see the search as an invasion of privacy similar to a form of assault and abuse that could potentially lead to emotional trauma and the eventual poisoning of their children's minds about school and education. The parents are also reluctant to get involved with this teacher.

3. What do you think about the students and parents' response to the search?

Some may try to dismiss the parents' and children's concerns as cultural backlash, but they have a legitimate complaint. Although the doctrine of "in loco parentis" (in place of the parents) has been used previously to show cause and to defend the decisions, actions, and authority of school officials over students at school, many courts are now limiting its applicability (Fischer, Schimmel, & Kelly, 1981).

4. What do you think about the locker search and the eventual strip search? Was it warranted? Are there other steps that might have been explored? What about the legal rights of the students? Were they violated?

The Fourth Amendment to the Constitution provides that "The right of the people to be secure in their persons, houses, papers and effects, against unreasonable searches and seizures shall not be violated."Lawful searches by school officials must be based on their moral obligation to provide a safe atmosphere conducive to learning for all students. Although school personnel are government employees, they are not charged with law enforcement. Therefore, the constitutional requisite placed on police that there be "probable cause" for a search is not always appropriate when referring to searches conducted by school officials. (*People v. Overton*, 20 N.Y. 2d 360, 229 N.E.2d 596 [1967]; *Horton v. Goose Creek Independent School Dist.*, 690 F.2d 470 (5th Cir.1982), cert. denied 463 U.S. 1209, 103 S. Ct. 3536, [1983].) A lesser standard of "reasonable cause" seems to be the prevailing test for most searches conducted by school personnel in a school setting. When assessing whether the school officials had sufficient cause to conduct a search, courts consider such factors as source of the information, the child's record, the seriousness of the problem being addressed by the search, and the urgency of making the search without delay.

Locker Search. The search of school lockers can be conducted by appropriate school officials if they have reasonable suspicion that dangerous or unlawful materials are concealed there. The appropriate school officials who plan to conduct the search must have "probable cause" to carry out such a search. This means that they have acquired evidence from highly reliable sources indicating that the student is concealing dangerous or unlawful objects. When dangerous or unlawful objects are found, several scenarios can play out in a court of law. In some courts, evidence gathered without a student's consent will be excluded; however, in other courts the evidence will be admitted based on the rule that school administrators may consent on behalf of their students (Fischer, Schimmel, & Kelly, 1981).One thing we do not know in this particular case is how reliable the fellow junior high school students are who reported and corroborated the story that they had seen the boys smoking marijuana and crack cocaine. We also do not know if these boys have prior infractions on their school records.

Strip Search.   It is important to note that the search of a student's clothing or body (i.e., strip search) merits greater protection, because it involves invasion of privacy and possible "psychological damage to sensitive children."The degree of intrusiveness of the search itself plays a significant role in determining whether the search conducted by school officials is legally permissible. Searches can involve students' desks, lockers, pockets, purses, packages, outer clothing, underclothes, and body; however, the cause for each search must satisfy progressively higher standards as the search becomes more invasive.

An opinion was issued by the Supreme Court in 1985, adopting "reasonableness under all circumstances" as the standard for all searches conducted by educational personnel. Reasonableness was reported to refer to two standards:

1. The school official has reasonable cause to suspect that the search will produce evidence that the student has violated the law or rules of the school.
2. The range or scope of the search is permissible when the actions of the search are reasonable and not excessively intrusive to the age and sex of the student and the nature of the infraction. (New Jersey v. T.L.O., 469 U.S. 325, 105 S.Ct. 733, [1985]).

5. What other discussion techniques might Jane use with her students to assist them in dealing with Amendment #4 of the Bill of Rights and the issue of the strip search in her building?

Three suggestions are listed next. Not an exhaustive list, it includes several ideas that Jane Powers might incorporate into the classroom to focus and develop discussion in the classroom. In each of the items, she would still be responsible for a significant amount of planning to help facilitate the discussion.

Partner Journals (Yopp & Yopp, 1992).   Journals can be vehicles for promoting thinking and preparing students to participate in discussion. Journals allow students to explore their own thoughts and ideas in writing before engaging in discussion. The act of journaling helps students to collect and organize their thoughts and can serve as a rehearsal of what the student might say during the discussion.

Because Jane Powers already incorporated one journaling activity into her lesson, she might consider engaging the students in another journaling activity such as partner journals. As the term implies, partner journals involve student–student interaction. Students are given a question, puzzling situation, or concept to address. They are given 10 to 15 minutes to respond in writing in their journals. (Time may be longer or shorter depending on the subject matter.) They then trade journals with a peer or partner. They read their partner's journal entry and respond to it in writing. Students can share later their exchanges with the whole class.

Think–Pair–Share. This discussion technique grew out of cooperative learning strategies. Students are asked to think for a few minutes about a question or issue associated with a concept being addressed in class. Next, they pair off with a peer and discuss what they think. Usually students are given about 5 minutes to share their thoughts. The time depends on the topic. The pairs of students then share what they discussed with the whole class.

The Fishbowl Arrangement (Arends, 1994). Students are placed in two groups. Each group has a specific role. One group discusses a particular issue. This group sits in a circle where all can see and listen to each other in an easy manner. The second group is responsible for observing the first group. They sit in a circle outside the other circle. After watching and listening to the group for 20 minutes, the second group must give a short report on what they saw and heard. The two groups then switch roles and the process begins again. The teacher serves as the facilitator of the discussion, posing questions and prompts and sharing comments when appropriate.

6. Whom might Jane consult to find varied approaches to help her students deal with the search?

There are numerous individuals, services, and support groups in the district, school building, community, and state agencies that Jane might approach for support. Within the school district, the teacher might meet with the school or district guidance counselor or psychologist. Classroom teachers are members of a larger team that might help these children feel comfortable in class and perform better in school.

REFERENCES

Arends, R. (1994). *Learning to teach.* New York: McGraw-Hill.
Cazden, C. (1988). *Classroom discourse.* Portsmouth NH.: Heinemann.
Fischer, L., Schimmel, D., & Kelly, C. (1981). *Teachers and the law.* New York: Longman.
Horton v. Goose Creek Independent School Dist., 690 F.2d 470 (5 Cir. 1982), cert. denied 463 U.S. 1207, 103 S. Ct. 3536, (1983).
In re William G., 221 Cal. Rptr. 118 (1985).
New Jersey v. T.L.O., 469 U.S. 325, 105 S.Ct. 733, (1985)
People v. Overton, 20 N.Y. 2d 360, 229 N.E.2d 596 (1967).
Reutter, E., (1985). *The Law of public education* (3rd ed.). Mineola, NY: The Foundation Press, Inc.
Yopp, R., & Yopp, J. (1992). *Literature based reading activities.* Needham Heights, MA: Allyn & Bacon.

10

The Unwritten Amendment: Freedom of Curriculum

Joanne M. Herbert
University of Virginia

M. Elizabeth Hrabe
University of Virginia

> **Editors' note:** Herbert and Hrabe draw attention to the importance of both case content and the process by which it is presented. They describe how racial prejudice and poor judgment interacted to create national controversy about democratic ideals when a San Francisco teacher took his students to see the movie *Schindler's List*. The authors did not possess first hand knowledge of the events, yet they recognized the educational potential of the story. Here they weave the story of Mark Rader (the San Francisco teacher) as it was presented in the popular press in a fictionalized story of New York City teachers facing similar problems. Their teaching note emphasizes the centrality of "knowledge" in the case-analysis process. Known public events set in a fictional context yield a provocative piece of curriculum for the education of teachers and suggest a strategy for creating other similar cases.

THE CASE

Lisa's Story

I have taught eleventh-grade history and twelfth-grade government at Bradley High School in New York State for 2 years. I'm beginning to feel at home in this urban environment, populated largely by minority students, most of whom are African American, even though I'm only 25 and not African American. The "only 25" bit makes me most uncomfortable. My colleagues must average 45, on a good day. On a bad day they look like I feel—about 60.

I'm not Jewish, either. That may seem like a strange thing to say, but several of the other women here are. I think they must have adopted me the minute I entered the teachers' lounge; it just took me a while to figure it out. I have never known a funnier, warmer group of people than my colleagues at Bradley High; several of them have included me in a group. They delight in their work and in giving me a crash course in what it means to be Jewish—it must be one of those unforeseen benefits of the job that my principal, Mr. Shapiro, told me about. If there is a downside, it would have to be that virtually every lesson is accompanied by "noshing." We have snacked and talked our way through more heavy food than I care to remember.

Our group went to see the movie *Schindler's List* one Friday night after an unusually difficult week, and the tone of the evening was considerably different from what I had grown used to. The movie recounted the true story of Oskar Schindler, a German entrepreneur living in Nazi-occupied Krakow, Poland, during World War II who managed to save hundreds of Jews from concentration camps by declaring them "essential workers" in his factory. The film definitively depicted the Holocaust by following the plight of Polish Jews from the liquidation of the Krakow ghetto to the death camp at Auschwitz.

The horror of the film lay in its portrayal of Nazi soldiers who perpetrated mass murder and genocide with the bloodless determination of bureaucrats. They repressed human instincts in mindless paperwork, essentially depersonalizing those they destroyed. In contrast, Schindler, who early in the film appeared to be an opportunist who used Jewish factory workers solely to increase production, began to realize the humanity he shared with the Jews after witnessing hideous violence on the part of Nazis. Schindler repeatedly risked his life and eventually spent his fortune to save Jews' lives. In doing so, Schindler embodied the heroism and morality latent in the most common people. The irony and justice of his act were that he used the same paperwork to hide Jews that the Nazis employed to kill them.

The 3-hour film was shot almost entirely in black and white to emphasize the bleakness of the story and to approximate the pictures we carry in our heads of period newsreels and movie footage from World War II, Nazi propaganda films, and depiction of the liberation of Jews from concentration camps. Color was used sparingly and symbolically: at the very beginning of the movie as ceremonial candles burn down while a rabbi sings, again in the red coat of a little girl symbolizing for me Schindler's dawning recognition of the humanness of the ghetto Jews and the awakening of his own conscience, and in the last scene of the film, which transports viewers to the present.

The use of black and white both dampens and underlines the visceral emotional effect of violence. Blood running black in the snow is effectively shocking. Killing of Jews appears matter-of-fact and impersonal. Deaths appear realistic; bodies fall according to the laws of gravity rather than in the choreographed slow-motion contortion of some recent films.

Roberta Yaspen, the literature teacher and the person to whom I felt closest, wept quietly during the film. As we left the theater, she and the others were visibly shaken:

Roberta: My mother told me stories about the Holocaust. She had narrowly escaped internment herself when she and her mother fled to Switzerland. Her father, my grandfather, was not so lucky. He died in Buchenwald.

Freida: I grew up horrified by the stories of the Nazi machine, and no less frightened by the thought that if it happened once, why not again? Still, I could never really, truly appreciate the pain in my parents' eyes when they spoke of all the people they had known who had disappeared. I must have been too young to fully understand. I think that like most young people I felt somehow immune to such tragedy. It could never happen to me, yet I had such a strange feeling.

Peggy: I know what you mean. When that look passed over my mother's or father's face—it could have been anytime, triggered by some random occurrence—I knew exactly what she or he was thinking. The whole thing was so ingrained in my family that the Holocaust—we didn't call it that—the murders seemed to define us in a secret way. It was something so horrible that we shared that we believed nobody else could possibly imagine who we were inside.

As we walked from the theater to the train that night, I resolved that I had to do more to teach my own students the importance of learning history. It wasn't just the old George Santayana quote about being doomed to repeat it if you didn't know it; history shaped our conceptions of ourselves in deep and personal ways. Suddenly, I said, "Hey you guys, I'm going to take my eleventh graders to see this movie!"

"Oh, I don't know if you should do that, Lisa," said Frieda. "The film is 'talky'—it's an idea picture—and it's in black and white—it's long, too. I don't know if your students would appreciate it."

"I think you might be selling them short, Freida," I countered. "I showed *To Kill a Mocking Bird* to my government class, and they liked it. The quality of the discussion it stimulated surprised me."

The next Tuesday I began organizing a field trip for my eleventh-grade history class to see *Schindler's List*. I had talked to Mr. Shapiro on Monday, mocked up a parent permission letter that night, and began to discuss the Holocaust in class the next day. I was jumping ahead in the curriculum—we hadn't even reached World War II yet—but I had to act while the movie was still in town. Little did I know that another teacher all the way across the country apparently had the same idea. That Friday night I watched the national news and learned about Mark Rader's class in Oakland, California. He, too, thought it would be a great idea to take his class to see *Schindler's List*—that is, until they actually went to the theater, and then, according to the news report, all hell broke loose. Watching television and reading the newspapers for the next few days, I slowly pieced together the whole of Mark's experience.

Mark's Story

On January 17, 1994, the Oakland, California, schools were closed in observance of Martin Luther King Day. A few days earlier, Mark Rader, a science teacher at Castlemont High School, had contemplated ways he might make the holiday meaningful for students. Castlemont housed about 1,400 students, most of whom were African Americans and Latinos, in Grades 10 through 12. Many students were low achievers, and fewer than 5% attended college after graduation. Although his teaching situation was a challenging one, Mark was excited by the possibility of making a difference in young people's lives.

A graduate of Wheaton College, Mark had flown full-time for the Navy for 7 years before entering teaching. Thanks to a quick credentialing program in California, he obtained an emergency certificate allowing him to begin his first year of teaching at Hayward High School. At the same time, Mark was able to continue flying for the Navy on a part-time basis with a reserve unit based in Alameda. After one year at Hayward High, he took a position at Castlemont, where he was made director of Oakland, an academy within the school that focused on international trade and transportation. Along with 11 other teachers in the academy, Mark planned a variety of activities to broaden students' experiences and to increase their confidence. Among other things, students visited a local winery and the NASA Space Center at Aims. They also went hot air ballooning and took a tour of United Airlines.

In his third year of teaching at Castlemont, Mark was still seeking ways to help students stretch and grow. After seeing *Schindler's List*, he hit on the idea of taking students to see the film. Apparently just as I had done, he viewed the movie as a powerful one that illustrated leadership and sacrifice—attributes he wanted to instill, particularly in his male students. Sure that students would not see the movie unless he took them, Mark proposed a field trip to the theater on Martin Luther King Day. He thought the experience might also be an appropriate way to encourage students to consider issues of racial injustice and discrimination. He sweetened the trip with the promise of ice skating afterward.

Because schools would not be in session, students would have to provide their own transportation to the theater. The Academy would pay for the tickets and transportation from the theater to the ice rink. Although 75 students signed up for the trip, Mark suspected only 50 would show up at the theater, so he figured one bus would take care of their needs. With the pending holiday, finding chaperones proved somewhat difficult. In the end, four adults, including Tanya Dennis, Dean of Students, and Aaron Grumet, a math teacher, offered to accompany the group on the field trip.

On the day of the field trip, about 70 students showed up at the theater 10 minutes before the noon-time showing of *Schindler's List*. As Mark handed a check to the theater manager, both were obviously agitated. "What do you mean, you didn't know we were coming?" said Mark. "My colleague called last week to reserve a section of the theater for our students." Although he insisted he knew nothing of Mark's phone call, the manager allowed Mark's students to enter the theater, ahead of a long line of patrons who had been waiting patiently to buy tickets for the show. As Mark moved past the group, many of whom were middle-aged White men, he overheard one of them say, "What are these kinds of kids doing here?" Mark thought to himself that the remark sounded racist.

Once inside, things got worse. The movie had drawn a near-capacity crowd, so it was impossible to seat students in a section together. Students were split up among the seats; Mark was near the front with a group of about 20 students, but several other groups were clustered near the back of the theater. During the first part of the movie, Mark began to doubt the wisdom of bringing students to the showing. As he searched the rows of seats, he noticed several of them were missing. Slipping out of the theater as noiselessly as possible, he moved toward the concession stand to hunt for stragglers.

After sending them back to their seats, he continued his trek; he found students in the restroom and in other movies—*Grumpy Old Men* and *The Pelican Brief*—in the multiplex. Although students moaned and groaned as he herded them into *Schindler's List*, Mark was optimistic that they would soon settle down. Admittedly, there were a number of scenes in the first hour of the movie that probably made little sense to students, but he knew if they stuck with the film they would get something out of it.

Fifty-five minutes into the film, a young Jewish woman engineer argued loudly with Amon Goeth, a Nazi officer, about the quality of a building's foundations, insisting that the structure be rebuilt. Goeth ordered that she be killed, and several movie patrons flinched as the woman was shot in the head from behind. The woman engineer immediately fell forward and flipped on her side. Mark grimaced as one of the boys from Castlemont said in a loud voice, "Oh, that was cold!" and laughter erupted from several of his peers. When the laughter continued for a good 30 seconds, Mark was incredulous.

Faces full of anger turned toward the students, and several patrons left the theater. Mark heard angry voices saying, "Be quiet!" Moments later, the movie stopped, the lights came on, and owner Allen Michaan asked all Castlemont students to go to the lobby. Mark was stunned and embarrassed as he and the students moved toward the door, particularly when several angry patrons gave a standing ovation at their departure.

In the lobby, Mark made his way toward Mr. Michaan, who argued that the patrons were so upset by the students' laughter and comments that he had no choice but to evict them. Some in the audience were Holocaust survivors; the behavior horribly offended them. One woman was weeping uncontrollably. Mark apologized to Mr. Michaan, and he and the other chaperones moved the group of students toward the front doors of the theater. Never in his wildest dreams had he imagined such a fiasco.

One of Mark's colleagues called to arrange for a bus, which arrived 20 minutes later. As they waited outside the theater, Mark noticed that most of the students seemed to be handling the situation quite well. The 10 or so students who had caused all of the commotion, however, were still laughing. The teachers, the dean, and Mark discussed their next move and finally decided they would cancel the ice skating and take the students back to Castlemont High. As the 70 students clambered into a bus designed to carry 55 passengers, Mark wished things had turned out differently. He also wondered what he should do next. Lecture the students on their behavior? Write a letter of apology to Mr. Michaan? Talk with fellow teachers about their perceptions of the event? Once they arrived at school, he left a phone message for the principal, explaining the turn of events.

The next day, Mark was ordered to go to Southern California to fly for a week. The timing could not have been worse. The principal thought Mark was running out on her. She took the media backlash, of which there was plenty. The heading on the front page of the Oakland Tribune read "Field trip to *Schindler's List* backfires. Grand Lake Theater ejects rowdy Castlemont students for laughing at Holocaust horrors." Castlemont students' field trip was also the primary topic on radio talk shows. The principal's phone rang nonstop; faxes and letters poured in from places as distant as England and Germany. Members of the press clamored for interviews. The school's normal routine was shattered.

I couldn't believe my eyes and ears when I read and heard the story of Mark Rader and his students. How fortuitous, I thought, that the movie had opened on the West Coast instead of the East Coast. Perhaps Mark's experience had saved me the pain and embarrassment of having a similar experience with my students. I wondered if my colleagues had seen the stories. How could they have missed them? What would this do to my plans to take my history class to see the movie?

When I walked into the teachers' lounge on Monday the gang was all there—in rare form:

Roberta: My heavens! Did you all catch the news this weekend?

Peggy: Are you kidding? Every time I turned on the radio or the television there was a reporter talking about that disastrous field trip in California! Unbelievable! Why in the world did he take them to see *Schindler's List* on Martin Luther King Day? How could anyone expect a group of high school kids to understand the connection? I don't understand it myself!

Freida: Lisa, I hope you learned a lesson. Like I said last week, you can't expect these kids to appreciate Spielberg's film. They're not like you; they're desensitized to violence, because they see it every day. Wasn't it just last week that those two high school kids were arrested for smashing a family's picture window and destroying their menorah? We've got trouble enough in this community without making things any worse. Take my advice and forget this trip. By the way, when you got permission to take the trip, do you know if anyone really paid attention to what you were proposing to do? Did they know the story line of the movie? Did they ask you where the movie fit into your curriculum?

Just then the 8:00 bell sounded and my colleagues and I hurried toward our classrooms. My stomach was churning. Frieda was right; our community had had its share of violence, and I certainly did not want to worsen the situation. At the same time, wasn't it my responsibility as a teacher to educate young people? I had been so mesmerized by *Schindler's List* that I couldn't believe my students would react any differently. Or would they?

I thought more about the field trip in California and wondered if it was a fiasco simply because students weren't prepared in advance for the experience. From news reports, it sounded as though Mark Rader didn't know which students were going to show up to take the bus to the theater. He mentioned to one reporter that he wished he had emphasized manners and courtesy before students went to the theater. He also talked about how teachers cannot relax for a minute on field trips, and that there are always unforeseen events. I never saw or heard anything, however, about what type of content instruction Mark provided before the students went on their field trip. How much did they know about the Holocaust? Were they studying about World War II at the time of the field trip? Did they have any idea what they were going to see, or did they think *Schindler's List* was just another movie?

I was scared, but I was not ready to give up on my idea of building *Schindler's List* into the curriculum. Mark Rader's experience, however, was a sobering one. I had already mentioned to a few students that I was planning the field trip, and they seemed excited. But were they enthusiastic for the right reasons? Was I putting myself professionally at risk to proceed with my plans?

I snapped out of my reverie as Mr. Shapiro's voice boomed through the intercom. "Attention students, there are a few announcements about today's after-school programs...." As students shuffled to their seats, I realized I had more questions than answers.

TEACHING NOTES

We wrote this case—or more accurately, case within a case—to focus teachers on the idea that life around them contains rich possibilities for teaching and learning about democracy. The story of Mark Rader is true; that is, we took the details from published reports of events in Oakland, California and from follow-up telephone conversations we held with Mr. Rader. The story of Lisa and her colleagues is largely fictional. To create our case, we needed more information and more freedom than the facts of Rader's experiences would allow. The overlay of Lisa's story helped us realize these possibilities. Parenthetically, we think this strategy might be useful in developing other cases based on real-life, widely publicized occurrences.

We often use a five-step approach to analyzing cases (McNergney, Herbert, & Ford, 1994; Herbert & McNergney, 1995). These include: (a) identifying issues and problems in the case; (b) considering perspectives or the values of the actors in the case; (c) making explicit knowledge that might guide one's (d) actions if you were the protagonist or some other actor in the case; and (e) speculating about the likely consequences of such actions. The five steps alert people to ways of thinking and talking about a case so it will make sense to them—that is, so they can prepare themselves mentally to deal with the case at hand and thus with similar situations in the future. The five steps are a system or an organized way of approaching an ill-formed set of real-life problems.

The system does not dictate a rigid prescription for practice. Instructors and students must decide where to enter (i.e., with which step they will begin), how much time to spend on the steps, and in what order to progress through them. The time available influences all these decisions. And time also interacts with student interest; people get bored if they spend too much time on a particular activity. For the instructor, tension exists between wanting to encourage students to consider all the steps and wanting to go more deeply into one or two areas. The tension seems especially high in this particular case.

We resisted the temptation to do too much too quickly with this case. Instead we tried to encourage students to spend more time seeking knowledge that might support reasonable teaching actions. We did so for two reasons. First, the knowledge step in the five-step process is key to our conception of professional practice. Professional educators possess and can use knowledge that nonprofessionals do not possess. This simple fact is one hallmark of all professions—no knowledge, no professional behavior, diminished likelihood of positive consequences. Too often, in our haste to have students solve problems, we give too little attention to reasons underlying their projected actions.

Second, the content of the case itself impels us to think carefully about how the Holocaust has influenced people over time and space. As human beings, we are obliged to "get it right." As teachers, we must try to deliver this knowledge so the lessons of the Holocaust will not be lost or forgotten. These demands require special knowledge not only of the events surrounding World War II and its aftermath, but of the pedagogy necessary to use knowledge of the Holocaust in classrooms. For these reasons, we emphasize the close relationship between the knowledge and action steps at the expense of the other three steps in the case-analysis process. Because Lisa and her colleagues want to encourage attention to issues they believe are vitally important to their students, as did Mark Rader, we begin with a brief consideration of teachers' freedom to express what they believe is important in their teaching by selecting and defining the curriculum they teach.

1. What do you know about teachers' freedom or lack thereof to deviate from "prescribed curriculum?"

In 1988, the Supreme Court ruled in *Hazelwood School District v. Kuhlmeier,* 484U.S. 260(1988) that principals could censor school-sponsored publications. The basis for the Court's decision emanated from a case involving students in a high school journalism class who claimed that their First Amendment rights were violated when the principal reviewed their material and removed two stories—one on divorce, the other on three students' experiences with pregnancy—from the school-sponsored publication. According to the Supreme Court, a student newspaper does not represent a forum for public expression when it is part of the school curriculum. Thus, school officials can censor material considered inconsistent with the educational mission of the school.

Since that ruling in *Hazelwood v. Kuhlmeier,* the U. S. Supreme Court has indicated a willingness to allow local school boards the final decision regarding the curriculum in elementary and secondary schools. However, if school boards' actions have the effect of contracting rather than expanding knowledge, judicial intervention is not uncommon. When deciding individual cases, the courts usually consider the educational relevance of controversial material, teaching objectives, and the age and maturity of the intended audience.

In 1989, a Fifth Circuit Court of Appeals ruling held that teachers cannot assert a First Amendment right to replace an official supplementary reading list with their own list of books without first getting administrative approval. Nor may a teacher delete parts of the curriculum if they conflict with personal beliefs. Such restrictions do not mean teachers are constrained to use a particular strategy, however. Teachers who want to assign controversial materials may usually do so as long as selected materials are (a) relevant to the topic of study, (b) appropriate to the age and maturity of students, and (c) unlikely to cause disruption (McNergney & Herbert, 1998).

Consider Mark Rader's case in light of the guidelines from these court cases. To what extent is *Schindler's List* relevant to the topic of study? Was it appropriate to the age and maturity of Mark's students? Is it appropriate to the age and maturity of Lisa's students? Are there other factors besides age and maturity that Mark and Lisa should consider? Are there factors in Lisa's situation that are different from Mark's situation and that should affect her decision about using *Schindler's List* in her curriculum? What are they, and how might they affect her decisions? How should Lisa use knowledge from these court cases about the extent of teachers' autonomy in curriculum decision making as she makes her final decision about using *Schindler's List?*

2. If you were in Lisa's or Mark's position, what might you want students to learn from viewing Schindler's List and studying the Holocaust? Where might you find objectives and information related to the Holocaust?

One of the legal guidelines about the use of controversial educational materials is that the material and objectives must be relevant to the topic of study. Ask students to consider how they would develop objectives and find supporting materials for *Schindler's List*. The following are some initial resources:

A document entitled "The Authentic Lessons *of Schindler's List*" created by Presseisen and Presseisen (1994) and produced by Research for Better Schools, Inc. with support from the U.S. Department of Education, Office of Educational Research and Improvement, lends direction to the lessons to be drawn from the movie *Schindler's List:*

- Understand the historical context of the film.
- Understand the central events of the Holocaust.
- Analyze the moral and political significance of *Schindler's List.*
- Recognize the central role of prejudice in creating the Holocaust.
- Understand the significance of the Holocaust to their own lives and the world today.
- Understand key theories on the causes of "rescuer" behavior.

The website for the United States Holocaust Memorial Museum in Washington, D.C. is a rich source of information about the Holocaust (http://www.ushmm.org/index.html). The site includes historical information from as early as 1933, when Hitler was appointed Chancellor of Germany, to recent events, including the U.S. State Department report on efforts to recover and restore gold and other assets stolen or hidden by Germany during World War II. An online guide provides teaching tips for educators who are preparing to teach Holocaust studies and related subjects. Sample curricula and lesson plans are also available from the following address:

Education Department, United States Holocaust Memorial Museum
100 Raoul Wallenberg Place SW
Washington, DC 20024
telephone: 202 488-0400.

Robinson's (1995) *Schindler's List Teaching Guide*, distributed by the Southern Institute for Education and Research, includes a brief chronology of Oskar

Schindler as well as questions to facilitate discussion about Spielberg's film. The guide can be accessed online (http://www. Tulane.edu/~so-inst/slindex.html).

3. What are some elements in the structure and composition of the movie Schindler's List *that might cause adolescents to have difficulties in accessing the plot? How might Lisa use this knowledge to prepare students to see the film and gain more from it?*

Schindler's List is a 3-hour film shot almost entirely in black and white. The first hour is largely preparatory, depicting Schindler setting up his factory. There is little dramatic action in the way that American teenagers have come to expect. Later in the film, deaths are portrayed as realistic and matter-of-fact. The film opens with the Jewish ceremony of the lighting of candles and chanting in Hebrew, of which most teenagers are ignorant. The film is long, "talky," about a time, place, and people who are remote from the experiences of American teenagers.

Ask students to consider what Lisa might do to help students prepare for a film with these characteristics. How do teachers prepare students to tackle a difficult text or concept? How might those strategies apply to viewing a complex film? What further knowledge does Lisa need about her students to help her in her planning?

4. What might a teacher have to know and do to prepare students to see a movie that depicts persecution of one people by another—a movie such as Schindler's List*?*

To understand the persecution portrayed in *Schindler's List*, students must think about the film from the perspectives of both history and art. Without some historical background, students will not understand many terms, allusions, and events in the film. Without some understanding of the artistic techniques and visual metaphors used, students may miss some of the power of the film as a visual message.

Understanding the Film as History. Robinson's (1995) *Schindler's List Teaching Guide* notes that *Schindler's List* is "at times a historically complex movie." The guide recommends that students know the meaning and significance of the following terms prior to viewing the film: anti-Semitism, Death Camp, Germany (point out on map and explain role in World War II), ghetto, Holocaust, Jews, Krakow, Nazi, Nazism, Nuremberg, Laws, Poland (locate on map and explain role in war), World War II (nations involved in the war and key events leading to the war: Nazi seizure of power, invasion of Poland, beginning of WWII, Death Camps Open, End of War).

CIVITAS (Quigley & Bahmueller, 1991) contains a concise and very useful outline for discussing the rise of fascism in pre-World War II Germany and its promulgation by the Nazis. The outline includes the role of geography in Germany's quest for security; Germany's military defeat and desperation at the close of World War I;

Hitler's development of Nazi ideology; Nazi techniques of rule; militarization; genocide; etc. The *Civitas* treatment of this period of history provides conceptual connections to similar events in history (e.g., the development of fascism in Italy and Japan). Perhaps more important, this framework for civic education links the events depicted in *Schindler's List* to contemporary life by pointing to the failures and successes of democracy in other parts of the global community.

Ask students to consider these terms and concepts and other historical facts and issues that students should know for the film to be meaningful. What might Lisa do before she takes the students to see the film to provide them with better knowledge of the historical context?

Understanding Film as Art.   Students may not think of movies as an art form. Like an artist with a painting, a director carefully composes a final product in line with his or her vision. Teachers may want to show a painting such as Picasso's *Guernica* and talk about the historical events to which these artists were reacting.

Teachers can talk about the composition of the film as art, the use of black and white photography both to emphasize the bleakness of the story and to approximate those pictures we carry in our heads of the period newsreels and movie footage from World War II, the Nazi propaganda films, and the liberation of the concentration camps. They might ask about the symbolic use of color throughout the film: What is the meaning of the little girl in the red coat? What is going on in Schindler's head as he looks at her?

Understanding Human Nature.   Besides knowledge of history and art, students will gain more from the film if they think about human nature. Schindler did not begin by wanting to save Jews; he wanted to make money and Jews became part of the plan to make money. By the end of the film, however, he risks his life to save Jews. Ask students to try to figure out when Schindler changes. What makes him change?

In the film, the Nazis describe the Jewish people as "vermin" and as "rats." Reducing the Jews to these animal images, the Nazis sought to dehumanize the Jewish people, to place them beyond the boundaries of human and moral obligation, to reduce them to the "other." The Nazis believed that this was the necessary step in the process of first isolating the Jews and then exterminating them.

Discuss the phenomenon of objectification of the "enemy," the need to depict one's enemy as less than human. Discuss examples in history: Native Americans during the opening of the West, Blacks by slave owners, Japanese, Germans, Vietnamese. How was America portrayed by the Iraqis during the Gulf War? How do the Israelis and Palestinians view each other, the Bosnian Muslims and the Serbs?

What do students know about objectification and stereotyping personally? Gangs? Terrorists who blow up an office building full of innocent workers and children in a day care center? Muggers attacking their victims?

Ask students to think about the use of language in their own communities. What are the words that describe different ethnic groups? Have students think about how rival sports teams/ schools are depicted at pep rallies and activities leading up to the big game. What about the kind of stereotypical divisions among students within a school: preps, geeks, jocks, etc. What words and characteristics are used to describe students in these different groups? Why do people need to feel superior to others? What do people need to belong to a group? Have students imagine how one might move from these "minor" types of stereotyping to the dehumanization and persecution of the Jews by the Nazis.

5. At the end of the case, Lisa is still committed to using Schindler's List as part of her curriculum, but she is now more cautious. She was sobered by Mark Rader's experience, and she has listened to the cautions of her older colleagues. What actions should Lisa take? How should she use the knowledge from the previous questions in her decisionmaking and her planning?

Sometimes even the best-laid plans go awry. Two months after Mark Rader's experience, Susan Gross took about 70 students, freshmen through seniors, to Chicago's Winnetka Theater for a daytime screening of *Schindler's List.* According to Susan, she worked hard to prepare students for the experience:

> We spent several class days discussing how Hitler came to power and how it all fell apart, and we watched the film *The Rise and Fall of the Third Reich.* We talked about the concept of ethnic purification, both in the past and the present. I even brought in song lyrics from contemporary neo-Nazi music and talked about the current Nazi mentality among the KKK and the skin heads. I wanted them to have a sense of context before they saw [the film]. I also told the students and their parents the movie had scenes of graphic violence, nudity, and foul language. I did as much as I could to get them ready. (Roeper, 1994, p. 11)

Despite her efforts, Susan's experience at the theater sounds hauntingly familiar. Students were restless during the first half-hour of the movie. Once the tempo increased and violence erupted on the screen, a few students began to laugh, particularly during a scene where female prisoners were stripped and forced to run around the yard of the Nazi camp like cattle while Nazi guards sorted out the old, the sick, and the lame for execution. "Here I was sobbing ... and some of the kids thought it was the funniest thing they had ever seen.... I'm not saying every single kid laughed ... but at times the laughter was so loud you couldn't hear the dialogue of the movie," said Susan (p. 11).

After the showing, Susan asked about 30 of the students to write down their thoughts about the film. While many of the responses were positive, a few were not. "One student said that I was violating her constitutional right to laugh at anything she wanted to laugh at, and another said she couldn't understand why anyone would be upset at her for laughing at the movie" (p. 11). A third student commented that the movie stirred up "a lot of lies and no good."

If either of us were Lisa, our initial reaction after reading about Mark and Susan's experiences might be to abandon our plans for viewing *Schindler's List*. However, when we reflect on our experiences as classroom teachers, we cannot recall a single assembly or program we attended when there wasn't "inappropriate" behavior from a student. (By the way, we have been to public meetings with adults who have also behaved rudely and irrationally.) Thus if we were in Lisa's shoes, we probably would not run scared from what we perceive to be an educational opportunity.

Like Lisa, we would seek administrative approval for the field trip and we would contact parents to explain the purpose of including *Schindler's List* in our course of studies. In preparation for the field trip, we would use resources such as those from the Holocaust Museum to help students understand the history of the Holocaust. We would also include Mark Rader and Susan Gross's stories as part of the curriculum to encourage students to think about problems and issues teachers and students in other communities faced during and after their viewing of *Schindler's List*. This would seem a great opportunity to talk about First Amendment rights and to compare our conceptions of more and less acceptable public behavior. In doing so, we would press students to consider situations from different points of view.

Do we think such action would help us reach consensus on beliefs about human rights? We would certainly hope so, or at least move us in that direction. At minimum, we would expect us to reach quick and certain consensus on the essential evil of the Nazi regime. Would our conversations lead to consensus on what constitutes more and less appropriate behavior in public settings, for instance in movie theaters? Knowing what we know about public behavior, probably not. But no doubt Mark's and Susan's stories would stimulate fascinating discussions about rights and responsibilities in a democratic society.

POST SCRIPT

An interesting postscript to the Mark Rader story, written by Mary Ellen Butler, appeared in the Greensboro, North Carolina, *News and Record* in June 1995. The fact that the incident in Oakland, California, created ripples in a Greensboro newspaper suggests correctly that Rader and his students had unknowingly stimulated a national controversy.

According to the Greensboro story, The *Oakland Tribune* proclaimed: "Field trip to '*Schindler's List*' backfires. Grand Lake Theater ejects rowdy Castlemont students for laughing at Holocaust horrors." The fiasco at the theater was also on all the local radio talk shows. When CNN and the other networks picked up the story, the Castlemont High School principal's telephone rang nonstop.

Butler reported that "Most callers conveyed the same furious message: This action was one more indication of how brutalized Black youth were, what a lousy job their parents and schools were doing of educating them, and how relations between African Americans and Jewish Americans were worsening by the day. Some callers were more anguished than angry. They were Holocaust survivors or relatives of victims. They wanted to tell the students about the grisly cataclysm that would forever stain the 20th century. In addition to phone calls, faxes and letters began to pour in, some from as far away as England and Germany. Print and electronic reporters demanded interviews" (p. F1).

When the principal talked with Rader and the students, they confirmed each other's version of the events. The students, however, said they knew little about the Holocaust. "One girl thought, before seeing the film, that the term referred to the atomic bombing of Hiroshima. As for hostility between African Americans and Jews, the students said they usually didn't know who was Jewish and who wasn't (p. F1)."

Four days after the original episode, the principal called a press conference. The students apologized publicly for their behavior at the theater. Shortly thereafter, California Governor Pete Wilson announced Castlemont would receive a "Courage to Care" award from the state for their responsible handling of the "unfortunate experience." The principal organized a diversity workshop for staff, followed by other meetings on cultural diversity, and capped with a day-long, school-wide teach-in on the African American Experience.

The media coverage of these events caught the attention of *Schindler's List* producer Steven Spielberg, who also visited Castlemont High. He used the visit to announce a national campaign to use *Schindler's List* as a vehicle to educate American high school students about bigotry, oppression, and the Holocaust. Spielberg returned later without a press entourage and talked with the students. According to the principal, his visit helped bring closure to the whole experience, as did the visit of Leon Bass of Philadelphia, a member of the all-Black 183rd Combat Engineering Battalion, who had helped liberate the Buchenwald concentration camp.

As the school began its next year, the staff inaugurated a new multicultural curriculum, installed new computer technology, and started a new program to lower dropout rates. Spielberg's production company sent prints of the movie and an accompanying study guide to 21,000 high schools in the United States. By January 1996, more than 2 million high school students had seen the movie and studied the guide.

REFERENCES

Butler, M. E. (1995, June 18). From conflict to consensus at Castlemont High School. *News & Record* [On-line]. Available: NEXIS Library: NEXIS File: NWSREC.

Hazelwood School District v. Huhlmeier, 484 U.S. 260 (1988).

McNergney, R. F., Herbert, J. M., & Ford, R. E. (1994). Cooperation and competition in case-based teacher education. *Journal of Teacher Education, 45*(5), 339–345.

McNergney, R. F., & Herbert, J. M. (1998). *Foundations of education: The challenge of professional practice* (2nd ed.). Boston: Allyn & Bacon.

Herbert, J. M., & McNergney, R. F. (1995). *Guide to foundations in action videocases: Teaching and learning in multicultural settings*. Boston: Allyn & Bacon.

Presseisen, B. Z., & Presseisen, E. L. (1994). The authentic lessons of *Schindler's List*. Philadelphia, PA: Research for Better Schools, Inc.

Quigley, C. N., & Bahmueller, C. F. (Eds.). (1991). *CIVITAS: A framework for civic education*. Calabasas, CA: Center for Civic Education.

Robinson, P. (1995). *Schindler's List Teaching Guide*. New Orleans, Louisiana: Southern Institute for Education and Research.

Roeper, R. (1994, July 30). Movie's grim message breaks this crowd up. *Chicago Sun Times* [On-line]. Available: NEXIS Library: NEXIS File: CHISUN.

United States Holocaust Memorial Museum (1996, March 13). *Learning about the Holocaust* [On-line]. Available: http://www.ushmm.org/holo.htm

11

A Case of Freedom to Learn: Balancing the Needs and Rights of All Children

Thomas D. Peacock
Clayton E. Keller
Helen Rallis
University of Minnesota, Duluth

Editors' note: Democracy for whom and under what conditions? No educational situations have forced these questions more openly than those involving children with special needs. In this case Christine, a teacher education student, views "Sean's Story"—a nationally acclaimed video production about a child with special needs who has been mainstreamed into a general education classroom. As students in the teacher education seminar discuss the video, Christine's thoughts and reactions are complicated by the fact that her own sister has Down Syndrome. Christine must face serious personal and professional questions about who wins and who loses when children with special needs are excluded (and included) in general education classrooms. Peacock, Keller, and Rallis raise provocative questions about the rights of all citizens.

THE CASE

Her Name Is Alice

There are seemingly insignificant, almost mundane events in our lives that take on deeper meanings as we grow older. These childhood memories become markers by which we gauge other moments in our lives. They become our own personal legends. This is one of them: In my childhood eyes, I remember my grandmother leading me down a hill near our old farmstead to a place where there was a natural flowing spring. We would go there often, and she would always tell me that this was the place her parents got their drinking water before the days of wells and indoor plumbing, and that before her parents homesteaded the land, the Indians probably came there for the cold, fresh water.

"I still make my tea with that water, Christine. And I come here to think, too," she would say to me. As I grew older and my grandmother passed on, I would sometimes return to that place when I missed her, and when I found myself caught up in the moment of my own personal problems. Time ran together in that place, and it served as a reminder that my life was part of a larger story that goes on forever. As my grandmother did, I would go to the spring to think. We all have our own personal, sacred places where things suddenly become more clear, where our questions are answered, and where each visit results in an epiphany. I wish I were there now.

Our farm is just outside of Brownsville, Minnesota. My father raised Guernseys, although by the time I was in high school the price of milk was so low he had to get a day job at the meat packing plant in Austin. But dairying is in his soul. My mother is a farm wife. She has her garden and chicken coop full of Rhode Island Reds. We have barn cats without names and two dogs that have been my friends through most of my growing up years. I went to school in Middle River, a regional school that serves several rural communities. I graduated near the top of a class of 50 or so. I dreamed of being a history teacher. Maybe my love of history came from my grandmother, who fostered in me that way of being that sees the past, present, and future all at the same time. Maybe I was influenced by the rusted and discarded farm implements that lay around our yard. Each of them was full of stories of hard work, sweat, triumph, and plenty of failure.

And I have a sister named Alice.

My dream of being a history teacher led me to the Duluth campus of the University of Minnesota, where I quickly became an ornament in the student center. Duluth is a long way from Brownsville, but an inner voice told me that for a period of my life I needed to be surrounded by pine trees and be able to hear the lapping of Lake Superior. College and I get along just fine. I make all the right moves. Written assignments flow from me as clean and fresh as the spring of my childhood. Tests are no problem. I am good at facts. Financial aid forms and I have become intimate friends. When I need familiarities, I jump into the car my father got for me as my high school graduation present and drive down I-35 back to the place of my childhood. I always exit onto Highway 218 just out of Owatanna and take the back roads the rest of the way. Past all the other farms, then on to a dirt road and over a rise, I see my home. I have this habit of checking the mail box before I navigate the long driveway that has always drifted over with snow in winters. Even when I was a young girl, there were times my father let me drive the tractor to plow us out.

Invariably, my sister Alice is the first one to run out to greet me.

"Cwissy's home. Mom! Its Cwissy!"

Alice is 5 years younger than I. My parents waited a while between children, but then again Alice seemed to come along unexpectedly. Two girls. One who dreams of being a history teacher. One who will in some ways always remain a little girl. My sister Alice has Down Syndrome.

During the fall quarter of my senior year, I took Secondary School Apprenticeship, the first class where we get some real experience in schools. When I was in high school, I did my share of tutoring junior-high students, so working with kids wasn't completely new to me. I try to spend 4 hours a week out in my placement site, a middle school located just off campus. My cooperating teacher is Mrs. Turner, a nice middle-aged homemaker who went back into teaching after raising her children. We share a common love of history. I help her grade papers, supervise a study hall, and work with students who are behind and need special attention. Although I am not officially supposed to be teaching lessons by myself, Mrs. Turner has turned the class over to me on several occasions when she had errands to do. For 2 hours a week, the Apprenticeship class meets on campus in a seminar, where we tell war stories of our apprenticeship experiences. The professors (the course is team taught) remind us of the relationships between the theoretical foundations of education and the reality of classrooms. That is a big order for many of my classmates, but not for me. I don't need reminding. My grandmother taught me all about things being connected.

We get 3 weeks in Apprenticeship Seminar on special education issues. The professors told us there would always be students in our classrooms who need special education, and that we must know something about the issues these students faced, as well as have a background on the laws and regulations regarding special education. Perhaps more important, we get an overview of strategies for teaching students with special needs, as well as engage in protracted discussions of classroom management issues some of these students may present. These past several weeks in seminar, I often thought of Alice. Last week when we discussed how we might adapt or modify our classroom lessons, a fellow student at the next table tried to be funny by mimicking the actor with Down Syndrome who was in a fast food television advertisement.

"Welcome to McDonald's. May ah hep you?"

I gave him the look my mother gave me the time I was in high school and she caught me sneaking into the house 2 hours after my curfew. Who would believe such insensitive jerks like that would be allowed in a teacher education program? Teachers are not supposed to be common mortals. I didn't say anything because I seldom speak out in classes, even when I feel there has been an injustice. My grandmother said I preferred to let others fill in my sentences, but I find a certain comfort in being quiet. I thought of what I should say, practicing it over and over again in my mind until I had each word memorized by heart, but soon the topic shifted, and it was time to think about something else. I've spent my whole life doing that. In that particular instance, I was also afraid I'd lose it and say something stupid like, "Stop teasing my sister. NOW!" I had to say that a lot back in Brownsville. When my sister needed me to defend her, my personal rules about being quiet were temporarily set aside.

For our third and final session on special education issues we watched a video, "Sean's Story," an ABC News Turning Point episode that describes what happens over the course of a school year as Sean, a boy with Down Syndrome, is integrated into a first-grade classroom in Maryland following a federal court order. The events of Sean's story are contrasted with those of Bobby, one of Sean's friends, another boy with Down Syndrome who attends a special education school. The documentary presents the turmoil over whether mainstreaming students with special needs either did or did not meet their social and educational needs, or whether mainstreaming may deprive other "typical" students of appropriate education. I made a point of sitting in the front of the room, close to the video monitor. It felt like Alice was sitting there in that room right next to me. At other times, particularly during difficult moments, it seemed my grandmother was also there; she was holding my hand.

The video began with a scene of Sean getting on the bus for his first day of school. Sean's parents were there to send him off, and his mother was crying because that particular day was a culmination of the fight she had to wage for the right to get him into a mainstream classroom. Her tears seemed to carry in them all the struggles she had waged over those years.

I don't ever remember my mother crying over Alice, but I remember the struggle she had with the school to enroll Alice at Middle River. The principal and special education teachers had recommended that Alice attend a special education cooperative program in Austin, but my mother insisted Alice attend school in Middle River. At Middle River, she insisted, Alice would get both a regular and special education. There were several meetings at the school about this issue, as well as numerous telephone calls with school officials, and finally she had to threaten to go to the school board. My mother told me she learned to be stubborn and to stand firm from being a farmer's wife. At the same time, I remember my mother wondering aloud what it would be like for Alice when she went to school. My grandmother reminded her it wasn't long ago that many children like Alice never lived long because of the accompanying health problems sometimes associated with Down Syndrome, and if they did live, they were institutionalized or kept at home, never to attend school.

I remember that first day Alice got in the school bus with me like it was yesterday. Some of the other students stared at her, the same way some adults stared at her when we went into town or at church. I remember asking myself if they knew they were staring and also wondering what they were thinking. The incident made me feel very self-conscious but protective of Alice at the same time.

Viewing "Sean's Story" brought up to the surface my own lingering questions about Alice's education. Was she better off mainstreamed into certain classes or was placement in special education classes only of more benefit to her? What was the impact of both Sean's and Alice's placement in mainstream classes on other students' social and educational growth? These questions made me question my own loyalty to Alice.

Early in the video, Kathy Epple (Sean's teacher), wondered whether her classroom was the best option for Sean. She thought he was not progressing academically. As the school year progressed, Sean's teachers modified his lessons and the curriculum he received, because he wasn't able to keep up with his classmates. During a November staffing for Sean, Kathy said in frustration, "I can't get blood from a turnip."

Meanwhile, Chris Reymour (Sean's physical education teacher) wondered aloud whether the extra time he spent with Sean was depriving other students of their education. "I'm spending valuable time (with Sean) that these other students need ... I have to stay with him all the time."

I never heard any of Alice's teachers say those kinds of things about her specifically. Then again, it was a small school, and everyone knew I was Alice's sister. If they did have their own views, I never heard them. I once heard two teachers complaining to each other about the placement of a student with an EBD (Emotional Behavioral Disorder) in their classrooms. They thought the other students were suffering because of the EBD student's classroom behavior. One of the teachers also remarked that the EBD student also suffered, because his needs weren't being met in regular classrooms. On another occasion, I overheard a couple of teachers make similar remarks about the children of migrant families that had begun to settle permanently around Brownsville. "Those children have so many needs, and many of them are so far behind. I'm spending all my time with them."

Those comments made me wonder whether the migrant students could sense their teachers' frustration. Did they feel unwelcome or unwanted at school? Some of the migrant students were teased by other kids because they spoke with a heavy accent and because of their dark hair and skin color. I wondered what it would feel like if every time someone looked at me, they were thinking how different I seemed to them. Did Alice wonder about the same things, or was that type of behavior too subtle for her to notice?

Early in the school year, Sean was hitting and kicking other students. A teacher made a remark that mainstreaming had resulted in her being hit and kicked many times by special education students. But as the year went on, Sean learned to control his impulses, and he used force less often. One little girl made a comment that it was hard in the beginning, "Because he hits some persons, but now we say no and he stops." When asked if Sean bothered him, another student responded, "No, Mrs. Spidero (Sean's teacher's aide) takes care of him, and she does a good job."

Alice also had some early trouble with kicking or hitting other students in school and on the school bus. Especially when she was in elementary school, some boys would be so mean to her. They would tease her unmercifully, making faces at her and calling her a "retard." Sometimes I got into trouble defending her. On more than one occasion my mother and father got telephone calls from the school or from other parents because one of us fought back or attacked others in frustration.

I remember it wasn't always thoughtless boys who angered or hurt Alice. She could start her own share of trouble as well. I carry a few mementos on my shins from our sisterly spats. Likewise, she was the target of my retaliations and more than one preemptive strike. I specialized in putting her face down right next to the cow manure.

Eventually, the teasing stopped. Alice learned to control her fighting as well. Today, my sister Alice is one of the kindest, most gentle people I know.

The video raised another lingering concern I've had about the appropriateness of mainstreaming or placement in special education classes only. Alice would most likely never be able to communicate for herself on these issues, either verbally or in writing. She would never be able to fight perceived injustices with her own words.

There was a particular moment in the video when Sean wasn't doing well either socially or academically in school. He said, "I have a sad face when I come here." The scene then shifted to Jasmine Shriver (Bobby's mother) as she explained the reason she kept Bobby at the special education school. "I feel self-esteem is very important for Bobby. If you lose that, you lose everything."

There were times I remember Alice being very sad. When she was in elementary school, I sometimes saw her sad face on the playground when she had been teased or when no one would play with her. Another time was when my grandmother died. I remember taking Alice down the hill to the spring where my grandmother would take me and told her what a special place it was. This was where I would come when I felt sad or had something to figure out. I told her this could be a special place for her, too.

The video continued with Sean's teachers and others debating the value of mainstreaming. However, by the end of the school year, Sean was doing fine in a mainstream classroom, both educationally and socially. One of Sean's classmates remarked that, "Sean is not someone to laugh at. He's just a regular boy."

Kathy Epple believed it was good for the other students to have a student like Sean as their classmate. "I want Sean to be successful. I want other children to take away an awareness that there are handicapped people in the world." When she was asked if she would do this again, that is, take Sean into her classroom, she said, "In a minute."

A happy ending, just as it should be. The lights were turned on and one of the professors announced, "Take a 10-minute break."

Movies and videos often present clear endings with clean pathways, but real life can be messy and unpredictable. I knew because of Alice that Sean's story didn't end there. Sean will grow into a teenager and be confronted with a new set of issues. Alice was never mainstreamed into algebra or American literature. She will never get to take physics. In high school, she has been mainstreamed into so-called nonacademic courses such as art, physical education (although she does have a program adapted to her capabilities), and industrial arts. When she becomes an adult, her options may be limited. What will the future hold for Sean? What doors will open or remain closed to him?

During break I went outside to get some fresh air, avoiding several of my friends with whom I would usually have shared a snack and a soda. It was a beautiful fall day, a light blue sky and a few sparse, wind-blown clouds. Off in the distance I could see Lake Superior. The reflective beauty of being outside, however, didn't help. I knew we would be discussing the video after break. "Shall I say something during discussion? Shall I talk about my sister Alice? What will I do if somebody says something disparaging about not wanting kids like Sean or Alice in their classrooms? I might get mad and say something I will later regret. What if someone notices that even I have questions about mainstreaming?"

I felt self-conscious when I walked back into the classroom. Doesn't it seem foolish to think the whole world is focusing on you? Isn't that incredibly self-centered? That's what anticipation can do.

The professors began the discussion of the case by having individuals retell the story. My friend Cathy, who always spoke up in class, volunteered readily, as usual. She mentioned that the superintendent (Mr. Berger) had implemented mainstreaming less than a year after the federal order despite the fact that the district had 2 ½ years for implementation. Some of the teachers, she noted, felt unprepared to have students with special needs in their classrooms. She argued that the district should have done some inservice training to prepare their teachers for the challenges they would face. She then focused attention on herself and the rest of us in class.

"I don't know about the rest of you, but I don't have the training to have kids like Sean in my classroom. This is all we get here in our teacher ed. program on special education. I don't think these three classes are even close to being enough to make me feel comfortable."

"What do others think?" asked one of the professors. When she asked that question, I thought she was looking right at me. I didn't want to say anything. Cathy didn't know about Alice. She didn't know that Alice might fit nicely into her classroom.

Another student reiterated what the video's moderator, Meredith Viera, had said about already financially strapped public schools being hurt by the need to shift scarce human and fiscal resources away from typical students to special education students. Sean, she noted, required special speech instruction, reading instruction, occupational therapy, a regular teacher, and a full-time teacher's aide to work on his educational plan.

I remember reading in the Minneapolis paper about the ongoing debate over financing special education. Schools got extra funding for special education students. Alice, like Sean, received speech and occupational therapy. When my mother had insisted that Alice attend regular school in Middle River, the principal said it would be more "economically feasible" if Alice went to the special education cooperative, where she would have ready access to all the specialists she needed. I remember my mother saying that Alice had every right to attend school in Middle River, as did every student in the attendance zone.

The only time I heard a teacher make a similar comment about students costing more to educate was when one said the school needed to hire a bilingual teacher for some of the migrant students. "Can't they just speak English?" she said. I remember thinking what a profoundly ignorant question that was.

We had a real debate in Apprenticeship over the issue of mainstreaming, or to be more precise, everyone else had a debate except me; during most of the discussion I was quiet. My colleagues seemed to believe they didn't have the training necessary to have students like Sean in their classrooms.

"I don't have any prejudice toward Sean or kids like him," remarked one of my classmates. "But I have no idea what I would do if Sean walked into my classroom right now. No idea. I feel the same way about some other things too, like multicultural education, and how to handle students who are severe discipline problems. Sometimes I think we are just being sent out into classrooms and fed to the wolves. It's sort of like you professors are teaching us to sing battle songs, like we should be for mainstreaming, for multicultural education, and for experiential learning, and all that other stuff, but we need to learn how to fight at the same time."

Typical male, I was thinking. Always using the marching-off -to-war metaphor, with little or no idea of what he is fighting for or against.

There comes a point when we either say something, or we don't. My time came when a student reiterated Meredith Viera's comments to Dee Begg (Sean's mother). Essentially, the student believed that Dee was "pushing her own agenda" in sending Sean into a mainstream classroom.

"You're not doing this for Sean. You're doing this for you," Viera had said and my colleague repeated with obvious enthusiasm.

That comment angered me so much! I was thinking of my mother. She didn't have a choice to have a so-called "normal" child. She had Alice, and she never complained. My father and she did everything they could for Alice just as they had done for me.

And I thought of Alice, of every time I went home to visit and how she would run out to meet me and give me a big hug. I missed her so much right now. I wanted to scream out to my classmates, to the world: "This is my sister Alice we're talking about. I love her very much, and she loves me. I want her treated like everyone else. I want her to have the same hopes and dreams and opportunities. We aren't just talking about Sean, who none of us will ever meet. We can't have some kind of rational discussion of what to do or not do."

I knew about the struggles other people have made throughout our history to have an equal voice in the American story—women and African Americans in particular. Just recently in an American literature class I had read *Snow Falling on Cedars*, a fictionalized account of the internment of Japanese Americans during World War II. I remembered one of my other professors reminding us of how Native Americans are virtually ignored in American history. I also recalled my tenth-grade history teacher writing something on the board and then telling us that if there was one thing we needed to remember about our American democracy, it was this: "No person is free until all people are free."

At that very moment in the Apprenticeship Seminar I wished I was down by the spring on the farm with my grandmother—that place where all my doubts are calmed, all my questions are answered, and each visit results in an epiphany.

The clock read 3:45. If I didn't say anything in the next 15 minutes, my voice would never be heard. I don't even remember raising my hand, but I remember looking up once it was there. It sort of snapped into place like it belonged up there.

"Christine, do you have something to add?" One of my professors asked me.

It seemed the whole room looked at me that day, like they knew all along I had something that needed to be said in a strong way. I had practiced every word.

"I have a sister," I began, "and her name is Alice."

TEACHING NOTES

What happens when the rights of an individual conflict with the rights of others? Do one side's rights—the individual's or the group's—take precedence? Why or why not? Satisfactory answers to such questions are critical if the rights of a citizenry are to be preserved and democracy is to flourish.

Questions like these are raised daily in schools throughout this country when students with disabilities are integrated into general education classrooms. Do students who are in special education have more rights than their nondisabled peers? What happens when the rights of special education students seem to conflict with the rights of their nondisabled classmates in general education?

In the video, "Sean's Story," the focus is on the rights of one versus the rights of the group, but there are other obvious and subtle issues present in the case. We frame the issues as questions that guide us to examine the case. We discuss the rights of special education students based on existing rules, laws, and recent court cases. We follow with another perspective on the rights of other students, teachers, and other members of society. Finally, we reframe the issues by proposing that the diverse and multiple needs of individuals and groups can be met by creating win–win solutions based on principles of conflict resolution.

The Rights of One Versus the Rights of Many

One can view "Sean's Story" and make an argument opposed to mainstreaming. The argument would most likely focus on either the inability of mainstream classrooms to meet the educational and social needs of special education students or on the contention that mainstreaming deprives other students of appropriate education. Certainly the situation raises a number of serious questions:

- Will special education students suffer academically in a mainstream environment?
- Will special education students get the individual attention they need when that commodity is in short supply in large, often overcrowded mainstream classrooms?
- Will the demand to give these students special attention deter teachers from giving adequate attention to the other students?
- Are typical students at risk academically in a classroom where children with special needs are mainstreamed?
- Do the low social skills (sometimes resulting in impulsive and/or aggressive behavior) of some special education students put other students and teachers at physical risk?
- When faced with the taunting of other students, academic failure, and low social skills, will the self-concept of special education students suffer in a general classroom setting?
- Should schools be responsible solely for meeting students' academic needs and leave the development of students' social needs to parents?
- Are classroom teachers adequately prepared to work with students with disabilities in regular education classrooms?
- Do students' special needs belong in special education classrooms or schools, with teachers trained in special education?
- Do school districts have a responsibility to offer professional development for their teachers on the needs of special students?
- Should staff development time be spent training school staff on mainstreaming issues and strategies?
- Are already financially strapped public school systems being hurt by the need to shift scarce human and fiscal resources away from typical students to special education students (many of whom need a variety of specialists)?
- Are supporters of mainstreaming right when they suggest that having special education students in classrooms with other students creates more and better opportunities for students who have disabilities?
- Does exposing typical students to special education students improve the acceptance of individuals with disabilities?

The Educational Rights of Special Education Students

Given the controversy about integrating students with special needs into the mainstream, what are the educational rights of students with disabilities? First, their disability status provides protection for their civil rights. All students with disabilities are protected against discrimination from participating in and benefiting from educational programs by virtue of the civil rights legislation of Section 504 of the Rehabilitation Act of 1973 (for programs receiving federal funding) and via the Americans with Disabilities Act (for all other programs).

Second, students with disabilities who meet certain eligibility requirements—that is, their disabilities adversely affect their school performance to a significant degree—are provided certain process and procedural safeguards by the Individuals with Disabilities Education Act (PL 101-476; formerly the Education for All Handicapped Children Act, PL 94–142). These safeguards protect special education students' right to liberty and their property rights to education, the same rights of every student. The United States Congress, however, deemed these extra measures as necessary protection for students with disabilities. Before the passage of PL 94-142 in 1975, access to public education (a property right) and the right to protest actions taken by school systems against them (a liberty right) were not provided consistently to students with disabilities (Turnbull, 1993).

The Individuals with Disabilities Education Act mandates a variety of educational components to provide these safeguards. Two safeguards in particular create tensions in "Sean's Story" and in many other cases of mainstreaming: (a) free, appropriate public education (FAPE) and (b) least restrictive environment (LRE). Students, families, and educators must determine how to meet and balance these separate but interrelated demands. Yet the ambiguity of these critical concepts fosters widely differing interpretations of the content and even location of educational programs for students with disabilities, as we often see in "Sean's Story" and elsewhere (See Kauffman & Hallahan, 1995; Lloyd, Singh, & Repp, 1991, for summaries of different positions on the debate over the Regular Education Initiative). Questions about the educational rights of students with and without disabilities, of their teachers, and of society only complicate matters.

States must develop the means to implement these federal safe guards. Minnesota provides an educational rule about FAPE with which the Individualized Educational Plans (IEPs) of all special education students must be in compliance:

> Children and youth with disabilities and who are eligible for special education services based on an appropriate assessment shall have access to free appropriate public education, as that term is defined by applicable law (Minnesota Rule 3225.0300 Provision of Full Services).

The determination of an appropriate education for a particular student in special education is made by a team of individuals, minimally composed of the student's parent(s)/guardian or a surrogate if there is neither, a special education teacher, a general education teacher, and someone, usually an administrator but sometimes one of the teachers mentioned, who can speak for the school district. These people produce the student's Individualized Education Program.

One of the major interpretations of an appropriate education came in the 1982 U.S. Supreme Court decision in *Board of Education of the Hendrick Hudson Central School District v. Rowley* (commonly referred to as the *Rowley* decision). The majority opinion defined "appropriate" as "personalized instruction with sufficient support services to permit the child to benefit educationally from that instruction" (102 S. Ct. 3034, 3049, 1982, cited in Osborne, 1996, p. 97). "Appropriate" does not mean "that the level of services must be such that the potential of the student with disabilities must be maximized commensurate with the opportunity provided to non-disabled students" (Osborne, 1996, p. 97).

Regulations about LRE provide additional guidance, but still leave the student's IEP team with responsibility for interpretation:

> To the maximum extent appropriate, children with disabilities shall be educated with children who do not have disabilities and shall attend regular classes. A person with disabilities shall be removed from a regular educational program only when the nature or severity of the disability is such that education in a regular educational program with the use of supplementary aids and services cannot be accomplished satisfactorily. Furthermore, there must be an indication that the pupil will be better served outside of the regular program. The needs of the pupil shall determine the type and amount of services needed (Minnesota Rule 3525.0400 Least Restrictive Environment).

The first three sentences contain a presumption that the special education student's education will occur in a regular educational setting. This does not mean, however, (a) that regular education is the only setting in which special education students should be placed or (b) that a special education placement that places a student with a disability only with other special education students for part or all of the school day can never be the LRE for a particular student.

The Rights of Others: Students, Teachers, Schools, and Society

What are the rights of the players other than the special education students in these situations? The U.S. Constitution, specifically the Bill of Rights, does not divide people by group. Instead it states that all people are created equal and endows them with the same rights, regardless of group membership. Laws such as the Individuals with Disabilities Education Act do not provide special rights to one group. Rather, they ensure that people within a group, usually a minority group, receive the same rights as everyone else. For example, Section 504 of the Rehabilitation Act of 1973 prohibits discrimination on the basis of a disability; the law does not give people with disabilities additional rights over others.

To ensure that minority groups receive the same rights as the majority group, laws specify through regulations the procedures to be followed. Because equivalent procedures and regulations for the majority group are not so clearly defined in their enforcement, however, people sometimes challenge these laws as providing unfair advantages. As we see in "Sean's Story," majority group members may perceive their rights as being violated by rulings that guarantee the protection of the rights of specific groups (such as the ruling that placed Sean in a regular education classroom).

"Sean's Story" illustrates how the status quo can be viewed by some as a right instead of as tradition or privilege perpetuated over time. It is important, therefore, to distinguish between *Rights*, with a capital "R," and *rights*, with a small "r," hereafter referred to as *perceived rights*. Our Rights are those defined by the constitution of the country and have been clarified by laws and court rulings. By contrast, perceived rights are better described as "wants."

Examining the Rights, With a Capital "R," of Others in "Sean's Story." The Right of every student, regardless of ability, disability, or any other defining characteristic to an education dominates the story. The Supreme Court decision of *Brown v. Board of Education* defined segregation by race unconstitutional. The ruling also stated, however, that education is a Right that must be granted to all students on equal terms. Students also possess is the Right to be safe. Teachers must exercise reasonable care to protect students from injury and foreseeable harm.

Examining the Perceived Rights, Small "r," of Others. Related to the real right to education is the perceived right of students to equal access to the teacher's time and attention. This issue is more of a concern to teachers and parents than it is to students, or so we assume.

While giving equal time to all students is not a defined right for teachers or students, teachers do have a responsibility to all students. For example, this responsibility is defined by the Code of Ethics of the Education Profession, developed by the National Education Association (1975). The code specifies that teachers should protect the freedom of all students to learn, should guarantee that all children have equal opportunities to learn, and should not "grant any advantage to any student." Some teachers believe they are failing to protect this freedom if they allow a special education student to disrupt their class or if they cannot spend as much time as they would like with other students because they are providing individual attention to one student. Furthermore, this attention to students with disabilities is interpreted as giving those students special advantages.

The issue of teachers' lack of training in special education is central in "Sean's Story" and is discussed more thoroughly here. Although teachers may think they have a right to be prepared adequately to work with students in their classes, no law requires that schools provide them with this training. There are, however, rules created by state education bodies governing requirements in the training of preservice teachers and recertification of inservice teachers. Similar standards are set for the accreditation of teacher education programs such as those of the National Council for the Accreditation of Teacher Education (NCATE). In "Sean's Story," these rules and standards are not raised as being relevant; rather, the discussion is about a broader view that teachers have a right to be prepared for the demands of their jobs.

School administrators are allowed to make decisions to integrate students with disabilities in general education classrooms. All that schools must do is provide a basic education enabling students to meet state standards. Students do not have a right to anything beyond this basic level. How funding is allocated, how schools are run, and how decisions are made about curriculum are decisions to be made by the school board. States delegate these rights to local school boards.

Teachers' Rights are clearly defined only in terms of academic freedom and free speech. They have the Right, in most states, to bargain collectively and to negotiate contracts. Once a contract has been negotiated, teachers may have recourse to claim a right to adequate training if, and only if, this right was included in the contract. This same argument is true for reducing class sizes if there are students with disabilities in their classes or for acquiring extra help to meet the needs of these students. The school is only required to provide teachers' aides if provision is made as a part of a student's IEP. This regulation protects the right of the student with a disability to equal education, not the right of the classroom teacher to certain instructional conditions.

The rights of parents and the broader society are limited to the right to elect officials at all levels. In nearly all localities, citizens vote for school board members who support their beliefs about their children's rights. Citizens also attend school board meetings to bring pressure on the board and school officials to listen to their concerns. In addition, they can demand greater funding and/or more attention be given to their children, but the granting of these demands is not a right.

Reframing the Issues: A Win–Win Solution

The issues presented in "Sean's Story" were settled with a partial win–lose solution. Sean was mainstreamed, but the schools were unprepared to work with students with special needs. We propose the issues in "Sean's Story" be reframed to a win–win proposition for all parties. If we accept that Sean and other special education students have the same educational rights as all other students, albeit with additional processes to safeguard those rights, then we may begin to accept that students with disabilities can attend general education classrooms. This assumes their IEP teams decide that these are the least restrictive environments where appropriate education can be provided.

Framing the question about rights as, "Can schools ensure the rights of an individual to a free, appropriate public education in the least restrictive environment while at the same time respecting the rights of others?" forces confrontation. Someone is destined to win at the expense of others. Moreover, such an approach is fueled by a scarcity mentality; that is, by the belief that power and wealth are limited by some imaginary constraint.

An alternate approach is to ask, "How can schools ensure the rights of all students to a free, appropriate public education?" This question recognizes all people as individuals with the same rights. The analysis is then framed in terms of individual rights instead of group rights.

Another way of reframing the issue could involve a different, peaceful way to resolve conflicts. This type of problem solving may require fundamental changes in culturally acceptable behavior, because it does not rely on the common adversarial American decision-making model. Quakers and many Native American tribes, for example, use a peacemaking model (Witmer, 1996). In a win–win scenario, everyone's needs are met: teachers are instructed on strategies to work with students with disabilities in preservice or inservice preparation programs. Resolution seeks individual and group harmony and to balance social, educational, and psychological needs.

An analysis of "Sean's Story" through this last approach must begin with an examination of people's needs and desires. Are these needs mutually exclusive? Can everyone's needs be met?

A win–win solution seeks to meet the needs of all, but it would require two actions. First, both regular education and special education schools would need to be kept open. Parents of students with disabilities would have a choice; what may be the least restrictive environment for some children is not the least restrictive for others. This would be one way of complying with a legal requirement to provide a full continuum of service arrangements available to special education students in a school district. Second, class size would have to be monitored based on the needs of its students and kept small. The greater the range of background, abilities, and disabilities in a class, the more teachers must take time to individualize instruction. Reducing class size would make it possible for all students to benefit by receiving more attention.

Exposure of students to diversity, especially when this diversity is valued, is a win–win situation. This exposure is advantageous to all and helps prepare students for the world they face outside of school. And when students graduate skilled in working alongside people different from themselves, we all win.

REFERENCES

Kauffman, J. M., & Hallahan, D. P. (Eds.). (1995). *The illusion of full inclusion: A comprehensive critique of a current special education bandwagon*. Austin, TX: PRO-ED.

Lloyd, J. W., Singh, N. N., & Repp, A. C. (Eds.). (1991). *The Regular Education Initiative: Alternative perspectives on concepts, issues, and models*. Sycamore, IL: Sycamore.

Osborne, A. G., Jr. (1996). *Legal issues in special education*. Boston: Allyn & Bacon.

Turnbull, H. R., III. (1993). *Free appropriate public education: The law and children with disabilities* (4th ed.). Denver: Love Publishing.

Witmer, S. (1996). Making peace the Navajo way. *Tribal College, 8,* 24–27.

12

Full Democracy by Students of Color: A Case From Two Urban Classrooms

Carl A. Grant
University of Wisconsin-Madison

Editors' Note: Carl Grant uses the term "case" as it is used in case study research. He takes a participant's perspective as he presents a case of two White teachers working in classrooms in which the majority of the students are Black. Grant forces readers to consider whether students and teachers from different ethnic and racial backgrounds can teach and learn effectively in our schools. He also wants people to think about how students can become participating members of a democracy if they lack opportunities for effective teaching and learning. As students of teaching read of Grant's two teachers, they will inevitably face provocative questions about pedagogy, teacher–student interactions, and curriculum. The kind of answers teachers offer could shape the nature of interracial, interethnic life in a larger democratic society for years to come.

THE CASE

I swear to the Lord I still can't see
Why Democracy means
Everybody but me.
(Excerpt from "The Black Man Speaks," Langston Hughes, 1943, p. 5)

Throughout the nation's history, people of color have struggled to participate fully in democracy. In the United States, "democracy" means different things to different people. For some, it is access to societal institutions and participation in the decision-making process including the rights to sit at a lunch counter and to vote. For others, such as myself, it means, in addition to access, the ability to benefit from what one has access to without the barriers of racism, sexism, classism, and other forms of marginalization. For example, in addition to being able to sit at a lunch counter, one is accepted and treated as an equal human being and a valuable customer, at all commercial establishments from fast food restaurants to private golf courses in country clubs. In addition to having the right to vote, one can participate in the democratic process at varying levels (e.g., as a voter, campaign assistant, or any type of public representative).

The historical struggle to participate fully in U.S. democracy occurred in many contexts, including the Black soldiers who fought and died in the Civil War, the Japanese American soldiers who fought and died in World War II while their families were interned in concentration camps, the Native Americans who chose to attend boarding schools to learn the White American ways, the Black children who walked through gauntlets to actualize *Brown v. Board of Education* and other desegregation mandates while Whites shouted obscenities at them, and the Chinese Americans who fought and won in *Lau v. Nichols* in 1974 to gain language assistance in schools for their limited- or non-English-speaking children.

Of the many struggles people of color have faced, the barriers to achieving an education preparing them to both acquire and contribute to the "diffusion of knowledge" in society have kept people of color from fully participating in democracy. According to Thomas Jefferson (cited in Glickman, in press), the "diffusion of knowledge" is crucial to improving the "human condition," which is why it is important that people of color are part of the knowledge diffusion process.

In U.S. society, the Bill of Rights in the Constitution gives meaning to how democracy should play out in everyday life; for example, "freedom of the press." The freedom stated in the Constitution for U.S. citizens is, for the most part, granted to students. However, schools and teachers are gatekeepers to students' career goals and simultaneously inspirers or barriers to students' opportunities to full participation in U.S. democracy. How teachers play out their role as gatekeepers depends on several factors, including their biographies and education, their perspectives on their students, the students' perspectives on their teachers, classroom management and discipline, and the curriculum and instruction.

To understand the influences of students' participation (especially students of color) in democracy at school, and how they are or are not being prepared to participate fully in democracy in later life, I conducted a case study of two teachers, whom I call Ms. Inger and Mr. Robertson. My purpose in this case is to examine the question: What are the barriers in U.S. classrooms to full participation in democracy by all citizens?

Methodology and Procedure

This case study was guided by explorative (Denzin & Lincoln, 1994) and interpretive (Erickson, 1986) methodologies. It is part of a larger study in which data were collected over 2 years. I visited and observed two classrooms more than 20 times. Each visit was between 30 and 90 minutes. The teachers and students usually participated in taped interviews after the observations. During the visits, I took field notes and examined instructional materials and student assignments. I analyzed observation and interview data separately, then compared them to determine the extent to which they were mutually exclusive or supportive. Data analyses included a content analysis and documentation of trends and patterns. When unexpected patterns and trends emerged, I followed up on these topics in subsequent observations and interviews.

Case Site: Lincoln Middle School

Lincoln Middle School, the site of study, is located in an urban community in a small midwestern city that is a 45-minute expressway drive from a major metropolis. The city desegregated its schools in 1978. Lincoln's students come from a working-class neighborhood. An automobile manufacturing plant, a small college, and several industrial parks are the major industries. I refer to the community the students come from as "A'ville." A'ville was often the initial residence of different ethnic groups that migrated to the city. For the past 2 decades, however, the population has been relatively stable. At the time of the study, the student population was African American (75%), Mexican American (15%), Asian American (recent immigrants from Laos and Cambodia, 5%), and European American (5%).

Biographies and Teacher Education

The findings of studies of teaching, teacher–student interactions, classroom management and discipline, and curriculum and instruction shed light on Ms. Inger and Mr. Robertson's practices in a local setting. Studies of teachers indicate that many teachers do not want to work in urban areas. Approximately 80% of the new teaching force grew up in suburban and rural settings and strongly desires to teach in those kinds of environment (AACTE, 1987, American Association of Colleges of Colleges for Teacher Education, 1988, 1989, 1990; Zimpher & Ashburn, 1992.) Studies of teacher education programs indicate that they have done little to prepare teachers for the changing student demographics and/or to increase their understanding about human diversity and social justice issues. In her study of teacher education programs integrating National Council for Accreditation of Teacher Education's (NCATE) multicultural components, Gollnick (1991) states, "In its review of the first 59 institutions seeking accreditation under the current NCATE standards, NCATE found only 8 (13.6%) of the institutions in full compliance with

[the] multicultural education requirements" (p. 234). Other research studies on multicultural teacher education (e.g., Grant, 1994; Grant & Secada, 1990; Grant & Tate, 1995) support Gollnick's findings. They indicate that multicultural education in teacher education programs is weak and/or superficial. These studies reveal that most teacher education programs are not preparing teachers to teach students so that they can participate fully in democracy.

Teacher One—Ms. Inger

Ms. Inger is a 37-year-old White female. She lives with her husband and two children. She earned her B.A. and the credentials for her teaching license from a small state university close to where she grew up. She completed a Master's degree in literacy at a nearby college of 5,000 students, most of whom are night students. The focus of her Master's thesis was whole language and literature. Ms. Inger reports that she did not take any multicultural education or ethnic studies classes during her undergraduate and graduate study. She stated, however, "In my sociology and education and society classes, I received information on ethnic minorities … Blacks and Mexicans, mostly." She also said, "I read two to three women studies books, and once did a paper on pink collar vs. blue collar wages." Ms. Inger has taught for 12 years, the first 7 years at an upper-middle-class, predominately White suburban middle school called Kennedy, and the last 5 years at Lincoln. Ms. Inger came to Lincoln because student enrollment at Kennedy was steadily decreasing and her position was cut.

CAG: How did you come to select Lincoln for your assignment? Were you assigned here?

Ms. Inger: I received word that I had to leave my school, the enrollment had declined. Also, I was told the district was doing very little relocating or hiring. Therefore, I needed to locate a school fairly close to where we lived. I didn't want to stop working. To be honest, my family has gotten used to my paycheck. They were hiring in this district and Lincoln was fairly close. I heard good things about the principal, and heard that the students were pretty good, no major behavior problems. So, here I am.

CAG: What are some of the differences between the two schools?

Ms. Inger: Three major differences: One, the students at Kennedy are more motivated and dedicated to their work; two, although the resources are about the same, at Kennedy there is more variety, that is, computers, a library with a large collection of books, after school activities, for example, clubs; many of the teachers have the responsibility for an after-school club; three, much more student diversity [at Lincoln].

CAG: Have you initiated the club you were responsible for [at Kennedy] here [at Lincoln]?

Ms. Inger: No, not yet.

CAG: How have you adjusted to the student diversity?

Ms. Inger: I am fine. At first, it was an adjustment. I had never experienced such diversity. The town I grew up in was predominately White. And, although there were a few Black students at my college, I never had close contact with them.

Studies of biographies and autobiographies are useful in understanding teachers and their teaching and determining how the acculturation process influences teachers' attitudes and behavior about the race, class, and gender of people of cultural groups different from their own. For example, several narratives by White teachers explain how their life experiences were often a barrier to the schooling of students of color (see, for example, Canfield, 1970; Decker, 1969; Parkay, 1983). Zeichner and Gore (1990) argue, "These interpretations and critical studies have begun to provide us with rich information about the ways in which teachers' perspectives are rooted in the variety of personal, financial, religious, political, and cultural experiences they bring into teaching" (p. 21).

Ms. Inger's View of Her Students. Becker (1952) and Sharp and Green (1975) observe that teachers have an "ideal client" in mind whom they wish to teach and they judge students on how they meet "ideal criteria." Rosenthal and Jacobson (1968) and Page (1991) believe that teachers respond more positively to students they believe smarter than to students whom they believe less smart. Additionally, teacher–student interaction studies report that students' race and ethnicity (e.g., Wright, 1992), gender (e.g., Sadker & Sadker, 1994), and/or social class (e.g., Gouldner, 1978; Rist, 1970) affect how teachers view their students (Grant & Sleeter, 1996). These findings are alarming because, with preferences for some students over others, teachers are working against principles of democracy they are responsible for upholding and teaching.

The students at Lincoln did not meet Ms. Inger's criteria of an "ideal client." Their race and class were generally different from hers. Although Ms. Inger always planned to teach, the students she planned to teach were very much like herself—White and middle class. Inasmuch as she had taught her "ideal clients" for 7 years before coming to Lincoln, she did not believe the students at Lincoln capable of much academic success. She believed that the way students performed in her class was the only way they were capable of performing. She also believed that her teaching methods and selection of materials were not problematic to the students' level of performance.

CAG: Tell me about the students in your class.

Ms. Inger: For the most part they are good kids. I get along well with them. They are very interested in their social life, much more than their school work. I really have to stay on them to get them to finish assignments and take this class seriously.

CAG: What do you think most of these students will be doing 10 years from now, when they are in their 20s?

Ms. Inger: Hopefully, most will be working, especially the boys. I suspect that a good number of the girls will have children.

CAG: What kind of jobs do you see them holding?

Ms. Inger: Hard to predict with all of the changes in society being discussed. But, probably some type of service or vocational job.

CAG: What do you think are their chances for going on to college?

Ms. Inger: A few, but for most, college will be difficult. Some, if they work at it, may attend a community college.

CAG: You and Mr. Robertson teach the same students. Do you compare notes?

Ms. Inger: Not really. We have discussed Girard a few times, but for the most part we don't do too much talking. There really isn't the time, and our prep periods are not at the same hour.

Ms. Inger, like a good number of teachers in urban schools, teaches in and for a system where students of color do not exist to succeed, a system in which code phrases and words like "at risk," "single-parent family," and "inner-city school" translate to mean low expectations and limited student capability for learning (see Swadener & Lubeck, 1995). The teachers may become socialized into the existing system much like medical school students and individuals who join a major corporation (Becker, Geer, Hughes, & Strauss, 1961).

Ms. Inger, a gatekeeper to access to full participation in democracy by students of color, is not aware of her authority and power or does not care to use it. Although her socialization, including her professional preparation, has at best provided her with only limited awareness of race, gender, and social class inequities, she has not attempted to educate herself about these issues. In a democracy, where such principles as "equality" and "justice" are cornerstones, teachers must accept the responsibility to seek and acquire the knowledge and skills (beyond what they have learned through teacher preparation) necessary to help all of their students to achieve the fruits of democracy.

Students' Perspectives on Ms. Inger.   Teachers come into classrooms with attitudes and behaviors toward students that are shaped by their biographies, education, and previous interactions with students. Similarly, students come into classrooms with attitudes and behaviors toward their teachers based on their biography and past school experiences (Grant & Sleeter, 1996). Students in urban schools, according to a study, do not expect too much of their teachers (Payne,

1984). Payne states, "There is little suggestion ... that a teacher should be intellectually stimulating, personally involved with students, enthusiastic, or even interesting" (p. 76).

The students in Ms. Inger's class extended to her the courtesy expected to be extended to a teacher, but they were not great admirers of her. Students would not miss Ms. Inger much if she left Lincoln. For some students, she is someone mainly performing a paid service, not someone teaching because of a "love for children" and a professional "desire to help children" (Lortie, 1975; Waller, 1932).

CAG: Tell me about Ms. Inger.

George: She OK, but I don't really care for her too much. She kind of phony. I don't think she really likes teaching here. Sometimes she tell us about the other school where she taught. How the students listened and did very good work. She needs to go back there.

Larry: She's OK; she can be pretty interesting sometimes. I think she misses her old school. Talk about it, tell us how well the students there do their work.

Marion: I don't know what to say. She's nice. I used to try and talk with her. She would talk some, but not too much.

CAG: Can you say what you talked about? And, did you say you stopped talking with her?

Marion: Yeah, I can talk about it. But, there's nothing to say. It just didn't go anywhere. Oh, sometimes I'd stop by her room after class, but she always acted too busy to talk.

The students' interview statements about Ms. Inger did not embody any meanings revealing caring, admiration, or respect. Similarly, they never discussed Ms. Inger as intellectually engaging and challenging or personally involved with them.

Students' discussion of Ms. Inger focused mainly on management and control, often in relation to her missing teaching at Kennedy. Marion's comments are representative of the frustration and lack of success of the few students who attempted to get to know or to get close to Ms. Inger. The students apparently understood that she was not upholding such democratic ideals as equality and fairness for all.

Educational literature is replete with reports that indicate "love for students" and "desire to help students" are the major reasons people enter the teaching profession, and that the intrinsic rewards teachers receive from students are very important to them. This literature, however, does not address whether the "love" and "desire to help" are the same toward all students. Teachers' life stories and studies (AACTE, 1990; Dilworth, 1990) suggest a hypothesis needing testing: Are the "love" and "desire to help students" teachers cite as reasons for becoming teachers extended, in practice, to all students, or more to students with backgrounds similar to those of the teachers?

Class Work.   Gay (1995) argues that, "Poor children, children of immigrants, and children of color generally have less opportunity than middle class children to acquire the cultural knowledge that gives access to positions of power and privilege in this society" (p. 54). Page (1991) states:

> In a variety of explicit and implicit ways they [teachers] signal the seriousness with which students should regard lessons or homework, the type of topic appropriate for students' attention, the degree to which students will engage with and contribute ideas, the respect they will accord peers, and a host of other activities. To define the student's role is one of the teacher's fundamental obligations and prerogatives. It manifests the teacher's greater authority and power in the classroom. (p. 33)

The lessons and classroom climate students experienced in Ms. Inger's class were not preparing them to take full advantage of benefits and opportunities (e.g., college education, career guidance) associated with full participation in a democracy. Scholars of education in urban setting and multicultural education argue that culturally relevant teaching (Ladson-Billings, 1994), multicultural curriculum (Gay, 1995), response to students' learning styles (Shade, 1982), and lessons taking into account the social context for learning (Moll, 1988) are important to teaching students of color successfully. In very few observations of Ms. Inger's classroom did I see students doing work related to the social context of their lives. There were no classroom activities helping to empower students (i.e., teaching students to pursue knowledge beyond drill and practice exercises) or enable them to take charge of their life circumstances. Mainly, the students read from textbooks and answered questions in response to their reading. She frequently used worksheets to teach grammar and punctuation skills. She discussed the importance of requiring literacy skills, but usually in connection with skills needed for employment and speaking "correctly." Trade books (e.g., novels) were in the room library, and students were permitted to take them home and to read them in class after they finished their work. She rarely used trade books in connection with lessons or to generate topics for study.

> CAG: Tell me about the work you do in Ms. Inger's class.
> Raphael: We stay pretty busy. She checks to make certain that you do your work. We do a lot of worksheets, although sometimes she lectures.
> Shirley: Sometimes we read books from our library. If we write a report on the book we get extra credit. But, most of the time we work on our grammar skills and other writing activities. It gets boring.
> CAG: Why so much time on grammar skills?
> Shirley: To help us speak correctly and to help us get a job.

Education for students of color must be more than acquiring skills and learning to speak properly in order to get a job. The purpose of acquiring an education is to develop one's total self (e.g., spiritual, emotional, academic, vocational, and leisure) to participate fully in life and help others to live fully. Gardner (1965) states: "Education at its best will develop the individual's inner resources to the point where he can learn (and will want to learn) on his own. It will equip him to cope with unforeseen challenges and to survive as a versatile individual in an unpredictable world. Individuals so educated will keep the society itself flexible, adaptive and innovative" (p. 26).

The education that Gardner advocates, which includes preparing individuals to "keep the society flexible, adaptive and innovative," is necessary to keep our democratic ideals (e.g., government for and by the people) viable in our ever-changing society.

Classroom Management and Discipline. Ms. Inger interacts with her students at Lincoln as if they were lower-track students.

CAG: Tell me about the rules and discipline in Ms. Inger's classroom.

Larry: She uses a system [Assertive Discipline] where our names are put on the board and we receive check marks if we do something she doesn't like. If you get too many checks you can be sent to the principal's office or home until your parents come up to school. She can be pretty tough.

Girard: She had me sent home a few times for not following her rules. I think it's stupid to put our names on the board and add check marks.

Anna: They are OK. I have had my name on the board a few times, but I have never been sent to the principal's office or had to bring my mother to school.

Robert: Pretty strict, until you learn how not to bug her.

Ms. Inger did not implement classroom management and discipline procedures to teach students the importance of self-control and self-determination in relationship to reaching their personal and professional goals and to contributing to our democracy. She was more interested in class discipline and control in order to have a peaceful day of teaching. Page (1991) argues that teachers expect trouble from students they perceive less academically capable and therefore emphasize discipline. On the other hand, teachers expect academically capable students to be "good" and therefore emphasize academic progress (p. 33).

King (1994) and Ladson-Billings (1990) recognize the importance of classroom management as a way to teach African American students two concepts important to full participation in democracy: responsibility and empowerment. King (1994) learned that successful teachers of African American students structured classroom social relations to help students assume responsibility for their own learning. The teachers saw their interactions with students as an opportunity to prepare their students to survive both the educational system and society rather than to "fit into it." Ladson-Billings (1990) reports that successful teachers of African American students developed an equitable working relationship with their students because they viewed education as an empowering force. Ms. Inger appears unaware of the importance of these concepts and teaches in ways that promote neither responsibility nor empowerment.

Teacher Two—Mr. Robertson

Mr. Robertson is a White, 35-year-old social studies teacher. He is married and has two children; he travels on the expressway for about 35 minutes to reach school. He has taught school for 10 years and worked at Lincoln for 7 years. He received his B.A. and teaching credentials from an Ivy League college and earned a Master's degree in U.S. History at a Big Ten university. Mr. Robertson reports that he received very little formal instruction in multicultural education during his college education. He noted that several years ago he happened across Howard Zinn's *A People's History of the United States: 1492–Present* (1980) and was amazed at the content. Since that time, he has purposely worked to teach himself about history and social issues from other people's points of view and has encouraged his students to consider multiple perspectives as well.

Mr. Robertson's View of His Students.   A growing body of educational literature (e.g., Nash, 1973; Ladson-Billings, 1994) reports that teachers who have high expectations for students of color and teach them because they want to be their teachers achieve positive academic and social results. Mr. Robertson holds high expectations for his students and believes that his responsibility is to see to it that they learn when they are in his class. He believes his teaching philosophy is in part based on his Protestant upbringing, which includes a strong work ethic.

Mr. Robertson: I have a responsibility to every student in my class. I know that when many of them enter my class, they come because they have to, not because they want to or because they want to learn. I am paid to see that they learn.

CAG: You seem to stress that their success is your responsibility, almost an obligation for their learning.

Mr. Robertson: Right, I was raised this way. If you take a job you do it well! (his emphasis) And, for the most part these are good students. They need to know teachers believe they can do good work and will support them. Teachers need to have high expectations.

CAG: Do teachers here have high expectations?

Mr. Robertson: It's hard to say for sure. Some, a few.

CAG: I have noticed Remez in your class before and after school. Why?

Mr. Robertson: According to his test scores, he's reading below the third-grade level, but he is much smarter than that. He is often overlooked because he's shy and stays to himself. I learned that up until he moved here a year ago to live with his aunt, he was a migrant worker, working along with his parents. He has good academic potential; I just want to see that he gets a chance to succeed.

CAG: As I shadow your students to other classes, I find that they don't seem to maintain their same enthusiasm and high regard for learning. Many say they are bored in these classes, but I rarely see that kind of attitude in your class. Why?

Mr. Robertson: Careful, Carl, today you seem to be pushing me to discuss other teachers.

CAG: Not really. I am really trying to get your comments on students' learning.

Mr. Robertson: Clever answer, but let's just say that I think everyone in the school needs to work harder, and be more committed to students' learning.

Several educational researchers report on successful teachers of students of color and provide critiques of education of students of color (e.g., King, 1994; Ladson-Billings, 1994; Nieto, 1996). The recognition and confirmation that successful teachers possess teaching qualities such as high expectations, intrinsic motivation and caring, consideration of students' social context and ways of leaning, fairness and respect, and the inclusion of parents and community members are common in this literature. This literature also reports that these teachers wish to empower students so that they may fully participate in democracy, a process that includes helping other marginalized people accomplish the same.

A study of a teacher like Mr. Robertson sharpens the focus on the research on teachers of successful students of color. Although Mr. Robertson employed many of the teaching qualities related to successful teaching, his concerns about social justice and democratic issues were more related to access and opportunities to civic responsibility (e.g., voting). He provided little formal instruction for his students related to educational and social inequities based upon race, gender, or class. For example, in a class assignment to study the mayoral elections, he encouraged students to seek multiple perspectives on the coverage of the elections, but he neither told nor encouraged them to analyze the two candidates' positions based on which candidate would best serve their community needs as working class people of color.

Students' Perspectives on Mr. Robertson.   A small but growing body of classroom research includes the attitudes of students of color toward their teachers (e.g., Grant & Sleeter, 1996; Lee, 1996; Payne, 1984). It indicates that when teachers respect students, are friendly to them, and treat them fairly, the students respond with positive attitudes toward the teachers (Grant & Sleeter, 1996). Nevertheless, years of frustration and boredom in classes and suspicion about the behavior and attitudes of teachers taught many students of color to approach teachers, at least at first, with caution (Grant & Sleeter, 1996). Interviews with Mr. Robertson's students suggest that they both like and respect him. Even students who initially had reservations about him grew to admire and respect him.

> CAG: Tell me about Mr. Robertson.
> Anna: My older brother had Mr. Robertson as a teacher when he first started to teach here. He tells me that Mr. Robertson was the one teacher who seemed to really care about the students. We don't usually agree on many things, but that's one thing that we do agree on.
> Willie: He doesn't put you down; he pushes you, but in a way doesn't 'dis' you.
> Walter: At first, I didn't like Mr. Robertson, but, he's all right. He is fair, give you more than one chance, and will let you do it your way, as long as you do it.
> Russell: I have learned more from Mr. Robertson than any of my other teachers. I feel a part of the class.
> Audrey: He told my mother that I was a very good student. He is the first teacher that I really think cared about me. He's great! I wish he taught all our classes.

During their school life, many students of color do not experience genuine respect for their minds and aspirations. This condition affects the students' self-concept and motivation and creates barriers to their full participation in democracy. The students in Mr. Robertson's class appreciated the way he respected them. He was fair, showed interest in them, and wanted them to do well in his class. However, the students' reactions to Mr. Robertson is also a commentary on the poor quality of respect they are receiving from other teachers. Mr. Robertson stands out to the students because he is the one teacher that they have experienced who is making genuine efforts to engage them. Teaching that engages students, however, is not necessarily teaching that is preparing them to fully participate in democracy. In addition to engaging teaching, students need assignments that empower them with the knowledge and skills enabling them to analyze their life circumstances and take charge of their destiny.

Class Work.   Scholars of multicultural education and education in urban settings argue that students need curriculum taking into account their backgrounds, interests, and social context (Gay, 1995; Moll, 1988; Trueba, Jacobs, & Kirton, 1990). Mr. Robertson used project activities (e.g., writing short reports, interviewing, gathering information from newspapers and television) and class presentations based on themes. He taught students how to do these things and encouraged them to use multiple textbooks and primary sources to obtain information. The classroom was very lively, and students moved freely about. They worked individually, in pairs, in small groups, and as a class. They did not hesitate to go to Mr. Robertson or to call on him for advice.

How students and teachers decide to pursue "knowledge" is a good determinant of successful teaching and learning. In Mr. Robertson's class, the students had a voice in deciding how they would learn, including students who would work together.

> CAG: What are you working on?
> Sonia: Mayoral elections in [name of metropolis] and how the different newspapers and television are covering the candidates.
> CAG:
> How are you doing that?
> Sonia: In our group, two members read one newspaper and watch one news channel [news reports from a large city were carried by three major networks], two other members read another newspaper and watch a news channel, then we compare notes.
> CAG: How are you getting the newspapers?
> Charles: My father and William's father work in the city and get them for us.
> Maria: We also listen to news reports on the radio. I listen to the SBBC [fictitious call letters], the Spanish-speaking station.

Although the students were involved in making decisions about the instructional process, when Mr. Robertson believed it was in the best interest of the students to have some activities pursued in a certain way or wanted to have certain students work with each other, he would tell the students.

> CAG: How was the decision made to do this activity?
> Mr. Robertson: We are supposed to study city government, and I thought this would be good way. So I introduced the ideas to the students. One reason I believe they like it is because they get to work together; there is some competition involved and it is more fun than reading about city government in the textbook.
> CAG: I see Charles and Mary are working together. Is that your doing?
> Mr. Robertson: Yes, both of them are leaders in their groups, but sometimes their groups need some space from them. Others students need to have the opportunity to lead. Besides, I believe they can learn from each other.
> CAG: Ben for the most part always seems to work alone.
> Mr. Robertson: I know, he is pretty much a loner. Whenever I try to place him with a group or get him to work with another student—for instance,

Lester, who he seems to be somewhat friendly with, and Doris, who he seems to respect—he always leaves them. Got any suggestions?

Robertson's method of teaching runs counter to how teachers teach as described in the research. In their studies, Cuban (1984), Everhart (1983), and Goodlad (1984) observed little student involvement, interesting activities, and variation during instruction. Cuban (1984) describes the main pattern of teaching as, "rows of tables and chairs facing a teacher who is talking, asking, listening to student answers, and supervising the entire class for most of the period—a time that is occasionally punctuated by a student report, a panel or a film" (p. 222).

In *After the School Bell Rings*, Grant and Sleeter (1996) indicate that many students of color were unaware of what they needed in coursework, study habits and skills, and intrinsic motivation to succeed in higher education. They had little understanding about how issues of race, class, and gender were affecting and would continue to affect their life opportunities. Furthermore, their family and community members have insufficient knowledge about pathways to success in higher education to help them. The students' lack of understanding about how White power and privilege control their life opportunities, their lack of knowledge about the pathways to success, and the lack of sustained support from teachers are all barriers to the students' full participation in democracy.

Rules and Discipline.   Nieto (1996) reports that, "Disciplinary policies often discriminate against particular students, especially in middle and secondary school, where they may be at odds with the developmental level of students and where they are imposed rather than negotiated" (p. 100).

At the beginning of the semester, Mr. Robertson and his students discussed classroom rules and regulations. The fundamental rule they agreed on is that everyone—students and teacher—is responsible for doing his or her best work. Everyone must respect everyone else; all must comply with school rules including no wearing of hats, coats, or gang colors. Absences and tardiness were unacceptable and rarely occurred. Students were permitted to move about the room, working with one another and/or in groups.

CAG: How were you able to get the students to come up with the classroom rules and regulations?

Mr. Robertson: They have heard about me before they came to my class. They know I will respect them and be fair. But, they also know that in order to work the way we do, we must have rules—respect for one another and for what we are doing.

Mr. Robertson's perceptions were underscored by statements from several students. The following from Gerard is illustrative:

CAG: Is it fair to say that it is pretty well known throughout your grade that sometimes you can be difficult?

Gerard: I guess that fair ... ya, it fair. But, it not always my fault.

CAG: OK, I accept that. I noticed that you get along very well in Mr. Robertson's class. You come on time, turn in your assignments, and seem to get along with Mr. Robertson and your classmates.

Gerard: I never have a problem with the students, not even the [gang members]. So far, they have left me alone, they know I am not interested. My goal is to play ball, pro [football] some day. Mr. Robertson doesn't hassle me. He has come out to some of my games. He also thinks he can play basketball. He's not bad. He has played with us a few times, after school.

CAG: Sonia, tell me about how you deal with the rules and regulations in Mr. Robertson's class.

Sonia: There are no problems He was tough at first, but as soon as we got to know him, and he got to know us, everything was good. He is easy to get along with, you can disagree with him, as long as you do it in a respectful manner. He treats us like we have brains, like we are somebody.

Bryk and Thum (1989) report that an orderly environment, a committed and caring faculty, and an emphasis on academic pursuits contribute to lower dropout rates. Similarly, Good and Brophy's (1994) message to teachers who believe they have problem students like Gerard is to "build close relationships with problem students as individuals, both to develop better understanding of their behavior and to earn the respect and affection that will make the students want to respond to change efforts" (p. 183). Order in a democracy is essential. The students in Mr. Robertson's class willingly accepted and complied with the discipline code that they themselves helped to establish.

DISCUSSION AND SUMMARY

Through education, ideals such as freedom and social justice become part of people's lives and everyday actions, and we learn to understand and accept these ideals. Muller (1960) states, "The success of democratic means depends upon the vitality of democratic ends—upon how deeply, even unconsciously, the proclaimed ideals are ingrained in everyday thought, feeling and behavior" (p. 157).

Reading this case suggests how and why Ms. Inger's teaching and actions with the students did not fully empower them to participate in democracy. Her responses toward the students were friendly but indifferent. She neither engaged them intellectually nor encouraged their pursuit of knowledge that would make a difference in their lives and prepare them to achieve their highest potential. Ms. Inger was more interested in helping the kind of students she had previously taught at Kennedy. Sharp and Green (1975) note that, although teachers display a moral concern and belief that every child matters, in practice there is a subtle process of sponsorship where they offer opportunities to some but not to others.

One can easily conclude from reading this case that Mr. Robertson was an excellent teacher for his students. He provided a style of teaching and assignments appealing to them. He treated them with academic and social respect and thereby earned genuine respect from them. He was also responsive to the students' parents and community members. It is important to understand that students of color attending schools in urban settings are "academically starved" for schoolwork that takes into account their learning styles and is not boring. Mr. Robertson understood this and took it into account during his teaching.

Although Mr. Robertson's teaching deserves praise, it falls short of what teachers can and must do to prepare students to participate fully in democracy. Thus, although Mr. Robertson's teaching was much more responsive to the students than other teachers, he did not consider, or only in a limited manner, the social justice issues students are facing or will have to face in future years. Mr. Robertson is preparing students for democracy, but for a democracy that has more to do with access to societal institutions and with becoming a knowledgeable voter and a good citizen. Mr. Robertson's teaching falls short of preparing students to benefit from what society has to offer. He does not impart a knowledge of the "cultural capital" (Delpit, 1995) they need to "succeed" in society, ways to gain that cultural capital, or the importance of such capital.

Students of color in urban settings must have an education that takes into account their learning styles, background, and social context; teaches them about their history, the history of other peoples of color, and the importance of examining issues from multiple points of view; analyzes and critiques issues of power and privilege and endorses the importance of social justice; and prepares them to take charge of their life circumstances. Knowledge of these matters is neither hidden or mysterious; it is readily available to teachers who want both to learn about it and how to teach it. Scholars refer to it by several names: "transformative" or "critical pedagogy" (Giroux, 1992; McLaren, 1994), "pedagogy of liberation" (Freire & Faundez, 1989), "culturally relevant pedagogy" (Ladson-Billings, 1994), and an "education that is multicultural and social reconstructive" (Sleeter & Grant, 1999). Articles and books in core subject areas on this type of education are available to teachers and other educators.

In attempting to answer the question, "What are the barriers in U.S. classrooms to full participation in democracy?" I have presented a description of two teachers and their teaching. Ms. Inger is the kind of teacher educational researchers have found to be the typical teacher in urban settings: one more interested in control of the classroom and skill and drill practices who does not intellectually engage the students. Mr. Robertson is a unique teacher from the perspective of much of the research on schools in urban settings. He is caring, engaging, and interesting to the students. To many traditional educators and researchers, Mr. Robertson is a successful teacher. However, for the increasing number of educators and researchers who subscribe to an education that is multicultural and social reconstructionist (also critical, transformative, culturally relevant pedagogy), he is not providing students of color in urban settings with the education they need to participate fully in democracy.

Teacher educators must continually be alert as to what they consider to be "successful" teaching for students of color in urban settings. They must recognize the barriers and consider the extent to which the gate to full participation in democracy has been opened to marginalized students.

Teaching Notes

This case or description of the teaching of two teachers provides opportunities for teacher education faculty and prospective teachers to discuss issues of the treatment of minorities in the classrooms and the implications of such treatment for living in a democracy. The following questions can guide students in considering relevant issues and matters:

1. As you review the material, what appear to you to be the similarities and differences between Mr. Robertson and Ms. Inger?
2. To what degree to you think the difference in gender between Ms. Inger and Mr. Robertson affected the conversations and actions that Grant describes?
3. I indicate that biographies of both teachers and students are important in understanding the dynamics of classrooms. To what degree do you agree with this? If you agree, how do you see yourself implementing principles related to the biographies of both teachers and students?
4. The demographics of American classrooms are heading in the same direction that has prevailed for the past two decades: rapid increases in the percentages of African American, Hispanic, and Asian American students and decrease in the percentage of European American students; continued large majority of European American teachers and small minority of African American, Hispanic, and Asian American teachers. Consider your own ethnic heritage: how do you see the preceding affecting you as you prepare to teach?
5. I note that "These studies reveal that most teacher education programs are not preparing teachers to teach students so that they can participate fully in democracy." To what extent do you believe that your teacher preparation program is preparing you to teach students so that they can participate fully in democracy? What does "participate fully in democracy" mean to you? Do you participate fully in democracy? If you do, how? If you do not, why not?
6. Consider what you know about learning theory and adolescent development. To what degree are Mr. Robertson and Ms. Inger acting on principles from these two fields of inquiry?

7. Consider the subject area you are preparing to teach and/or the level of student that you are preparing to teach. What aspects of either relate to empowering students to participate fully in democracy? How is preparing students to participate fully in a democracy part or not part of your thinking about teaching?
8. Review the conversation with the students. What is revealed in them that you might see as hints of actions they might take to change the situation they are in? What do they say that indicates they have a conscious or unconscious desire to acquire the necessary skills and knowledge? Life in a democracy implies the need for personal actions, and schooling is a major part of lives of the students in this case.

Students might also role play an improvised segment related to the case. The following is an example:

DIRECTIONS: For the duration of the class hour, you are going to role play a scene adapted from the script of the case.
CHARACTERS: Ms. Inger, Larry, Anna (from Ms. Inger's class), Gerard, Sonia (from Mr. Robertson' class).
CONTEXT: Students from the two classes have been talking out of class and have concluded that both Ms. Inger and Mr. Robertson are trying hard to teach the students, but that Mr. Robertson is having much more success. Ms. Inger, concerned about her teaching and wanting to do better, heard of the discussions and decided to meet with four students and see what might emerge from a friendly discussion.
TASK: Conduct a 20 to 30 minute discussion in which each individual has ample opportunity to express opinions, ask questions, and make suggestions. Ms. Inger will lead the discussion. The rest of us who are watching and listening will observe the conversations and behaviors for clues and insights about the issues from the perspectives of the students and the teacher. We will keep in mind what we learned about group process, role playing, and related matters. We will also be conscious of how the activity does or does not promote effective participation in a democracy.

REFERENCES

American Association of College for Teacher Education. (1987, 1988, 1989, 1990). *RATE I, RATE II, RATE III, RATE IV. Teaching teachers: Facts and figures.* Washington, DC: American Association of College for Teacher Education.

Becker, H. S. (1952). Social class variations in the teacher–pupil relationship. *Journal of Educational Sociology, 25,* 451–465.

Becker, H. S., Geer, G. B., Hughes, E. C., & Strauss, A. L. (1961). *Boys in white: Student culture in medical school.* Chicago: University of Chicago Press.

Bryk, A. S., & Thum, Y. M. (1989). The effects of high school organization on dropping out: An exploratory investigation. *American Educational Research Journal, 26*(3), 353–383.

Canfield, J. (1970). White teacher, black school. In K. Ryan (Ed.), *Don't smile until Christmas.* Chicago: University of Chicago Press.

Cuban, L. (1984). *How teachers taught.* New York: Longman.

Decker, S. (1969). *An empty spoon.* New York: Scholastic Book Services.

Delpit, L. (1995). *Other people's children: Cultural conflict in the classroom.* New York: New Press.

Denzin, N. K., & Lincoln, Y. S. (1994). *Handbook of qualitative research.* Thousand Oaks, CA: Sage.

Dilworth, M. E. (1990). *Reading between the lines: Teachers and their racial/ethnic cultures.* Washington, DC: Clearinghouse on Teacher Education.

Erickson, F. (1986). Qualitative methods in research on teaching. In M. Wittrock (Ed.), *Handbook of research on teaching* (3rd ed., pp. 119–160). New York: Macmillan.

Everhart, R. (1983). *Reading, writing, and resistance.* Boston: Routledge & Kegan Paul.

Freire, P., & Faundez, A. (1989). *Learning to question: A pedagogy of liberation* (T. Coates, Trans.) New York: Continuum.

Gardner, J. W. (1965). *Self-renewal: The individual and the innovative society.* New York: Harper & Row.

Gay, G. (1995). Bridging multicultural theory and practice. *Multicultural Education, 3*(1), 4–9.

Giroux, H. A. (1992). *Border crossings.* New York: Routledge.

Glickman, C. (in press). *Democracy as education: Essays on the fundamental revolution of public schools.*

Gollnick, D. (1991). Multicultural education: Policies and practices in teacher education. In C. A. Grant (Ed.), *Research and multicultural education: From the margins to the mainstream* (pp. 218–239). London: Falmer Press.

Good, T., & Brophy, J. (1994). *Looking in classrooms* (6th ed.). New York: Harper Collins.

Goodlad, J. I. (1984). *A place called school.* New York: McGraw-Hill.

Gouldner, H. (1978). *Teacher's pets, troublemakers, and nobodies. Black children in elementary school.* Westport, CT: Greenwood.

Grant, C. A. (1994). Best practices in teacher preparation for urban schools: Lessons from the multicultural teacher education literature. *Action in Teacher Education, 16*(3), 1–18.

Grant, C. A., & Secada, W. G. (1990). Preparing teachers for diversity. In W. R. Houston (Ed.), *Handbook of research on teacher education* (pp. 403–422). New York: Macmillan.

Grant, C. A., & Sleeter, C. E. (1996). *After the school bell rings* (2nd ed.). London: Falmer Press.

Grant, C. A., & Tate, W. F. (1995). Multicultural education through the lens of the multicultural education research literature. In J. A. Banks & C. A. McGee Banks (Eds.), *Handbook of research on multicultural education* (pp. 145–166). New York: Macmillan.

Hughes, L. (1943). *The Black man speaks. In Jim Crow's last stand* (p. 5). New York: Negro Publication Society of America.

King, J. (1994). The purpose of schooling for African American children: Including cultural knowledge. In E. R. Hollins, J. E. King, & W. C. Hayman (Eds.), *Teaching diverse populations: Formulating a knowledge base* (pp. 25–56) Albany: State University of New York Press.

Ladson-Billings, G. (1990). Like lightning in a bottle: Attempting to capture the pedagogical excellence of successful teachers of Black students. *International Journal of Qualitative Studies in Education, 3*(4), 335–344.

Ladson-Billings, G. (1994). *The dreamkeepers: Successful teachers of African American students.* San Francisco: Jossey-Bass.

Lee, S. J. (1996). *Unraveling the model minority: Listening to the voices of Asian American youth.* New York: Teachers College Press.

Lortie, D. (1975). *School teacher: A sociology study.* Chicago: University of Chicago Press.

McLaren, P. (1994). *Life in schools: An introduction to critical pedagogy in the foundations of education* (2nd ed.). New York: Longman.

Moll, L. C. (1988). Some key issues in teaching Latino students. *Language Arts, 65*(5), 465–472.

Muller, H. J. (1960). *Issues of freedom: Paradoxes and promises.* New York: Harper & Brothers.

Nash, R. (1973). *Classrooms observed: The teacher's perception and the pupil's performance.* London: Routledge & Kegan Paul.

Nieto, S. (1996). *Affirming diversity: The sociopolitical context of multicultural education* (2nd ed.). White Plains, NY: Longman.

Page, R. N. (1991). *Lower-track classrooms: A curricular and cultural perspective.* New York: Teachers College Press.

Parkay, F. (1983). *White teacher, Black school.* New York: Praeger.

Payne, C. (1984). *Getting what we ask for: The ambiguity of success and failure in urban education.* Westport, CT: Greenwood.

Rist, R. (1970). Student social class and teacher expectations: The self-fulfilling prophecy in ghetto education. *Harvard Educational Review, 40*(3), 411–451.

Rosenthal, R., & Jacobson, L. (1968). *Pygmalion in the classroom.* New York: Holt, Rinehart & Winston.

Sadker, D., & Sadker, M. (1994). *Failing at fairness: How America's schools cheat girls.* New York: Scribner's.

Shade, B. J. (1982). Afro-American cognitive style: A variable in school success? *Review of Educational Research, 52,* 219–244.

Sharp, R., & Green, A. (1975). *Education and social control: A study in progressive primary education.* London: Routledge and Kegan Paul.

Sleeter, C. E., & Grant, C. A. (1999). Making choices for multicultural education (3rd. Ed.). Upper Saddle River, NJ: Merrill.

Swadener, B. B., & Lubeck, S. (1995). *Children and families "at promise": Deconstructing the discourse of risk.* Albany: SUNY Press.

Trueba, H. T., Jacobs, L., & Kirton, E. (1990). *Cultural conflict and adaptation: The case of Hmong children in American society.* New York: Falmer Press.

Waller, W. (1932). *The sociology of teaching.* New York: Wiley.

Wright, C. (1992). *Race relations in the primary school.* London: David Fulton.

Zeichner, K. M., & Gore, J. M. (1990). Teacher socialization. In W. R. Houston (Ed.), *Handbook of research on teacher education* (pp. 329–348). New York: Macmillan.

Zimpher, N. & Ashburn, E. (1992). Countering parochialism in teacher candidates. In M. D. Dilworth (Ed.), *Diversity in teacher education* (pp. 40–62). San Francisco: Jossey-Bass.

Zinn, H. (1980). *A people's history of the United States: 1492—present.* New York: Harper Perennial.

Author Index

Subject Index